SCHIZOPHRENICS CAN BE GOOD MOTHERS TOO

SCHIZOPHRENICS CAN BE GOOD MOTHERS TOO

Q S Lam

muswell hill press

London • New York

First published by Muswell Hill Press, London, 2015

© 2015. Q S Lam

www.muswellhillpress.co.uk.

British Library CIP Data available
ISBN: 978-1-908995-15-5
Printed in Great Britain

I dedicate this book to my parents, especially my mother who overcame great challenges to bring four souls into the world. May it elucidate a mother's complex mind, arming my children with the vital stuff they need to mentally dodge all the muck that life hurls their way.

The truth is rarely pure and never simple Oscar Wilde

Contents

Foreword

Everyone has an internal thought process: that silent other self who speaks to you; the one you debate with. Once mine starts, it doesn't cease. Imagine someone standing a centimetre from your face screaming very unpleasant stuff about you for hours on end, especially when it is time to sleep. That's what it is like inside my head. Rather than use the ubiquitous term *mentally ill* I prefer to describe myself as having *a different sort of brain* and I have, for many years, been seeking a different sort of psychiatrist to help me.

TrActor – located in Brussels, with a sister organisation vzw KAOS that specialises in creative projects with a mental health focus – is a hospital, a place for patients to gather, talk and seek appropriate care. Set in the grounds of a converted church, it also has an atelier for exhibitions. Privately funded, modern and unique in its approach and ethos towards mental health, it is unlike most mental health organisations I have encountered during my long journey seeking help for my own brain issues.

Based at TrActor, Dr Erik Thys is a psychiatrist, artist, musician and President of vzw KAOS. I first went to see Dr Thys proposing an alternative patient/doctor experience. No longer happy being the passive patient sitting in a room, pouring out my woes – a process that left me disempowered – I sought a doctor that I could work with. Making use of my creative skills and the insights I had acquired about my mental health condition over the last twenty-five years, my objective was to employ what I had learnt to aid others with mental health problems. Being useful and making a contribution, I believed, was more effective at keeping my mind healthy in the long term. KAOS holds exhibitions for artists and provides an innovative range of treatments that are often creatively based, participatory, and designed to encourage the patients to be as independent as possible, while providing mental health support.

Initially, Dr Thys seemed bemused that I was interested in working with KAOS; I felt like saying: "You don't understand, psychosis has left me ravaged, destroyed my confidence and killed my dreams for the future, so give me a chance and let's collaborate together to help your patients."

When Dr Thys saw my thirty-foot long scroll, entitled *A Soul on a Scroll*, which took five years to complete, his eyes widened with wonder.

I thought maybe I had finally found the right doctor, someone potentially whom I could work with, talk to, be myself and who understood the importance of making art for my continued mental welfare. There have been times when I have felt disappointed with Dr Thys, but we have usually found a way to move on from these awkward moments, stay in the present and continue to find meaningful ways to collaborate. At the same time, TrActor and KAOS have both tried to support me – creatively and mentally – as best they can within relatively limited resources. It is touching that they have taken me under their wing – a British born Bangladeshi who doesn't speak Flemish and speaks only rudimentary French – and tried to assist in a way that transcends a more conventional, mental health care plan.

Unable to recall when, exactly, I proposed to publish a book about art, psychosis and motherhood, it has been an organic process. First came the drawings and paintings I did after my postpartum psychosis in 2010, then the poems and finally the essays. Very little literature exists about art and psychosis and how art can be used as a tool to keep the mind balanced. My strategies involve art, writing, exercise, nutrition, sleep, identifying and avoiding triggers, and having the right support system in place. There are insights I have gleaned about my mind, such as why I am predisposed to psychosis and how I have, without medication, averted repeat psychotic episodes that I want to share with others, especially mothers. Mothers who have psychotic visions are often vilified or judged. They live in dread of having their children taken away, although many of us will recognise that there are times when children need to be protected and difficult decisions may have to be made. Many suffer in silence and deal with their condition in isolation, despite the fact that the cause of their visions is often related to sleep deprivation, chemical and/or hormonal changes, and not a reflection of dubious maternal skills. I, too, have struggled to find the right support – during both my pregnancies and in the postpartum period – with the complex array of mental health problems I suffer from, which I wrestle with on a daily basis, from the second I wake up to when I finally go to sleep. Many of the strategies I have created have been self-generated and I want to share them, because they work for me and for my beloved children; although there have been some hairy moments, when the symptoms have started with such rapidity that my mind has slipped towards the psychotic void until, somehow, I pull back and stop an escalation. This ability to press the mental pause button in my head is something I have learnt, by recognising distinct patterns, which mark the beginning of a sudden mental deterioration. Often it's as if I am teetering on the brink of madness, but never take the plunge and manage to cling onto a cliff of sanity with my fingertips.

The book consists of fourteen essays that explore various themes including psychosis; the impact of psychosis on my mind; the reconstruction of my mind post-psychosis; and why, perhaps, I was already predisposed to psychosis due to my history, which I describe as *mental mapping*. I also try to dissect and demystify psychosis, investigating other important questions about the role of psychiatrists and hospitals and whether they assist or impede recuperation. Often the partner, living with the mentally afflicted, is overlooked, which is why there is one essay that explores the destructive impact of psychosis on relationships. I explore the possible reasons why some mothers, including myself, have visions and hear recalcitrant voices instructing them to harm their children; and I address the question of whether or not mothers with serious mental health conditions are capable of being good parents. Another essay, deals with a difficult subject: should mentally unwell mothers be left alone with small children; what are the risks posed to both mother and child if psychosis strikes; and what can a mother do to protect herself and her children in such trying circumstances? The final three essays were, arguably, the hardest to write. *Schizophrenics Can Be Good Mothers, Too* required a degree of honesty that was eviscerating. The penultimate essay argues that my mental health issues are *A Sane Response to an Insane Situation* rather than purely because of some inherited defective gene. To conclude the end of my journey, I assess *Where I Am Now?* It was a meandering and protracted wrestle to cut the umbilical cord and finally set this book free from the brambles of my brain.

The essays can be read sequentially, or plucked out of the book and read in no particular order. I wanted each essay to work as a complete, cohesive entity, to paint a comprehensive picture and investigate the issues raised lucidly and candidly. Admittedly, I found it difficult revisiting the psychosis and have dealt with it in a fragmentary manner, which, although unsatisfactory, was the only way my brain has allowed me to process the memory. The poems explore the dark matter of psychosis more effectively, I think, than chunks of analysis. Using both methods I hope the reader gleans a greater understanding of the subject as a result.

The extensive artwork featured in the book complements the narrative and reflects how art has been a constant companion during times of mental uncertainty. It also assisted as part of my recovery from psychosis. The act of drawing both my children consolidated that crucial maternal bond, diverting my mind from black thoughts and strange voices. Words and the act of mark making, either with a brush or a pen, remain an important alternative strategy to medication. I hope the book is useful to doctors, psychiatrists, mothers, partners and families of those who are mentally afflicted and that it provides much needed insights into a difficult and, more often than not, misunderstood subject.

Finally, my decision regarding whether or not I should publish under my real name or a pseudonym has been a long and complicated one.

Of course, I would like to be brave and say, "This is who I am". There is no shame in suffering from psychosis or having a mental health issue, but I am thinking about my children. Would they like everyone to openly know? If I put myself in their shoes, I think not. And how much do I want my children to know, when my anonymity can only be partial. We live in a confessional age with a propensity to share every detail of life. Privacy and anonymity are being flung aside, as if they are no longer of any intrinsic value. Although I want to share my thoughts about these complex issues, my mother's instinct is to protect and shield my family. Hence my decision to publish these essays under a pseudonym. I would like to think, though, that just as I paint and draw in a multitude of styles, the same is true of my writing and therefore it is appropriate to have this other self and any subsequent essays or books that I write about this subject will always be under the name Q S Lam.[1]

CHAPTER 1

The Reconstruction of a Shattered Mind

There was never a genius without a tincture of madness.

—Aristotle

For me, insanity is super sanity. The normal is psychotic. Normal means lack of imagination, lack of creativity. Jean Dubuffet (French artist and sculptor)

As I sit down to write this piece, my mind has come to a standstill. Is it because I am attempting to write about the experience of psychosis and its impact on creativity? After ruminating on the above quotations, the first thing that came to mind was a short poem.

Genius or Nutter

Genius
Or
Nutter
"You are mad, bonkers, insane"
They all said
Hissing and laughing
"They are mocking you,
You are nothing," Fred said
The skinny girl was alone
Sitting at her desk
It was two
Maybe three in the morning
She had a paintbrush in her hand
For a few minutes she did nothing
Apart from stare at it
Long and hard

Then she
Wet the white skin
Of the paper that seemed to beg her to do so
And let the first blob of colour drop
Watching as it fell
Almost in slow motion
The colour imploded
More followed, one blob after the other
The colours were colliding
Dancing
It was beguiling
She was high
"A painting a day until I die," she said
"Never leave home without that sketchbook
Always a pen in the hand, wherever
Keep making the marks
Don't listen
Don't stop
Keep on going until the very end
They can hiss and mock all they like
I'll show them
You can't break me"
She knows they want to
Snap her in two
And then bury her in a hole
But she keeps on emerging
Like a curious worm
From its warm home in the darkness
That's where she's
Keeping the splinters safe
Then one day
Everyone will see
Her vibrant, rich spew
Thousands of works
Waiting patiently
To be seen
She'll keep on
Not caring
What people think
Even when they stare
And say she's weird
You see

You have to be a little mad
To put bits of your soul out there
In the universe.

I have lost count of the number of times people have called me mad and it used to dismay me, because mad seems more pejorative than complimentary It's not something you write proudly on your CV. I habitually look at artists – past and present – labelled as mad and the common denominator linking them together has been their never-ending desire to create and keep on creating until they dropped down dead.

To Be Mad

What is mad though?
The word has lost its meaning
Genius, too, is overused
You can inspect the work
The person
The mind
The flow of ideas
Geniuses are usually called so posthumously
Because when alive
They are threatening mavericks
Often ostracised
Marginalised
Impecunious
It is that very exclusion that fuels
The drive to create
It is that desperation
Which makes the brain burn
Melt and mutate into a different sort of brain
A brain that orders them to keep on creating
When they would rather sleep, eat, or watch TV
And do what the normal do
Often, it's a compulsion
To get the *hot stuff* out
Because keeping it in
Makes the mind heavy
And it all starts leaking
Then pouring and gushing
It's the gush of stuff that confounds

It's the gush that propels them forward towards the blue
It's the gush that is – the violent jolt to the brain – keeping them alive.

If you have ever suffered from psychosis it is an extraordinarily visceral, intense and scary experience. Being plunged into a parallel world that is so vividly realistic and complex can leave you trapped like a spider without legs in a viscid web peppered with golden flies. There is also the chance that you might not come back to the real world. The world cast under the burning fog of psychosis is alluring, complex, vivid, replete with patterns and narratives that suck you in and make your mind swelter as it frantically searches for answers and tries to decipher a myriad of codes. When you are neck deep in glittery psychotic waters, it makes you believe you are special, almost messianic. You have ultimately been selected out of billions as the chosen one. Your whole life suddenly makes sense and has a razor sharp purpose that starts to slice you up.

Living life post psychosis is like going to mental war on a daily basis, walking a fine tight rope in a delicately balanced mind, ducking and dodging the bullets that come firing hourly, daily, monthly, yearly. You respond by firing bullets of logic back to dispel a succession of irrational, emotional reactions with varying levels of success. What is your main ammunition? Not medication, not counselling, but simply creating every single day, in some shape or form. When Dubuffet said that "insanity is super sanity" he might have been referring to the extreme lucidity you experience when psychotic – and, yes, trying to be normal can be more taxing than the psychotic world conjured up by a dangerously deft mind. Adhering to social norms becomes a strait jacket that leaves you choked. Everything seems to be dripping in mendacity. Being creative is the only thing that seems real because it comes from within, it's tangible and indelible, and it doesn't lie to your face.

When I saw the work of the octogenarian Japanese artist, Yayoi Kusama, at the Tate Modern in 2012 I was extremely curious because I had never heard about her before. Suddenly her spotty, vibrant world was ubiquitous. What was more beguiling was her open admission that she was mentally ill. In 1975, fearing her own suicide she voluntarily elected to live in a mental hospital. Continuing to reside there, the hospital is five minutes' walk from her purpose-built five-storey studio. Doctors have diagnosed her with anxiety disorder or obsessive-compulsive disorder (OCD). Kusama does not define her mental illness as such, which makes it something mysterious, amorphous, and less threatening, perhaps. Candid about her hallucinations and the impact of them on her life, she spoke in a quiet, deliberate manner. There was a pervasive intensity and youthful energy in her art that is often absent in the work of other artists I have scrutinised.

She's influenced Andy Warhol and Damien Hirst – been a true pioneer – and yet she almost disappeared into obscurity after being both embraced and then unceremoniously rejected by the art world. It was the desire to create that saved her. She even said that, "If I didn't have art I think I'd have killed myself long ago." Her openness was confounding. Kusama didn't seem to care what people thought of her wonky mind.

Seeing video footage of the artist with her crimson hair, producing her art in a studio swamped with colourful large canvases, was like looking at myself. There was a fanaticism about the way she painted: it was all in the detail and she seemed to enter a trance-like meditative state as she made her marks. This is essentially what painting is, a succession of mark making. Kusama has an expansive team of dedicated assistants, but I work totally alone in my studio insistent on creating everything with one pair of hands. This insistence is not in order to take all the glory. It is simply because physically rendering art can have a profoundly calming impact on the brain. Kusama said in a recent BBC4 documentary *Polka Dot Superstar: The Amazing World of Yayoi Kusama*, "I was pottering at home, limping…now I'm here (in my studio)…I have no problem I can paint and keep going and going." Through the power of painting Kusama was searching for a path to live.

Creating allows you to become immersed, lost and transported outside the walls of the mind. I have observed the same emancipation when a toddler seizes a pen and begins the lyrical, spontaneous process on a rectangular piece of blank universe. The child doesn't know that it is paper, only that there is an open slice of space which he can plunge into and have a splash about with colours. The need to make your colourful imprint on the world starts early, then.

The parallels didn't end there; Kusama is a prodigious writer, publishing seventeen novels.[2] I too have written novels, volumes of poems and have published eight books. There are unpublished novels, novellas and another three volumes of poetry, hoarded like junk, on my hard drive. The desire to write became more acute as my mind unravelled. It was a strange development, but another way of unloading the heaviness that made the mind bloated and ready to burst like a bladder that needs imminent release.

If someone had told me twenty years ago that I would have experienced psychosis, I would have been alarmed and probably incredulous, since I was a calm, diligent and determined child. Despite a turbulent childhood, with the premature death of my father as a baby, the adversity that my family faced seemed commonplace, especially since my mother was first generation Bangladeshi. The immigrant experience is usually one of struggle, isn't it? Yet, when I look at the patterns of behaviour within my lineage the diagnosis doesn't seem that strange. It was still a shock though.

Personally, I find labels very unhelpful. If you meet someone and after a few months of amiable exchange they abruptly divulge, "By the way I have suffered from psychosis," the reaction is one of alarm or bafflement. Nowadays, being bipolar or depressed has become pervasive; being schizophrenic remains hugely stigmatising; and being diagnosed with a condition that combines all three – mania, depression and schizophrenia – is heavy to swallow and difficult to digest. Do you choose to be open? Or wear a mask, which will inevitably crumble? Do you hide away or surround yourself with empathetic people, who see beyond the labels and do not back away? Sometimes I wish I didn't have a diagnosis. It was almost easier stumbling in the dark, pretending everything was fine inside. However, for years I knew that something was very fundamentally wrong. The longer I lived with the symptoms, the more steadily entrenched they became by certain life events and dubious life choices, culminating in two intense, prolonged psychotic episodes that ripped my life apart. It is quite normal these days for people to spew every titillating detail of life's traumas, but it is what you do with all the shit that counts. This is often how it appears to me, great big piles of stinking shit that need to be cleared out of my head before they contaminate other aspects of my life.

When I was sifting through the wreckage left in the aftermath of what was, in effect, a mental tsunami it was like trying to sellotape tiny fragments of my mind back together. Stupendous art is like a "knife in the eye",[3] the heart and the soul. Continuing to create saved me.

For years I have shunned medication, because I have always known that medication might stunt my creativity. There are divisive arguments here: is it easier to live with a mind that is different (and falling apart at the seams), or to take medication, which promises to normalise pathways that have gone awry? Despite all the medication out there, I would rather live with the mind I have – sometimes wrestle with it, engage in long fights with it, even try and throw it in the bin, but principally use what it spews and fashion whatever it offers – however disturbing – into something tangible, indelible, arresting, lyrical and even beautiful. Yes, there is beauty in shit, if lit in a certain way.

Since 1999 I have been running a non-profit arts organisation[4]. My struggle to become an artist has been fraught with obstacles that I have managed to surmount. Yet if you see what *we* have managed to produce, in spite of these – and there have been many – it's a significant output spanning art, photography, films, books and extensive international art projects. I say *we* because people often think that my work is by a collective of different artists. Perhaps it is: there is something alchemic about creating art and often, after I have completed an artwork, I have no idea how I arrived at the final piece. Over the years, several alter egos have emerged and other selves that I hide behind. It would be fair to say my creative output is the result of more than one mind at work, real or otherwise.

There's a heap of new work that needs to be uploaded onto my organisation's website. Eventually I will get round to it, but it's the creating that's of most interest; what happens afterwards is immaterial. Tracey Emin said in a recent interview in The Guardian (8th October 2014) that – "There are good artists that have children. Of course there are. They are called men." – suggesting that to have children and be a great artist are somehow mutually exclusive. I can attest to the fact that having children is certainly time consuming and the hours that could be spent painting or thinking are spent changing nappies, wiping and perpetually clearing up. What constitutes a great artist? I continue to make art every day and motherhood will not stop me from aspiring towards greatness. Children grow up, creativity becomes stronger with age and experience: case in point Barbara Hepworth and Louise Bourgeois were both mothers and two of the greatest women artists that ever lived (in my opinion). Bourgeois' fame came in her 70s and her legacy remains staggering and more potent than ever. Motherhood consolidated their work and made it speak with a poignancy and depth.

Ironically, when I was at my most unwell, and not yet a mother, I embarked on my most ambitious piece of work to date: *A Soul on a Scroll*, spanning 30-feet.

In 2008 life was uncertain and getting more and more arduous, I was mentally war weary and embroiled in multiple conflicts on every front, internally and externally; there was no safe haven apart from the whiteness of a canvas or paper. I can't quite remember when I started to write very small. It began instantaneously and the desire to write smaller and smaller took root in my sketchbooks.

Writing very small was cathartic, a way of dumping the accumulated mental rubbish I was hoarding in my head that fuelled the hallucinations, the manic episodes, the daring risk taking that plunged me in sticky, smelly, very deep black holes. Rather than spew this stuff to people, I spewed it on the page. Writing in a hand that was barely visible to the human eye created a deliberate obfuscation offering some protection. I could reveal without fear, the content remained private, because it was almost indecipherable, yet was out there floating in the universe. The image making was also spontaneous. There was no pre planned grand design, one bit connected to the other reflecting my state of mind at that precise moment. The thought that I was making something truly epic was empowering. At the same time the work could be carried in a plastic bag or shoebox. There was something reassuring about that – making epic art that could be kept close like a trusted friend. Nor was it impinging on the environment in a pernicious

Image 1. *Detail from Sketchbook 101* (acrylic ink and pen on paper, size A5, 2008). When I re-read some of the writing in these sketchbooks it can be disturbing and intriguing. Discovering expressions such as, "The sun rose like a fist" is like finding a small gem in the detritus of my thoughts.

Image 2. Detail from *A Soul on a Scroll* (mixed media on 30-foot scroll of paper, 2012)

way, requiring exorbitant production and installation costs.[5] At every level, making the scroll was exciting, calming and challenging. Sometimes creating art has left me frustrated, irate, disappointed and afraid. Being afraid of creating a bad piece of art can be more catastrophic mentally than dealing with what life hurls at you. But with my scrolls, there are no mistakes; you just keep on going, until you reach the end.

The central image is kept securely entombed by parallel walls of text that lead the eye on a long dance in the central core of the artwork. Never tiring of creating these scrolls, I have made seven to date and am currently embarking on my eighth and ninth. The eighth is named *Sorrow on a Scroll*. It will depict many of the major historical wars, past and present, into one seamless hell, juxtaposed with tiny images of anodyne celebrity. The ninth one I am making with my son is called *Squiggle on a Scroll – Part 3*. My son creates squiggles and I transform them into magical landscapes roaming with dinosaurs, monsters and anything he requests me to draw.

Image 3. Detail 2 from *A Soul on a Scroll* (mixed media on 30-foot scroll of paper, 2012)

It was completing *A Soul on a Scroll,* which had the most palliative impact on my mind. Like a man who has been rendered impotent, or a woman who is infertile by no fault of their own, the collapse of my own mind left me wracked with guilt and a sense of inadequacy. People can be cruel and unsympathetic when you exhibit mental shortcomings, which is why so many suffer quietly and then erupt uncontrollably, to devastating effect.

In 2010, the same year of my second psychotic episode, I made an animation film for the UK Film Council. My film, *White Wall* is about a little girl who is trying to reach the end of the world to make sense of the darkness she carries within. Completing the film temporarily mended my broken mind; I was pregnant at the time of production and knowing I had a new life growing inside my belly made me dare to hope for the future. The strategies I have evolved, to stop the escalation and descent into psychosis, work – although the mental mapping of my mind is a life-long process. In March 2011, I had my first showing of work after the psychosis of 2009; this was a monumental step towards my mental recovery.

As part of my first solo exhibition in Brussels, at KAOS, in 2012, I created a new scroll with patients suffering from schizophrenia and other mental ailments. Working intensely on the scroll for three months, after completion we all gathered together, the patients and I, drinking tea and eating home-made cake, to talk about the experience. Patients remarked that it was working collectively on one piece of art that was empowering and exciting. Some had been sceptical at first, but by the end they couldn't believe what they had created. The completion of *A Forest of Minds* was a feat considering all the mental obstacles stacked against us. I also overcame my own in-built preconceptions about the mentally ill.

Image 4. Original sketch for UK Film Council funded animated film *White Wall* (pen and ink on A4 paper, 2010). Drawn on a beach in Bali, conceiving the film aided the process of mental rehabilitation from psychosis. The little girl wants to find meaning in her life and runs to the end of the world to discover it.

Image 5. Detail from *A Forest of Minds* (mixed media on 30-foot scroll of paper, 2012)

My latest scrolls are at the embryonic stages and will probably take many hours to complete. I will keep on making scrolls until I am a toothless, silver haired old lady. Seeing people's expressions of wonder when they look at the work dispels the fog in my head, albeit fleetingly. I can hold onto those reactions, store them in a safe place and replay them to remind me of the work that I have done and counter what my mind spews, which is usually a non-stop barrage of potent false narratives.

Creating art soothes the heavy throb of my brain flooding it with a *breathlessness* that comes from truly being alive. The dark forces that we carry within secret pockets inside can seep out, tying knots around our ankles, making us stumble and fall. Taking out a pen or brush, playing with colours, creating marks, writing tiny text, these are all things I can do instantaneously to fight back. Whether with paint, pen or words, art diverts and keeps the mind entranced. Gerhard Richter said, "It is better to paint than not to paint". I would agree with that. Tracey Emin said, "As I get older, my art is what drives me, and it will till the end of my life." My mother also once told me, "The mind is like a universe" and I would agree with that too. Sometimes the mind can also become a prison. I find ways to unlock that prison door and take a stroll in the universe of the mind with a pen and paintbrush in hand, discovering all that is hidden within its dense and often mouldy folds. Sometimes I think having this sort of brain has made me see and sense things more acutely – to have compulsions that others do not. This realisation makes it less cumbersome living with a mind that is not deemed normal – but then what is normal? There is no normal, just seven billion very different roaming and colliding minds. Just as no thumbprint is the same, no mind is either, or ever will be. Adhering to social norms is a crude way of defining a mind that is kept in check. To me that could be perceived as another prison that we voluntarily step into.

Seeing video footage of the Yayoi Kusama, diligently working in her studio surrounded by vibrant and vivid canvases, didn't appear extraordinary: actually, it seemed reassuringly mundane. Only the trance-like state of her face and the slight twitches of her mouth gave any indication of an inner intensity. Sometimes, I fast forward five decades into the future and see myself in a room, sitting at a desk working on a scroll. The room is empty, apart from a neat pile of scrolls created over a life time. There is a large window; light is seeping through; the sky is cobalt blue, cloudless and clean – like a mind without walls that is free and limitless.

Even if no one ever sees the scrolls that I am making, there is the promise of someone discovering them and stepping into a series of thirty foot mini-universes – that very prospect is tantalising, keeps the mind moist, stops it from becoming brittle and crumbling into dust.

It is something to strive for.

CHAPTER 2

The Shattering of a Mind

After finishing *The Reconstruction of a Shattered Mind*, writing another essay exploring how and why a mind implodes in the first place was a logical progression. There is the common assumption that a massive life changing event, or trauma, or an unexpected rush of anger is required to precipitate the shift into a mental realm that is other; or an accumulation of stressful events that climaxes in the mental crash. Certain minds are more predisposed to psychosis than others. My own mind was genetically more vulnerable, perhaps. But it is not just a genetic predisposition; a combination of factors all conspired towards my first psychotic episode. It's a complex puzzle that I have been trying to piece together, often in the dark.

My old tutor, at the London School of Economics, Dr Chun Lin reminded me of the importance of highlighting the devastating nature of mind disorders and their corrosive impact on life. She actually saw me when I was in the throes of psychosis in 2010, at a restaurant that I thought I had to smash up at the time. I wrote, in an email to her that "I must have appeared disturbingly deranged?" She did not reply to this question, I understand why, because it is an awkward question. It is a question that people would rather not answer. Some experience a one-off psychotic episode; others, like myself, have to live with the prospect that, given a set of specific circumstances, it could strike again. Triggers are pervasive. Now that I am stable again, this is how people want to perceive me. The periods when you are not are something that you have to deal with on your own, implementing innovative ways to re-emerge sane again.

Persistent mental struggle could be seen as a plausible response to stress, the strain of modern living, sustained isolation, losing the art of conversation, problematic relationships and the pressures of motherhood. Having children can be the glue or the undoing of, what were before, perfectly palatable unions. Why? Because the pillars of support needed to raise a family are threadbare. The problem, then, is the world we live in, coupled with the climate of innate social intolerance towards the mentally ill. Inroads are being made to change this via social media, websites and chat room forums, but for those of us that shun that level of openness, it's a solitary, mental grind each day.

The day before I wrote this essay, I was dangerously close to psychosis. It was as if I sensed a precipitous displacement of the tectonic plates in the brain, and I braced myself knowing it would be a rough ride. During this period I involuntarily wrote down what was happening in my mind. I say involuntarily, because someone else was commanding that I do this: the critical voice in my head. His full name is Frederick Vladimir Pucco. Here is a fake biography I wrote for him when I first exhibited as four artists: Sophie the Cloud Catcher, Mia the Diva, Fred the Devil and myself, in 2007 at the Truman Brewery in east London.

Frederick Vladimir Pucco

Frederick Vladimir Pucco is of Russian aristocratic descent and studied at The Russian Academy of Arts in Saint Petersburg and the Royal College of Art in London before being expelled, from both, for trying to burn down the colleges. His predominant theme is the "unfathomable". He has shown internationally in galleries around the world including the Guggenheim and Tate Modern, but despises the art world and the supercilious cretins that run it. Fred is as old as the universe – he refers to his father as "Darkness" and his mother as "Hell".

Fred is on a mission: "William Burroughs said that 'The magic universe is dying' – I will suck every last sparkle until there's nothing left but mould and rot."

Fred created the biggest sculpture on the planet – a giant platinum diamond encrusted penis that could be seen from the moon and made Damien Hirst's skull look like a piece of piss. He is also a performance artist extraordinaire, making three hundred toddlers cry for three hours while laughing continuously. He skinned a dog alive before stapling the skin back on for kicks. Gargling with bleach before brushing his teeth, he did not flinch during the whole process. His paintings are small, delicate, occasionally dainty and his draughtsmanship masterful. He usually paints and draws blind folded with his hands tied to his back, wielding the pen and brush with his mouth alone.

Some dismiss Fred's work as malevolent and devilish, but he has retorted with infamous insouciance: "The world is sick; my work just reflects the devil in all of us. People are afraid of darkness, they think it is something dirty but I think it is beautiful. Darkness is the closest we will ever get to enlightenment."

Fred has caused mayhem in my life, but he provides the fuel to spur me on, even if it is hurtling towards the precipice that is as clear as day. Fred makes precipices seem like the best place to be in the world. He dreams of making me jump off one with a firm hand on my shoulder willing me to do it. Imagine that: living with someone telling you to press the end button, in a voice yelled through a speaker directly into your ear with insidious fervour. My invulnerability to Fred's persistent battering over the years has often puzzled me. I don't particularly have a zest for life, nor do I often wake up *happy*. If anything Fred is offering me a solution – that's what he says, and yet something has sustained me, without medication. My mind has undergone many implosions, but how many more can it withstand? If you could put my mind under the microscope, it would be a luminous orb crammed with decades of memories, playing out like miniature movies individually projected in tiny bubbles that move randomly. This orb, with a diaphanous outer skin, is held together with needles, safety pins, flimsy black thread and opaque tape. This orb is so fragile, it is ready to break with the slightest tremor and, when it does, those bubbles come tumbling like stones rolling down a steep hill. Interestingly, my mind descriptions change, but they are essentially visual variations of the same theme, a mind that is on the verge of shattering.

Since my first two psychotic episodes in 2009 and 2010, and subsequent postpartum psychosis, I have experienced recurrent symptoms that are so precise it seems unbelievable that the brain can go into autopilot, flying straight in the direction of the blazing, psychotic gorge.

This is my attempt to summarise these symptoms factually, as they rapidly play out, paying particular attention to their sequence. By focusing on the precise order of the symptoms, it certainly helps me believe that I can climb into my head and press the stop button, rather than be a helpless bystander.

The Cumulative Stages that Lead to Psychosis

I was due to go to Oxford to contribute to a panel discussion about art and mental health at Pegasus Theatre in Spring 2011. Although sleeping well the night before, I was so apprehensive about the trip that I set off too early, which left me loitering and getting more agitated. I should have rested on the train, instead I was drawing, watching a movie, reading and writing: in effect, warming up my brain. It was a humid day, the tube was crowded, people moved fast – resembling angry ants – and the train to Oxford was packed. There was an obstreperous American, with a face like a sunburnt lumpy potato that was vexing; I tried to focus on the play of light on the leaves that caught my eye out the window. At one point I moved away from the inadvertent source of heat to my brain.

An amiable red haired girl picked me up. Engaging in small talk taxed my brain because as I was trying, in earnest, to be professional, inside I was getting stressed. Arriving at the theatre it was dark and cold, like the pit of an empty cave. People were already seated. Three of the women on the panel gave me a limp handshake and paranoia started to set in. To calm my nerves I went to the toilet, washed my hands and tried to make myself look polished. When I sat down, taking out a bag of nuts and several pens I started to draw. Throughout the discussion, keeping my head down, I drew and ate nuts until it was my turn to speak. Eating something prevented my blood sugar levels from plummeting; my mind however was getting hotter. I spoke loudly and clearly, although my hands were shaking. Describing my *sort of brain* to the audience, I revealed how after giving birth I had heinous visions that involved my child – there was horrified silence in the audience – before I frantically cited the strategies I implemented to counter them. Wishing I could have pressed the rewind button almost immediately, it all came out very fast and loud like a train. I tried to explain that after giving birth the combination of sleep deprivation, the massive hormonal changes, and even breastfeeding, can cause psychotic visions, and they are just that – not rooted in reality. Experiencing such visions doesn't mean you are a psycho. Unfortunately, by speaking candidly about such things, you could be perceived as one and that label sticks brutally. Revealing such thoughts and visions to health care professionals risks having your child removed[6] if they do not know your history and, even if they do, women remain painfully mute, terrified of the consequences, not knowing whom to trust, not knowing where to get help, or if help is even available. Throughout the rest of the discussion I privately lamented my openness and Fred was soon on the scene saying that the audience were staring at me, thinking I was a potential baby killer. Trying to push Fred away, he stayed within close proximity from thereon. Afterwards we all ate some food and more chitchat ensued with strangers. The stress levels were rising; I still had to pump milk, then there was the play and dance performance to watch. My head began to swirl from the energy emanating from the stage and my case seemed to be getting heavier after I'd been carrying it around all day. Tired and dehydrated, it was time to lie down and rest, but I didn't do either. The more I tried to relax and engage, the more Fred derided me. Talking to people became increasingly arduous. Finally, at 10.30pm a lady escorted me to the Bed and Breakfast accommodation where I was staying. The closest place for food was a fish and chip shop, not the type of food I usually eat. I had to eat alone, except I wasn't alone; Fred was right there, pulling me apart, laughing in that hideous cackling way of his. It was getting late. I called my friend Laurence to avoid engaging with Fred; talking began to hurt my brain and eyes. Knowing I had to be up at 4.45am to pump milk and get the 6.27am train back to London, I put the phone down and then Fred appeared. The whole night my mind was racing as Fred told me to write things down and to do it now because it was of paramount importance.

I saw plays unfold in my head and movies in 3D. The flight of ideas soaring in the vast open sky of my mind was becoming denser and I wanted to catch them all before they got "stuck to the bottom of the pan".[7] Many ideas sadly flew away or were lost, disappearing as they hit the ground. It was distressing watching them fall through the ceiling and then shatter in miniscule fragments onto the carpet. Losing these ideas was sending my mind in a panic; I became greedy for them all, wondering if I could conjure them back from the shards. I got up, took a shower, pumped milk and went downstairs. The lady running the B&B said she would make me some breakfast, but it was eerily dark and deserted, apart from Fred, who was following me everywhere. A bleary eyed lady eventually appeared and I ate a little breakfast, before getting into a cab. Knowing I hadn't had enough sleep, Fred was going to try and steer me towards the edge. Although I wanted to be silent and close my eyes, Fred forced my mouth open and I became voluble and overly convivial to the Ugandan driver, gleaning his whole life story in five minutes. The symptoms were beginning, due to the stress of participating in the event and being plunged into a new social situation. Paranoia quickly set in, aggravated by irregular eating and poor hydration. The subsequent heat in the brain contributed to the insomnia, which encouraged the flight of ideas, which led to a loss of inhibitions, a pronounced desire to be open and talkative, depleting precious energy reserves, leading to further exhaustion and increased mania. Arguably, I shouldn't have gone to Oxford, but then what kind of a life would I have; one of tip toeing cautiously, avoiding all potential pitfalls? That is no life.

Often, it does seem as if I am standing at the edge of a cliff, looking down, with Fred emphatically instructing me to jump. When the symptoms of psychosis ensue, Fred pushes me and I fall towards those boiling psychotic waters below, which would burn my brain to cinders if I reach full descent. Somehow, my rational self manages to stretch out an arm and grab a branch to stunt the fall and I begin my slow ascent away from danger. Each day I never know how close I will get to falling again because Fred is never far away with his taunts and demands, some of which are perilous and scary. It's a stressful and precarious way to live, yet there are merits to living such a life, namely, the possibility of creating something great and true.

With each psychotic episode the symptoms leading up to it are unerringly similar. Equipped with this knowledge, I understand what is unfolding and how to step out of the landmine that my head becomes. It can be a perilous place, with infernos ablaze. What do you do when you see a raging fire? You flee and, when your mind is incinerating, you employ every method to escape *mentally*. If the mind is indeed a "universe", as my mother often describes it, then it is possible to escape somewhere shady, sip something refreshing, and watch the ebb and flow of the sea. If you can't find a way to be calm, then being silent is another strategy and if you can't shut up, then physically walking away – from the potential confrontation you find yourself seeking with another person – is vital. Once Fred has lit the match to start the fire, he's playing games, looking for a fight, wants your blood, to mess with your life, and, ultimately, destroy you. It is just sport for him. What is difficult to accept is how the smallest of incidents can start the blaze – very much like the flutter of a butterfly wing in Cornwall can cause a cyclone in Chittagong.

On the train from Oxford back to London I should have slept. Mentally exhausted, Fred insisted I capture the morning light and take photos with my iPhone out the window, which would have drawn unwanted attention. Surrounded by men in suits, who resembled clones, I was vigilant. Deciding to do a deal with Fred I agreed to take five photos and after that he had to let me sleep. This did not happen. After reaching Paddington, I rushed onto the platform, surrounded by robotic expressionless figures with complexions' the shade and consistency of mashed potato. Fred ordered me to film them; I ignored him. With another train to catch, determined to sleep, I reminded myself of the ramifications of excessive tiredness – this was my reality check. The memory of previous psychotic episodes was enough to keep me trying to fend off Fred. Upon arrival at Kings Cross I marched into two shops spending one hundred and fifty pounds in ten minutes on superfluous items. Knowing what the symptoms meant, the cognitive part of my brain stepped up the tussle with Fred, who was trying to steer me down paths that would further exhaust my mind and start the inexorable spiral towards psychosis. The pattern was all too blatant. Reiterating internally, *you have to sleep and drink*, these two simple measures could prevent an episode. We often forget how thirsty the brain gets. It's not just the body that needs water.

Settling down to sleep, once I boarded the train, I immediately noticed that the stones on the track gleamed like jewels. Fred promptly instructed me to capture the morning light and take photos throughout the journey, or film. Each time, Fred planted some ludicrous, energy draining, suggestion in my head I fired one *bullet of logic* after the other, to dispel them and avoided conversing, to beat him at his own game. Unfortunately, as I closed my eyes and tried to escape the torrid, atomic mental invasion, the man behind me, talking on his mobile phone, sounded like amplified screams in my ear. By now my brain was acutely sensitive, as if someone had stripped the skin off my body and was avidly rubbing lemon and chilies into the flesh. At first, I politely requested that he keep his voice down, speaking with closed eyes. He ignored me. Asking a member of staff to intervene, he ignored her, then I called my husband and said, "I am trying to sleep but this selfish bastard behind me doesn't give a shit. He doesn't understand that I have to sleep *now*..."

Shouting with complete abandon, indifferent that I was being openly abusive about the man in question, he promptly became quiet. In fact the whole train went quiet. When I lost my inhibitions and stopped conforming to normal social codes of behavior, I was in trouble. Such was my rage; I could have lost it there and then. Knowing I couldn't risk having an episode in a public place, I held it together until I reached home, realising my husband would be leaving, imminently, for a meeting. I had to look after our son and click back into gentle, patient mother mode. Really I needed to go to bed, but that was not possible.

Although relieved to be at home, everything I touched became distorted and transformed into one of the toxic hallucinations that were flooding my brain with increasing alacrity. As they ensued, I began to slide mentally even, deeper.[8] Dismissing them curtly is the method I employ to deflect these visions, mentally flicking them away, as you would a fleck of fluff with a finger.

If I see something that could harm the baby, rather than my brain creating a protective response, it tells me to do the antithesis with an accompanying gruesome image. My explanation is that the synapse connections in my brain are incorrectly wired, which creates the gross confusion. How else can they be explained? The persistent application of logic to the implacable onslaught of such visions is my strategy. In short, I never allow my mind to give them any credence at all.

My answer was to turn on some music and sing to my son (The Cure's *Spiderman* in this instance). At the same time, Fred was telling me to write things down and I obeyed, while trying to feed my son. Deciding to create some art with him, despite my exhaustion and precarious mental state, when my back was turned he scribbled on the sofa as if it was a canvas. Ironically, the sight of orange crayon on our cream sofa was the jolt I needed to bring me back to the real world. The time it took to remove the stain strangely cooled down my head. Perhaps it was the mundaneness of the task, which created the diversion. Changing my clothes and making myself look aesthetically presentable, we went for a walk and did ordinary things, as I waited patiently for my husband to return. Believing that danger had been averted, after feeding and getting our son to bed I sought my husband out and turned on him. Ever since the psychosis began, this has become habitual.[9] When I have been sanguine, I've told my husband that it is Fred who is looking for a fight. The stuff that comes out of my mouth is poo. It is the voice of Fred and not my own. Fred's words are not grafted to anything real. The best way to react to these odious rants is with a placid voice. Aggressive vituperation will only pour petrol onto the flames that are already raging in the brain. It is what Fred wants, it is why people with this *sort of brain* lose their friends, can't hold down jobs and alienate members of their family. It is these deeply unpleasant moments, which scare people away and make them forget the times when you were kind, generous, articulate, temperate and lovely. As the anger ensued, my husband, who was also exhausted, gave me a weary look. Locked in an internal skirmish with Fred, my husband was in the firing line. He was going to get hit by the bullets spewing, like a machine gun, out of the toxic hole my mouth had become.

Fred's voice can be so powerful and convincing, I simply yield to his commands: for example, writing inappropriate emails, very fast, one after the other, with Fred booming in my ear to press the send button, to devastating effect. If I manage to resist the urge to send emails, Fred will then tell me to start cleaning, working, writing, painting or drawing. Contrary to what people think, the work created during this stage of the mental condition can be quite incoherent and there is the risk that the artwork *fails* because of my rapidly diminishing cognitive abilities. This is when computers, iPads and mobile phones are hazardous and need to be turned off because they create too much mental heat. A *hot* brain is a sign that the symptoms are starting.

In order to sleep I had to cool down my brain. How do you do that? Once I started talking about the numbers 3, 6, 9 and searching for patterns within them, then psychosis was beginning. The allusions to these numbers started during my first major episode. You can find patterns in anything; patterns are grafted in nature and form the very foundation of the universe. During psychosis the identification of these numerical patterns made me believe that I was verging on genius. Using my rational and logical sense, I recognised that this was, actually, a sign of deterioration. The gush of ideas, numbers, memories past and present; the recollection of painful life events and the compulsion to reconnect with dubious characters was all too evident. Fred was telling me to seek these people immediately. If I obeyed Fred, the crash would have been harder, deeper and more damaging. My response was to do something mindless, watch something light, read something vacuous, anything that would act like a cold spray of water or better still an ice cube melting on the brain. If I didn't sleep another night, then the onset of psychosis was inevitable because the pattern was blatant and the symptoms, uncannily, unfolding with machine-like accuracy. To ensure that this did not happen I took half a sleeping pill; an emergency precaution. Using them very sparingly, preferring to try every other technique but this one, when the sleep deprivation becomes endemic, the sleep medication manages to pull out the power cord from my brain long enough for it to shut down for a night of restorative sleep. I go through long periods of not taking any sleep aid, such as now – mainly because I am breastfeeding and do not want to contaminate my milk. I also believe, almost fervently, that abstention is preferable to potential addiction to seemingly innocuous pills. The next morning I felt fine and engaged normally with my husband. We didn't refer to what had happened, knowing it was Fred's mischief. Better to move on and climb into a new day with wide-open eyes. My brain was tepid; there was always the chance it could boil over. Writing this essay creates heat for example: anything that requires concentrated brain energy is potentially precarious after such a close call.

A typical scenario is my proclivity for working after midnight. Deciding to call it a night and prepare for sleep, a decision which ensures that danger has been placed in a mental cupboard for the night, that drawer could be slyly opened by Fred's hand. It could all start up again, almost instantaneously, if I wake up and start writing or drawing when I should be resting my brain. My brain requires generous doses of slumber; sleep is more effective than medication. Sleep repairs the damage caused by Fred's manipulative games. Blinking rapidly, it takes a long time to sleep. Reading something embarrassingly trite to create a mind diversion usually works, but it takes an hour, sometimes longer. This is why I sometimes have to nap, when I can, to make up for the precious lost hours.

The following day felt like drowning in a grey puddle. Gone was the dizzy high, replaced with a phlegmatic hue, like walking around with a damp sack over my head. Trying to be blasé about the whole affair, the impression of having all the answers had faded. I didn't have the answers. I was fallible and as close to back to normal as I could ever be. Understanding what had just transpired, the symptoms don't scare me anymore. My strategies work, but I also know they can fail. The positive aspect of this mini episode was that I wrote a very detailed account of what was happening in my mind. The downside was that the intensity of the experience was painfully exhausting for my brain. Although inured to these rages, each time this happens it drains my husband's energy and it's never good if my son hears or sees me ranting. My husband tries to shield our son from these rants, but in the aftermath he becomes terse and my son subdued. Seeing these changes in both of them makes me more determined to have more *good* days than Fred days.

What is the state of my mind right now? It is a fractured, fragile mind – a mind that can be easily shattered by Fred's incessant orders or the onset of psychosis, if I allow it to strike again. This is why I lead such a disciplined, controlled life; otherwise I can find myself only a few steps away from mental collapse. There are only so many times you can reconstruct the mind. Without an inordinately patient and tolerant husband (who often uses silence to deflect whatever comes at him from Fred's caustic tongue), dealing with the condition this way would not be possible. A more relevant question is how did my mind end up like this, was it inevitable? Or could certain interventionist measures, implemented earlier, have resulted in quite a different mental landscape?

CHAPTER 3

Mental Mapping – Why Do I Have This Sort of Brain?

To try and fathom why I have this sort of brain, I began a process of mental mapping. Mental mapping involves charting pivotal moments in your life, from childhood to present day, as succinctly as possible. Drawing a map of the mind, punctuated with key events and mood fluctuations that have caused dents in a life's trajectory, can help a person understand how they arrived at the now. Treating the past as something dead is irksome. When people say, "Forget the past because you can't change it" this is an unhelpful platitude, because without an inspection of personal history, how can we learn about our psychological evolution? An exploration that is not a facile victim/blame approach, but rather an objective mental delineation can give you the insights and apparatus to create a mind that is not at the mercy of malevolent forces – in my case, the Freds of this world – but a mind armed with the tools to fight back. That is not to say you will not suffer lapses and terrible days, but there is always the prospect of climbing out of the treacherous, hostile pit the mind can become.

After I experienced psychosis, I created my own mental map. Written in a few hours and comprising bullet points, it factually described, in ten thousand words, those pivotal life-changing events: childhood traumas, teenage traumas, and adult traumas. Riddled with drama, it seemed to get more dramatic with each passing year, until my mental crash in 2009. An avid reader of artist's biographies, I often skip to the end and read the chronology to get an overview of their life first; a mental map is slightly different, because you solely focus on events that have instigated a change in your mental state. Just as a doctor might analyse an X-ray, a mental map provides a clear and concise overview of someone's mental make-up, allowing you to detect patterns in the peaks and troughs. An ongoing, lifelong exercise, a mental map enables you keep track and avoid the traps we naturally step into. It is not a journal, going into detail or complex analysis; it just reminds you of the seminal moments that contributed to where you have ended up now. Finding myself in repeat scenarios and situations which perplexed me, after creating my mental map I was able to understand how and why I ended up in the same unsatisfactory place. Life can become one long habit: having a mind disorder can play out the same tired narratives and destructive patterns of behaviour, with the same devastating outcomes. The only difference is that I now understand what is going on up there; the evidence is in the mental map. It reminds me of things to be aware of every day.

Other people don't have to go to such lengths to navigate through the spikes, poking out the walls of the mind without drawing blood. For them, it's comparatively effortless. For some time I have been working on a *Bookofminds* – a visual archive of people's minds. The idea is to collect mind descriptions, which I will visually interpret and display in a *Bookofminds* and then transcribe onto a scroll. At each exhibition, I participate in, I politely ask members of the public to kindly pop a *mind description* in my black book. To help people grasp the concept I say: "If you could describe your mind visually, what would it look like at this precise moment in time?" Each answer is very different. It gives me a fascinatingly brief insight into people's state of mind.

After asking my husband to describe his mind visually, he replied:

"My mind is like the sea.
It's a calm and sunny day and
I am drifting in a small boat
With a white sail,
Watching the waves
And feeling the tingle of the sun on my nose."

By contrast, I said:

"My mind is at war and
My soul is definitely a restless one
With an ever-fidgeting foot,
My mind has blood stained walls
With gaping holes that collapse habitually.
My mind is a tumbling down house,
Crammed with cupboards bursting with memories that
Refuse to be binned.
My mind hoards and revels in the details.
It is like one of those bag ladies
Getting heavier and dustier over time."

When he described his mind, I felt envious. He often says that he never dwells on the past, preferring to remain in the present. For him, the past is of no use and he doesn't hoard memories in the way that my mind does. It's as if he has a very good drainage system and flushes his mind out each night before he goes to sleep, adding a generous squirt of bleach to keep it fresh and clean for the next day. He is a *glass half full* person, focusing on the now and all that is good in life. During the twenty odd years I have known him, he has never been acutely depressed, the only person that has caused him anything verging onto *mild morbidity of thought* is me. He leads a disciplined life, wakes up early, works hard, putting everyone first before himself – in fact you could call him selfless. He has retained all his friends from childhood, is respected and popular and understands the importance of conforming to social mores.

The source of this unerring sanguine outlook is evidently his mother. She is irrepressibly vivacious, with blue eyes that literally sparkle. She enjoys each day to the full and once told me, "I am satisfied with my life."

In fact, she is constantly laughing and persistently jovial. My husband comes from a stable Swedish/Norwegian family. This is despite the suicide of his paternal grandfather. Such a tragedy could mark a family and even cause its unraveling. They seldom talk about it. I have often wanted to find out more. My father-in-law has obliged, but the darkness that lurks in the family is kept neatly tucked away. If I told my husband that he should create a mental map of his mind he would probably scoff at the idea, dismissing it as ridiculous, because he is happy with who he is and his life. I, on the other hand, think that if you are not in control of your mind, if it has forces within it that could be harmful to you and others, then creating a map is another tool to have when the cruel voice in my head named Fred strikes. And he can strike at any time.

Over the ensuing years I have seen my husband as the rock while I am the crashing wave trying to break it into in a thousand pieces. This force within is the burden of the disorder, which lashes out and wants to break everything that is real and worth cherishing.

To explain why I have this mind, it is crucial to look to past life events that have shaped it. Like my husband's family, mine too has suffered a big dose of tragedy. Could I argue that my family was genetically predisposed to develop a mental affliction, it just needed a series of traumas to switch the gene on and set it in motion? That would be overly simplistic, although there is some substance behind the hypothesis. There is a dubious gene on both my late father's and mother's side of the family. What evidence do I have? My mother has lived apart from her siblings for decades and yet they exhibit uncannily similar irrational mood patterns, especially her sisters. Observing this when I was working in Bangladesh and staying with my maternal relations, contact with my paternal aunts also gave me ample opportunity to scrutinise the familiar shape of their minds. One paternal aunt and uncle have both been deemed mad. There are similar threads in mood with both my mother and sisters, intermittently, over the years. These threads are coarse, jagged and adulterated; consisting of prolonged invectives and debasing monologues with repetitive themes. Making these observations, I force myself to acknowledge that my uncle (married to my maternal aunt) was not far from the truth when he said, "There is a genetic mutation in your family."[10]

What is a genetic mutation or defect? Genes that explain why mothers end up murderers and their off spring murderers and so on. It seems offensively crude to make such a supposition.

For the sake of argument, even if we did have a mutant gene, I would still argue that the mind is resilient, will fight back and try to repair itself until it finally caves in, not able to withstand the barrage of kicks over time. This is how I see my own mind, as a child. I constructed a cocoon around it, to withstand the blows delivered within and without, retreating into a carefully constructed Lego utopia, engaging in obsessional drawing, becoming compulsively spick-and-span in the quest for external order to counter the chaos of mercurial family life. I sought solace in solitary games or fantasy children's literature to try to get away from the source of mental heat. When I was a child, I believed that, through sheer determination, the tide would turn in my favour. Flowers would soon flourish in the garden of childhood and the tangle of thorns that was once tall and threatening, would wither. My spirit as a child was indomitable, much stronger than it is, now, as an adult.

When did the first kick begin?

It starts during conception when you are handed your genetic code, when the foetus is given its initial nutrition via the placenta, and after a baby emerges from the warm safety of the dark, watery womb, making its first scream in response to the glaring light and startling cacophony of the outside world. It starts when an infant hears the word "no" and doors start getting slammed and exploration begins to diminish. It starts when cortisol is released in the brain when an infant's cries are ignored. It starts when undeveloped minds are exposed to sly pressures and the allure of technology. It starts when a trauma rips a family apart and has to be held together again with flimsy string. Life acts like sandpaper on the soft skin of a newborn and some heal better than others.

The Mental Map of One Bangladeshi Family

In Chapter 1: *The Reconstruction of a Shattered Mind,* I briefly referred to the death of my father when I was a baby. I did not reveal that my mother also tried to commit suicide when she was pregnant with her second child.

She overdosed after discovering a letter revealing that my father was still in contact with his first love, an English woman, in which he neglected to mention his wife and child. They managed to move past this event. My mother was young; she'd married him in an impetuous midnight marriage. Several weeks later, she ran away with him (despite completing her BSc in Chemistry at Dhaka University and in the middle of studying her Masters of Education degree) and began a new life in the UK, far from friends and family. Uprooted, she tried to make a grown up life when she was not yet a woman. My mother believed that women in Bangladesh were often subjugated; escaping to England was her way of forging a new independence. Vividly recalling her own mother's apocryphal stories of growing up in Pathuakali, my mother was born after the death of her twin brothers. Grieving for them as she raised my mother, even though she bore three more sons, my grandmother yearned for the ones that died. My mother cites the loss of her twin brothers as the reason why she always wanted to be a boy, because she felt women were not valued in Bangladesh. She also witnessed my grandfather's wrath[11] and my grandmother's timidity and helplessness, because of her complete dependence on a man. Tragically, my mother also experienced some serious abuse as a child, although she never elaborated on the specific details. All these factors contributed to her desire to leave a country in which, she believed, women were certainly not destined to flourish.

Ironically, my mother yearned for daughters; it was my father who desperately craved for a boy. His disappointment each time she bore another daughter was evident and subliminally, she felt like a failure for not providing him with a precious son. I wrote a novel entitled *Gungi Blues*, published in 2008 (although initially conceived in 1996 and completed in 1999/2000) by Chipmunka Press, which is loosely based on my mother's journey. An attempt to ingest the struggle that she endured and overcame to grow into the person she became, it was a way of trying to unravel the complexities of my mother. I could write a better novel now because my focus would be less on what happened in her life, but more on how events impacted on her internal mental map and how that, in turn, shaped the mental maps of her children.

My middle sister was the first of my siblings to show signs of having a *different sort of brain* during infancy. Did my mother's overdose damage my sister's brain? Our local GP assured her that it did not, but how could he be sure? Why did she sleep so much as a baby, only waking to be fed, seldom crying? A docile lump for the first few years of life – some babies are just incredibly easy. Why did she cease to listen, become angry and stop smiling as a toddler? Was my mother's overdose the first trauma, setting the demise of her mind in motion? It is just conjecture on my part, yet her behavior patterns remain the same as when she was a five-year-old. Because no one has given my sister a credible explanation, she, like me, has embarked on her own analysis.

My middle sister is, and can be, extremely charming, funny and generous. She has an infectious giggle and often, when we have spoken on the phone for hours, I would be entranced, hanging onto every word she said. Whenever I complemented her, she would angrily say, "Stop calling me a genius," but, in my eyes, she definitely was. Extremely articulate, effortlessly erudite, she was frustratingly indifferent to her talents. It was very difficult to watch the rare orchid that was my sister pull out her petals and relish burning them one by one. Family was not a cosy, safe nest growing up – can family ever be that? Clearly, my mother was never the same after the premature loss of her husband. He was thirty-five when he died from a heart attack and she was in her mid-twenties. Rather than return to Bangladesh, a widow with three daughters, she remarried her husband's best friend to ward off other, more insalubrious suitors. He, in effect, became our new father.[12] She had to learn to love him and he had to learn to love us. A couple of years older than my mother, he found himself with the daunting responsibility of a ready-made family, while also grieving for the loss of his best friend. Just before he died, my father lay in his hospital bed totally distraught. "What will happen to my wife and children?" he asked frantically. My stepfather reassured his friend agreeing to take care of us, never imagining that he would die. It was an extraordinarily selfless gesture. But this radical change in life was a colossal shock for him. My stepfather recently told me, "I was just a boy (inside) when I married your mother."

When my mother returned to employment, after several years of staying at home to look after us, she used to catch two buses to work in Oldham as a social worker and my stepfather worked night shifts at Norweb (an electricity firm). Both were acutely sleep deprived, with three children under the age of five, one of whom had inexplicable anger issues. Warning my parents that it would just get worse, it was the school teachers that suggested my parents consult a psychiatrist, because they couldn't understand why my middle sister was so *different*. None of us could.

Often indignant, sullen and withdrawn, in childhood photos of us, you can see the growing malcontent in her eyes. There were times of laughter, pleasure, reveling in imaginative games (there were an abundance of those), creating comedy sketches that sent us into belly aching giggles, but these moments of bliss were transient, because the smallest of incidents could send my middle sister into an incandescent rage. Many childhood, teenage and adult years were spent trying to unpick the cause of her unhappiness. I even made a film about her.

Image 6. *Sisters Should Always Try To Love Each Other No Matter What* (poster paint on paper, size A3, 1987). Painted when I was fourteen it depicts a bony, elongated hand clasped around the neck of my middle sister, the water gushes through her brain, a futile attempt to wash the anger away. The glasses belong to my big sister. The anguished face contorted in a teardrop is mine.

I remember reading the infamous first line of *This Be The Verse* in an anthology of Larkin's poetry when I was at school. It has stuck with me ever since.

They fuck you up, your mum and dad.
They may not mean to, but they do
They fill you with the faults they had
And add some extra, just for you…
This Be The Verse by Philip Larkin (1971)

The same poem influenced my final MA film *Weakbladder* (shot on 16mm). Depicting the story of a very unhappy girl, the protagonist is under enormous pressure from her father to excel at school, is berated constantly by her mother who lavishes more time and attention on her plants, and is bullied, mercilessly, by two classmates in particular. One afternoon the girl is in the library perusing the shelves and stumbles upon the Larkin poem, captivated by that line she unwittingly places the book in her bag not realising her nemeses have witnessed the theft. In the next scene she's in an examination room, about to sit an important paper, overcome with nerves she wets herself, everyone in the room starts to snigger. Her humiliation is palpable. She's subsequently expelled from school for both failing the re-entrance exam and stealing. Her father is livid; the girl is distraught and in a fit of rage cuts up her mother's beloved plants. Incandescent her mother throws the girl out. The final scene depicts the girl walking forlornly in a dark forest intercut with an animated figure walking in a parallel, luminous imaginary universe. The journey ends when both the solitary animated figure and the girl collapse and sink into a ground that is peppered with mushrooming cyan blue flowers. I thought the film was about my middle sister, but it is also about me, trying to convey that sense of not fitting, of not knowing where to turn or whom to trust, and home being a hostile, lonely battleground. Needless to say when my middle sister saw *Weakbladder* she was implacable, swearing and railing against me asserting that I had shown an acute lack of sensitivity. It was actually my way of trying to fathom her torment and show empathy through the universal medium of film.

To return to Larkin's poem I paid scant attention to the last two lines:

> *...Get out as early as you can*
> *And don't have any kids yourself*

At the time I didn't understand what these lines really meant, but I do now. Having said this, I don't regret having children and if everyone followed Larkin's advice where would we be?

After many hours of tortured deliberation I have concluded that the issue with my middle sister is mainly with her brain, the same issues that I have with my own. Although I use the diagnosis of *schizoaffective disorder* to dissect my mental issues, my middle sister is broadly dismissive of doctors and their theories. Seeing a plethora of experts in the field of mental health, very few were able to help her. She would assert, "I am fine, there is nothing wrong with me," although she now concedes that we (my sisters and mother) are blighted with mental health issues. She often thinks the *experts* are the problem and she can out-talk and outwit them with ease. However, during a relatively recent correspondence with her she seemed surreally happy and almost a new person after trying Neuro - Linguistic Programming (NLP). Finally she'd found an "amazing therapist" and had learnt to accept that it's, "okay being me and if other people have a problem that's their issue not mine." My eldest sister recently saw her and remarked, "She's so chilled out, it's unbelievable." Has my middle sister found a way out of the darkness that has overshadowed much of her life?

Emotional detachment is critical when writing a mental map. Being emotional about the past is unconstructive; extrapolating the key events that have impacted on your life and subsequently influenced the map of your mind can make living a little *easier*. The causes of the emotional upheaval in my family are clear for anyone to see.

We can often become entangled in the past. I frequently observed how my middle sister strangled herself with narratives that were tired and jaded and didn't enable her to climb out of the holes she dug. She refused to accept that the patterns, which play out in petty family altercations are just that, designed to keep her entombed in the giant holes she willingly steps right into. She would often say to me, "Change the tape and listen to another tune", equipped with an array of wonderfully articulate insights, but unable to implement them herself. Then I would do the same as her, just as my big sister and mother would, too. Living in the past, rather than enjoying the now, was a mental tendency that reigned supreme.

Fred is an amalgamation of my mother, stepfather, sisters and the dominant males that have featured in my life. Sometimes Fred even sounds like them, particularly my middle sister. It's transference. Of course Fred does not exist, yet he is very real, because my potent past, which others can forget, is intruding on the now.

Battling with her chronic mood swings, I could see the split within my mother. Usually immaculate and softly spoken to invited guests, when they left and the door shut, the transformation began instantaneously. The strain of constructing the veneer was too much. My mother simply had no energy to engage with us.

Reverting to my own mental map, I had an obviously rocky start. The initial years were lugubrious and cloaked in my mother's grief. While my big sister remained amiably aloof throughout my early childhood, the relationship with my middle sister was problematic for as long as I can recall, despite a deep desire for closeness. With only thirteen months between us, her rejection was persistent and blatant. I was a plaything, useful when she felt like it, discarded when she grew bored or irritable; she could reel me in with her charm and wit and I would come bounding like an excited puppy, but then she could stamp on my tail and tell me to go to hell. The day she pulled a knife on me, during one of our petty fights, made me realise that this was not normal sibling rivalry. Anyone else would have given up, but this misplaced adoration persisted right until the psychosis of 2009. These inchoate destructive patterns (namely an addiction to rejection), formed in childhood became very difficult to redraw.

Apparently, I cried persistently as a baby, something my stepfather still mentions, almost implying that I inadvertently contributed to my biological father's death, because my cries kept him awake. Perhaps this is another false narrative that I have concocted and clung onto in order to lash myself with. From a young age I shunned all physical contact, loathing cuddles and kisses. A baby dies if it is not held – did I set the slow death of my mind in motion then? None of us have memories of playing with our parents or being read to by them, although my mother asserts that she did read books at bedtime. My only memory of these nascent years is of anger, yelling, abuse and violence in the form of smacking, hitting – whatever you want to call it – which I found unpleasant and demeaning. From a practical point of view, they provided everything we could need, within their limited means. There were always plenty of books that appeared mysteriously or regular trips to local libraries and we were given delicious, often elaborate, home cooked meals.

In terms of provision, I can't fault my parents, but emotionally it was deficient. Any calm, happy memories were superseded by the predominant colours of childhood: grey, red and black. My preferred state of detachment was a defense mechanism because life at home was chaotic. In response, both my big sister and I become fanatically tidy and self-reliant. We were seeking order in the messy world of home to detract from the internal mental mayhem that bubbled like a hot spring. This quest is something that has stayed with me. During psychosis, this desire for order becomes almost maniacal. On the whole, especially when I am tired, *tidiness* is a daily obsession.

Similarly, when my sleep deprived stepfather and mother used to hit me, I refused to cry or be broken. A resilient child, I never caved in, while my middle sister would scream unreservedly with the first slap or kick. How many knocks can you withstand until the walls of the mind, already precarious with unstable foundations, fall? For me being deemed "thicker than a brick" by my stepfather was beyond demeaning; being bullied at school another knock; being hit by my stepfather in front of my class mates – because I was taking too long to put on my laced up shoes after the school play *Goldilocks* – another. These were the first triggers that perhaps flicked on the gene lying dormant from birth, creating a whole library of hundreds of shameful memories to be stored, meticulously, on those empty shelves of a developing and mutable mind. Useless to recall and yet the mind clings to them as a child clings onto its favourite toy. For my big sister, she too held out for a long time. In her formative years she could do no wrong. Initially top of her class, winning an array of prizes and attending an eminent private school, then she started making questionable choices. My stepfather came down on her when she didn't get the expected "top" grades. I vividly recall him booming, "Best bloody school in the country, bloody waste of money" and it left me petrified. The irony is, her grades were very good; they just weren't what my stepfather had expected. Now he regrets his inflated response.

The continued traumas that punctuated my big sister's life were dramatic and sent her crashing in her thirties. Four-years-old when our father died, she was never told that he had passed away until much later. She was prohibited from seeing his dead body and never mentioned him again. His death plausibly had the most profound impact on her, since I was too little to notice anything. Yet, my big sister has no memories of him at all. My mother later told me that our biological father once said to my big sister, whom he doted on, "If you are naughty, I will go away and never come back". Is it not strange that, after such a close paternal bond, she acted as if he had never existed once he died? Did she blame herself as a child for the fact that he had gone? Whatever my theories, his death was profoundly traumatic for her. When I see how her life has played out, I wonder if it can all be traced back to this seminal loss. What I could not have foreseen was her own mental unraveling, such was her robustness as a child. She had also constructed her cocoon and, like mine, it had flimsy, thin walls. I recall visiting her to spend time with my niece and nephew in Barcelona. We'd been estranged for some years, ever since I had become mentally unwell. As soon as we met, I saw the same mental malaise in her eyes, heard it in her voice, felt it in her body language. It was tragically familiar.

The affliction that we have is specific to our family. It cannot be called depression, or bipolar disorder, or schizophrenia. It has such an infinite range of nuances, but when you have experienced it, you know it to be real. My mother does not like to use the term *mentally ill*. She is adamant that no doctor has ever diagnosed her as such; instead they said she was suffering from stress and grief. Rather than get bogged down in psychological semantics, I assert that a mental fragility[13] has plagued my family and continues to do so.

We all had this propensity for mental undoing, starting with my mother; as children, it was my middle sister who succumbed first, then me, then my big sister. Was it inevitable? Different circumstances may have constructed sturdier walls to withstand the force of grenades falling from the vast, open skies of life. There are some things that I believe the mind just can't withstand, such as the murder of your child, or the knowledge that your German grandfather was a Nazi who exterminated thousands of Jews. You can live life, but the mind is always straining under these heavy shadows of truth. What happened in my life and to my sisters and mother was tragic, but there are others who have endured the unthinkable and not mentally caved in like we did.

What often left me baffled, during my work in developing countries, was seeing extremely poor people having the resilience and drive to keep on moving forward, despite having little by way of clothes or food. Mentally, I became much healthier in these terrains. The sight of others, far less fortunate than myself, catapulted my brain into another gear, tossing me out of the tepid, solipsistic waters I liked to bathe in. The climate of abundance in the West breeds more narcissism and a victim mode of thinking. I am being harsh, but there is nothing like the sight of poverty to eject you out of your head. Having said that, relatively affluent people living in such countries, quickly become immune to the sight of suffering, just as the public becomes desensitized to inveterate reporting of war, rape and murder. What concern humans the most are the wars raging in their own heads first. Wars exacerbated by the strains of competitive daily life. These internal wars, that are raging in millions of minds at a micro level, reflect the wars occurring at a macro level. I see Fred in the impassive faces of dictators and oppressors; deranged and impervious as they brandish their guns and fire their rockets. Mental peace for one is one step towards mental peace for all.

The disorder's evolution could be perceived as a painting with many layers that become darker and more cracked with each application of the paint of life events. The smearing of ever-thicker impasto layers can't conceal what has transpired underneath. I sometimes refer to each day as a blank canvas – what kind of painting do you want your day to be? The colours signify your mood and the brush strokes are the words spoken and deeds done, to form the image of the final painting that is your day. We always have an opportunity to make a better painting the next day. Often I am creating the same painting, ripping it up and throwing it away, only to paint a replica of the one that preceded it in my head.

The first colour of my malady was a light and recurrent melancholy that followed me like a hum in my heart. It was always there. Even if I was laughing, the hum would return, reminding me that it needed attention. This sensation of chronic sadness was with me as early as four-years-old. Those emotions deepened perennially, despite my efforts to banish them away.[14] In my teens, my mother invited a psychologist to speak to all three of us. My big sister and I were staunchly resistant, the thick oak doors guarding the secrets we hoarded in our heads, remained shut. All I cared about was academic excellence, not emotional health. Work hard and you will be rewarded – this was my mantra. Excelling as a student seemed to be the key to flee the *saga of hell* that I equated with home. An extraordinary determination sprouted from nowhere, allowing me to get up on stage and perform in front of the whole school. I even won the Shakespeare Prize after a recitation of the famous soliloquy from *Macbeth*, "Is this a dagger which I see before me…" Little did I know, I would see daggers in my own head wielded by the hands of Fred.

My dogged desire to succeed was born out of a fear of failure and the pressure I heaped onto my bony shoulders became repressive. By the time I was seventeen this meticulously neat world of diligence and perfection was an acutely shallow one. My mind needed one final kick for those doors to open. It took a sexual assault (the first of a series), when I was seventeen and studying at Central Reference Library in Manchester, to instigate the mental crumble.

My parents didn't know what to do or how to respond to the first sexual assault. With no support or counseling, my weight plummeted and my brain went blank. Offered a conditional place at Oxford University to study History at Somerville College in 1991, I never told Oxford what happened either. I just struggled on. I attended Loreto College, which was in Moss Side, an insalubrious part of Manchester, rife with gangs who travelled in cars, often loitering outside the bus stop opposite the college. At sixteen, I was perceived as a desirable, sexual object. Men felt they could talk to me, look at me, honk their horns and make comments about my body and spew salacious remarks. It was enraging to see a man expose his penis on the bus, while seated adjacent to me. It was repellent to see another man expose himself while grinning, as I walked through the park with my sister. My first model agent in Manchester, Peter Martin, was jailed for drugging and raping the models; I had a lucky escape.[15]

These events happened thick and fast, one after the other. At college I had three different English teachers, two art teachers - who picked on me inexplicably - and a history teacher who was at first very encouraging but, after getting into Oxford, I received no extra tuition and became alienated, engaging in self-study instead. There was nowhere safe to turn, no one to talk to about the stuff at home, the bullying at college and the assault. I never informed Oxford about what had happened to me because I didn't know if this was an option, if they would listen or if it would make any difference to their decision. My mother was not culturally predisposed to talk about life, love, men and what to expect or how to be. When I was sixteen, my emotional maturity was probably that of an eight-year-old.

Against this backdrop I believed going to Oxford would make me a brand new person, becoming the painting I wanted to be. It was the wish of my late father that one of his children studied at Oxford: imagine having that hanging over your head? Instead, after dropping one grade[16] and abruptly losing my place, I became disillusioned. Swallowing the pain, I tried, stoically, to digest the bitter disappointment only to suffer a second sexual assault on a bus, months later. This time, I took the man to court and lost the case, which was devastating, reinforcing the belief that the good were punished and the bad rewarded. Perhaps it didn't pay to be good, then. My parents were extremely upset when they realised the Oxford dream was over, but then did I ever really want to go? All I wanted to be was an artist, an ambition they were ill equipped to encourage. To placate my parents, I completed my art foundation course at Manchester Metropolitan University half-heartedly, before going to the London School of Economics (LSE) to compensate for the Oxford failure. I concluded that the LSE was the next best university in terms of stature and surely going there would make them proud again. I remember getting my acceptance letter and feeling nothing much inside. At the LSE the mental condition took proper root and made a permanent home in my head.

The mental cracks that had formed years ago deepened after the assaults and losing my prestigious university place. There was no protective cocoon, into which I could retreat now. Unlike my husband, whose mind was open and empty with a view of the sky and the sea, mine became that old, rickety house, and the hoarding of memories on those dusty shelves continued. Perhaps early intervention could have led to the demolition of the house and the reconstruction of a spacious, new one, flanked by trees on a hill, with the view that I craved.

My mother – although this sounds like a contradiction – was and remains a formidable woman. Mine is not a sob story: it was her indomitable spirit that was passed onto her daughters. She often says, "I am happy that you are alive." To be alive was an achievement in her eyes and good enough. She was a pioneer workwise, wanting us to have autonomy and make our own choices. Although she tried to teach us Bengali (I later learnt the language phonetically during my work trips to Bangladesh), we were not taught to be and think like our Bangladeshi peers – that sense of our family being different was apparent. When I moved to east London I observed the Bengali community (who are mainly from the region of Sylhet) with a degree of bewilderment because they stick together, have their own vernacular, specific social mores, created a parallel community of shops and services, run the town hall, erected signs in Bengali and made themselves visible to the world. Not accepted by our fellow Bangladeshis, we were hybrids neither Bangladeshi nor British, just some one-off species that had no tribe and without a tribe you are rootless. My son already has a greater affinity with his father's side of the family; contact with my own is erratic and fractured (although much better now than it has been in years you never know when communication might cease for whatever reason, peripheral or otherwise).

I have received wonderfully humorous birthday cards from my middle sister, laced with the same humor we shared as children.[17] When I see the handwriting, my eyes light up. One card might have a cow on it and inside she's written, "Moooooo – you bloody cow", which makes me smile. If I picked up the phone and my sister and I spoke, would it just descend into a row? Sometimes it has. The last time we spoke we didn't row, but I soon became disenchanted by the conversation. Calling my middle sister is an irregular occurrence. Often I am overcome with sadness that these birthday cards, the odd text, erratic email correspondence (that on occasion can be unbearably rebarbative) and infrequent phone calls are the sum total of my relationship with her these days. Then, out of the blue, I will receive a heartfelt text or a passionate email with letters highlighted in bold, full of superlatives, hyperbole and positive affirmations and I dare to hope that we will meet, not fight and all will be well between us.

A stable family base produces a solid mind. Family is where the first clashes start; my family remains a peaceful war zone these days. It sounds paradoxical, but although there are times of ceasefire and calm, it remains a place I do not feel safe or understood, not knowing if I will get a bullet fired from an angry mouth that shatters my mind in an instant.

Avoiding triggers to stay well – and there are many – daily life becomes a stroll in a neighbourhood of invisible toxic atoms, excluding the ones in your head. Many might not have the will power to implement such input strategies, preferring to pop a pill as the solution for their mental woes, but in the long run is popping pills sustainable? Keeping a succinct version of your mental map in your pocket arms you with the vital knowledge to recognise those familiar, tired old narratives. It equips you to dismiss them, because knowledge of your mental map plants one foot in the real world, while psychosis transports you into an acidic web of narrative traps.

Only able to see one member of my family at a time, otherwise there is a risk that I can be triggered, in 2013 I resumed contact with my big sister. We started with consistent email contact, then we skyped (that was a breakthrough moment) and finally she visited. We didn't fight because she understood my triggers. There were times when I became manic, when I didn't want to sleep and insisted on talking about family stuff – topics that create mental heat– but I didn't relapse. Since the birth of my second child, she promised more visits, even if real life can get in the way.[18]

My stepfather also visited to help with the baby. Nervous about this initial meeting, since he has often inadvertently triggered me, the resumption of contact has been slow and cautious because psychosis is destructive and creates strong dissonant notions that are hard to dislodge. Now, after much hard work, my stepfather has a greater understanding of the key triggers. He rarely questions why things must be done in a certain way, he just does it, knowing that it keeps me calm even if he finds it challenging at times. Appreciating his efforts, I have tried to relax a little, not wanting this mental health condition to dominate my life. My mother, too, has persistently sent me beautiful cards and letters, which have become very precious. In these letters she apologises for the past.[19] Her apology has certainly assuaged the pain and helped immeasurably to dislodge the dominant, false threads, which are beginning to fall away. It doesn't take much for them to return though. Like weeds they grow back just as quickly as you pull them out.

The Obsessive - Compulsive Disorder and melancholia as a child developed into the depressive symptoms as a teenager. It is glib to talk of suicidal thoughts, or wanting to jump out of windows and in front of tubes etcetera, because I have experienced them time and time again, so much so that they have become an incorrigible recurrence. Fred's suicide bid doesn't scare me anymore, because I get the game; just as I get the games we play as a family and the games we play in relationships. It's easy to become lazy and make the same moves. It's much harder to be motionless and quiet and not yield.

At the LSE they had counselling facilities. Perhaps they could have encouraged me to plot my mental map. I was nineteen, there was a potentially bright future ahead, but I kept everything locked in a dark mental dungeon, refusing to talk about anything inside, believing it was a sign of weakness to be open. I recall a vivid incident when I was staying as a student in halls of residence at Commonwealth Hall. Dreary, with penitentiary-like corridors that reverberated with the slightest sound, the cleaning lady used to knock loudly on the door to empty out the trash. That knock was full of anger and felt like a slap each morning. That's when I just wanted to sleep in the darkness and the room became my burrow. I was so unwell I couldn't even go to the toilet. Such was my apathy, I would excrete in plastic Tescos bags and throw them out of the window. Surely, this was a sign that something was acutely wrong. Being incapable of completing a task as rudimentary as walking to the toilet filled me with increasing levels of self-loathing, and yet that corridor became a place I was afraid of, with its concrete walls, harsh light and the unsmiling face of the cleaning lady, whose mop resembled a gun.

I had met my husband to be within the first four weeks of starting university, he often says, "When I met you, you were not like you are now, you were *very* different. You used to make me laugh all the time and you were fun."

That person does exist inside, but she often gets smothered in the dirt that Fred keeps hurling at her. After leaving university I completed an MA (after being awarded a Channel 4 bursary). It was during this year that I dared to try to paint again.

This decapitated, blue nude was the part of a series I started after four languorous years at the LSE. I recall the hours spent staring at the blank canvas being intimidated and fearful of destroying the surface with an imperfect mark, not knowing where to start or if I even had it in me to make art that would be considered any good. The words of an opinionated ninety-year-old German art collector still reverberated in my head. I'd met him when I was nineteen, as a student in London, and nervously showed him some of my art. He announced dismissively, "Some people were born with a paintbrush in their hand and others were born with a pencil, you are the latter." I effectively stopped oil painting upon hearing his damning verdict.

Image 7. *Emaciated, Headless, Blue Nude 1* (acrylic on canvas, size 50x54 inches, 1997)

One evening, after months of inertia, I attacked that intimidating white skin and overcame my fear. The desire to create is within and if the desire is there nothing can impede you.

Shortly after film school I was elated to get into Art College to finally study a Fine Art degree at Chelsea School of Art and Design. Unfortunately, both the experience of film school and art school were littered with an array of tough challenges. And although I was, at long last, pursuing my ambition of being an artist, I was steadily becoming a little worse mentally each day, aligning myself with a coterie of the wrong sort of people in London and setting myself up for a colossal fall.

My brain became an entirely different beast when I smoked marijuana and skunk in my late twenties and early thirties. This intermittent, weed habit marked a turning point, contributing profoundly to the change in my mental condition. It was only when I began smoking that I identified Fred the Devil, Mia the Diva, and Sophie the Cloud Catcher. I was a puppet being controlled by all three at one point. Everyone adored Mia, because she wore makeup, high heels and was impeccably stylish and a riot. Mia is another creature, divorced from myself these days, although she pops up if I need to hide behind her glossy painted exterior. Sophie kept me dreaming and drawing clouds and trees. Fred was making me work, write, paint late in the night, ripping me apart, telling me to do things and then waging war in my head. Smoking weed/skunk, whatever it actually was, inched me closer towards psychosis. I was experiencing mania and hallucinations with excruciating lows and euphoric highs that left me aching for another suck of a spliff to get to that delicious, mellow, soaring place again.

For an exhibition I completed in 2007, entitled *Schizophrenia Part 1*, I exhibited as Sophie, Mia and Fred creating fake biographies for them. Here are the biographies of Sophie and Mia.

Sophie Cloud

Sophie Cloud, originally from Romania, studied both in New York and London, at Chelsea School of Art and Design and the Royal College

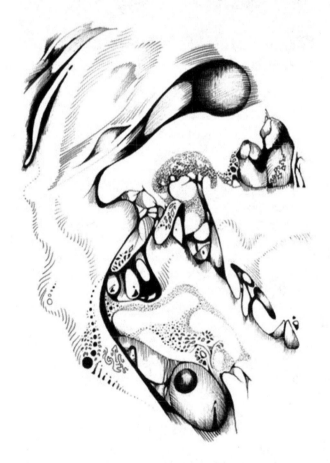

Image 8. *Brain Drawing* taken from my book *The Cloud Catcher*, which follows Sophie's quest to live in the sky and catch clouds (pen and ink on paper, size A5, 2007) I have at least five sketchbooks of these drawings, rendered in black and white meticulous detail. Creating them helped to navigate through some dark times.

of Art. She now lives and works in London. Her work focuses on the realm of the fantastical and imaginary. Taking inspiration from her name, Sophie is obsessed with clouds, the sky and nature. She predominantly creates landscapes in inks.

Sophie is also an activist and a performance artist. She famously rescued one thousand blue bells from a greedy dragon, has been known to console depressed butterflies and attempted to sew 100,000 clouds together to make the biggest cloud in the universe. She flew to the moon to spend time with a schizophrenic mouse that no longer liked cheese and just wanted to eat other mice. This experience inspired the film "On the Moon".

Some of her fantastical landscapes are on permanent show on the moon and a cloud floating over Pathuakali, Bangladesh.

Mia S.F. Heels

Mia Heels is half Brazilian, one-quarter Italian and one quarter Indian. She studied at Goldsmiths and the Slade, dropping out of both courses citing the degrees as "a load of cack". She is more famous for her looks and never-ending legs than her art. She is already a legend on Brick Lane and can be seen wearing outrageous outfits, in vertiginous red stilettos, cycling at break neck speed. For Mia, every day is a performance, a show and a spectacle. She recently starred in the yet to be released "Portrait of Madness" shot in Bangladesh, Nepal, Thailand, Vietnam, Cambodia, Miami, Malaysia, Indonesia and New York.

Mia's work deals with the body, sex, glamour, glitter – and explores the anthropomorphic qualities of the dildo. (In short she likes to poke fun.) She sees the body as something deeply aesthetic, but also metaphysical. Her work explores yearning, longing, desire, the body simply as object, the body as something powerful, the body as a source of pleasure and armour.

Mia doesn't like rules and this is reflected in her performance art, which is deeply socio/political, with maverick anarchic undertones and a dose of misandry. She famously castrated one thousand paedophiles and made them eat their own balls. She thrust a cucumber up Tony Blair's arse and was incarcerated for the trouble. She spat at the Queen because she thought she should experience abuse, as people do on the streets. She dressed up as Superwoman and whipped all the men's penises that happened to bulge at first glance of her while playing Capoeira on Brick Lane. Mia is quite a handful in real life; her art keeps her focused and temporarily out of trouble.

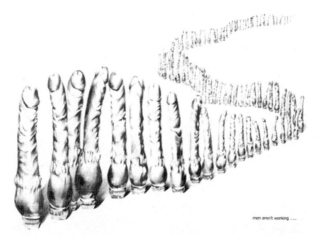

Image 9. *Men aren't Working* (pencil on paper, size A2, 2003). This dildo series examines the anthropomorphic qualities of the dildo with an ironic slant. Featured in different forms – ironic, menacing and provocative – this particular drawing was inspired by the 1979 Saatchi & Saatchi Conservative election poster campaign *Labour Isn't Working*.

Reading these pseudo biographies makes me realise I was slightly out of control, but I can't help grinning at the slight anarchism of my alter-egos.

I'd dabbled with weed briefly at eighteen when introduced to the drug by my first boyfriend. The world was an insufferable and unfair place; it didn't pay to be diligent and virtuous. (Losing my place at Oxford and being sexually assaulted turned my value system upside down). Smoking weed gave me the release I needed, but very soon I decided to stop, after sensing the changes in my mind with each puff. While studying at the LSE and throughout my first ten years in London, I abstained from any sort of drug and alcohol, even though I was in frequent contact with people where it would have been easy to experiment. It's almost unfair that after years of avoiding noxious substances, despite being offered them regularly, that smoking marijuana would change the neuroplasticity in my brain. It was a common assumption in the 1990s that weed was a mildly innocuous pleasure. Ironically, since I was a child I've been deeply suspicious of drugs and alcohol. The latter is a depressant, while drugs shave your neurons to shreds and screw up your brain. I didn't want to tamper with mine. In a moment of weakness I lapsed aged twenty-eight; that is not to say I wasn't culpable: no one put a gun to my head to smoke weed. It wasn't until 2009 that I finally gave up the drug. Although an occasional smoker, the times that I did smoke were corrosive enough.[20]

Could I then argue that those people with families who have a history of mental malaise should avoid any type of drug or alcohol? – I would say yes. My former psychiatrist, Dr Bass, told me, "Smoking weed is like cycling with the brakes on." I had sought help, but no one could help me, because I was not changing my life style of not sleeping, not eating properly and engaging in irresponsible and risky behavior, it is textbook stuff. I was also in London, away from my husband for long periods of time – in total eight years, on and off. I was cycling all over the city at odd hours, at breakneck speed, going through red lights while flashing obscene finger gestures at cab drivers, running on empty, travelling abroad for my work, surrounded by people who were more draining than nurturing, and often getting into fracas with strangers. The crashes had started to become more frequent and it was Dr Bass who diagnosed me with *schizoaffective disorder* in 2003.

I am arguing that mental health problems are generational, exacerbated by unfavourable socio economic factors. Without early intervention or networks of support, they can take seed, grow rampantly and permeate the future generations in your family. Since all my biological sisters are mothers now, I am determined to curb the spread of mental malaise. For that to happen you must start the hard work at the beginning of your children's lives.

The mind is a labyrinth and mine is a gigantic one, with aromatic flowers and spikes growing side by side. There are more flowers growing now and this makes me optimistic about the future.

Perhaps it is I who has major issues and an insurmountable block regarding the family. Although there is nothing like the birth of a baby to

Image 10. *My Dear Nephew* (oil on canvas, size16x14 inches, 2010)

melt a stubborn heart, familial contact remains detached, preferring the safe medium of email or the telephone rather than face-to-face contact. I also have minimum contact with my husband's family.[21] Is family the issue then? My husband says it is the *illness*, which keeps me away. This estrangement could go on for years, without having any compulsion to challenge a stale status quo. These barren years bleed into decades and then, it's too late. I don't want that, but I don't know how to find a way back into the fold, or if I could ever handle the *pressure* of acting normal with my in-laws. If only I could be myself and talk openly – that seems a remote and even unthinkable prospect.

The family featured heavily within my second psychotic episode. Calling my middle sister out of desperation, she hung up on me. Despite this seemingly callous response, my distress for the safety of my middle sister and nephew became overpoweringly acute. I believed that I was the only one who could save them; this *psychotic* narrative was steeped in my childhood dream of being close and dear friends with my sibling.

Image 11. *If God Existed He Might Look Like This Dude* (oil on canvas, size 16x14 inches, 2008). During the psychosis I kept staring at this painting believing that God was speaking to me through the eyes of this dreadlocked stranger.

Image 12. *100 Year-Old Soul* (oil on canvas, size 10x10 inches, 2009). During the psychosis the many portraits I'd executed of the homeless, the elderly and the destitute came to life and all the characters in the paintings began to speak to me. In that moment I felt their pain and it made me angry. I was on a mission to save all these lost, abandoned souls.

Of course I could not save her: she didn't want my input. It is only after I came out of the psychosis that I understood what the narratives meant. They were plucked from rusty strings deep within my subconscious, playing an intoxicatingly seductive melody that left me in a psychotic trance that became a frenzied dance and then an internal war, where I felt everything was at stake. It was all heightened to a hyper-visceral dimension. Believing that the whole of east London was full of clones and that my family, especially my mother, had been persecuted, all my childhood and adult memories were sewn together into this tremendously lyrical coherent story. My flat became my church and my paintings were infused with a profound resonance.

I talked to Rothko and Van Gogh and they were empathetic. Fred told me that if I completed certain tasks within a specific time frame then all the world's atrocities would be erased, we would return to *year zero*, life would finally be the utopian perfection I'd always dreamt of. If I failed, then all of history's atrocities would be inflicted upon my body.

Fred said I had to run naked down Brick Lane and I was hell bent on doing so to achieve this utopian fantasy. My husband, as a last resort, called the police. Taken to hospital barefoot, they wouldn't allow me to put on my shoes and while sitting in the ambulance I was utterly petrified and naked, apart from my husband's overcoat. Hard to write, there is an acrid taste in my mouth as I do so, the memory of both episodes remains palpable. The urge to remove your clothes during psychosis is very common, as if you want to strip yourself bare and be nailed to the cross as some sort of martyr intent on saving the world. The allusions to Jesus and God during my psychosis were potent, which is strange since I am agnostic and not at all religious (many psychotic episodes have these quasi-religious overtones). Nietzsche was right: *God is dead.* After psychosis, however, I wonder if there are other forces that come into play, an acute sensitivity to things that go unnoticed. When we were waiting to be assessed my feet looked blackened and my toes appeared like claws. The sounds were excruciatingly loud; I could hear Sylheti (a Bengali vernacular) seeping through the walls like a flood and see Bangladeshis, with rubbed-out eyes, staring at me through the spaces. I decided to stay reticent, my husband did all the talking and finally we were released. He let me wear his shoes, while he walked to the cab in his socks.

A Dissection of Psychosis is the topic of the next essay, where I try and plot what have to be the two most traumatic incidents in my mental map and which have impacted on every aspect of my life in its dull aftermath. Just as the survivors of an earthquake reconstruct a new town after the obliteration of the old one, I am doing the same, still clawing onto the memories of the mind that was dismantled and thrown away during psychosis. Even thinking about the details of both episodes generates heat that can whisk me back there. I have lost count of the number of times I have tried to write coherently about each episode, until finally being able to break through the fog in 2013. Of course, I had to write about both of them meticulously to exorcise them from my brain and stop the haunting of psychotic memories. Medically advised not to do so, I didn't heed the advice. I just decided to write about it all very slowly and carefully, like learning to walk again after both legs have been broken.

Motherhood, when you have mental health issues, is harder still. Along with dealing with the day-to-day tasks of keeping a home and nourishing a life, there is very little relief. Minds need time to replenish and rest. There is always the dread of more darkness, smothering the little light we try to covet. Nevertheless, I am lucky; my life could have been very different today. My husband told me that if he hadn't been there during my second psychotic episode, I would have been sectioned under the 1983 UK Mental Health Act.[22]

It is torture to write such things down, especially about members of my own family (and I have since edited more personal details because it seems like an unpleasant and unethical exposure, like a man flashing his private parts to an unsuspecting stranger). I also think that my writing is a gross simplification of life history events with massive holes that would take a million words to fill. This essay attempts to provide a rudimentary outline of what are extremely complex lives, to support the idea of mental mapping, a technique that could be used to not only help you explore your mind and the deep rooted causes of eventual psychosis, but maybe even prevent future generations from developing the condition. Psychosis is an intrinsic and dramatic part of my mental map, an event that has to be examined and documented in order to be laid to rest.

Despite the voluntarily imposed distance between my family and I (which is slowly beginning to diminish), my mother's letters (brimming with her eccentric idiosyncrasies) and now regular phone calls/Skype chats[23] all provide emotional nourishment - and I appreciate any amiable contact I have with my sisters. At least with email exchange, however heated, there can be no shouting voices and, just this morning, I was looking at old birthday cards, one had a chimpanzee on it, another had a

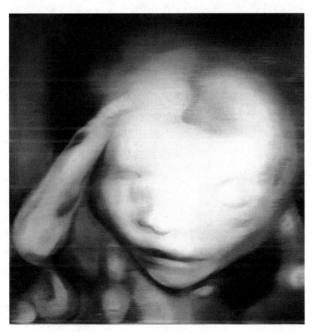

Image 13. *The First Son* (oil on canvas, size 10x10 inches, 2010) is based on his fuzzy 3-D scan in the womb. I made this painting to begin a dialogue with my baby before the birth; to try to connect and cut through the wall that had grown around my heart after the psychosis of 2009.

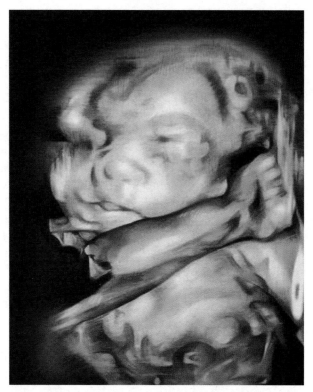

Image 14. *The Second Son* (oil on canvas, 10x10 inches, 2014). Also painted from a 3-D scan it was my unique way of trying to bond with my unborn child and penetrate the strange waves of negativity that were at times overwhelming.

drawing of a dog sniffing a fellow dog's bum. This is my family stumbling towards the right direction with our *unique sort of minds*. It was not easy being severed from the family; their absence left a damp, large, hole in my soul and a deepening ache.

Lapses are just around the corner, but the systematic implementation of my input strategies works. Keeping a mental map, adding to it, scrutinising it, keeping it close to remind me of what is real and what Fred has fabricated, writing a journal from my son's perspective, drawing and painting him, as I am doing with my second child and taming the beast with its sharp and hungry teeth makes me less like a helpless victim at the mercy of these violent shifts in weather, heightened by seemingly trivial, small events.

Just as I found it hard to feel much after the third month of pregnancy, my second one was even more challenging emotionally. Employing the same strategies, namely painting and writing, I made this painting to reach out, to say *sorry*, to explain to my unborn baby that I was struggling and fighting to stay well. Armed with my paintbrush and pen, "Everything will be ok," I told my baby.

Stephen Fry once wrote to me: "All I can say is that mood is like weather – completely real but guaranteed to change."

Having sat out this storm, as I have sat out many others, my sisters and I have let turbulence ravage our minds, tearing them to shreds and our lives, too, because we didn't know where to seek shelter. Life is a constant process of reconstruction and renewal. My son is a new life – a baby leaf with delicate fur lining and shiny green trim – that needs a mother who is able to help him build a strong wall, covered in ivy to stop that sleeping gene from growing into a sharp toothed giant who can bite and chomp and stamp all over him. My second child will need the same protection. The walls of my mind quiver daily, yet I diligently patch up those walls and keep them standing with thread, pins and magic tape, even though I know they can topple with the touch of a finger. I don't want to live amidst the rubble and dust, I dream of roaming in a mind that is a verdant, abundant garden with herbs, flowers, birds and bees.

Maybe the seeds of insights planted within this essay can assist others, similarly afflicted, pluck out the ugly, rotten plants that are ravaging the mental landscapes of too many people, leaving their minds derelict and starved. For some it is too late. I accept that if psychosis has been allowed to breed, inflicting recurrent episodes, it does corrode a mind down to a mental skeleton, because psychosis is like grievous bodily harm to the brain.

This rampant weed, worm, gift, curse, whatever it is, is here and I have tried to befriend and tame it and, instead, allow it to leave its violent footprint on my work. It is my intrinsic goal, as an artist, writer, wife and mother, to ensure that my children are sturdy and well on the inside first. If I can protect my children from Fred, then everything that my family and I have endured was worth it, because it has given me precious insights that can only be gleaned by experiencing them first hand however hideous, destructive and acrid.

Below is a poem taken from my book, *Eternal Pollution of a Dented Mind*, first published by Chipmunka Press in 2008, which deals with some of the themes of this essay. I have since reworked them.

To end, I recall something an elderly psychiatrist told me (the first one I, properly, spoke to). He said assuredly, "You will be alright because you are bright and have the tools to beat it."

I didn't quite grasp what he meant. Now, I think he was saying that, in my case, art and words were the best tools to tame the unsafe jungle of my mind. Slowly the poems began to form, then pitter-patter and rain heavily, to wash away Fred's excrement smeared on flimsy cardboard mental walls.

Poems, prose and fragmented lines can convey something tighter, leaner and closer to the truth than neat blocks of writing, bloated with too many words. Words can fundamentally get in the way of what I am trying to say. A poem, stripped down, comes closer.

A Small Cloud

A small cloud has been hanging over her
For as long as she could remember
Today the tears fell
Like slender rivers
The mask slipped off and fell to the floor
There she sat in the middle of the ocean
The dolphins were singing
And she didn't sing back
She threw small daggers at them
A little dolphin winked and squeaked
Opening her eyes.
She wasn't so alone anymore
Perched on a small rock, she stared out at the ocean
Kicked down the door of her mind
To take a gentle stroll.
What did she see?
More closed doors, not a shaving of light
Only a small cloud floating stubbornly
And a broken plate
"Chuck it away," a distant voice whispered
The landscape on the plate
Painted with such tender care
Faded now
Just an outline
"Time to paint a new picture," the voice whispered again
And step into a new landscape
With fresh things left to discover
She broke the locks of all the doors in her blurry mind
The clutter and debris spilled out
A constant noise that had been hurting her head
Grew louder
When all she longed for was a
Searing silence and calm
Not the ceaseless clamour that gave her a

Bloody headache everyday.
All those wasted words and
Meaningless chatter
That torments our tired minds
Instilling the panic
The fear to try and
Take risks
To suffer small deaths
When all she needed was
Silence
To soothe her heart
And stroke her mind
With a gentle finger.
She decided to embark on a new journey
One she wanted to make years ago
This sense of isolation
She carried with her since she was tiny
That bewildered girl
Tugging at her mother's sari
As she ignored her.
Her family was not
The warm tribe her heart ached for
Siblings
What to make of them all?
Some were allies
Others indifferent
And then there were the ones who
Stamped and stabbed her
To simply worsen the pain
She wished she could chuck all the garbage
Fastidiously catalogued
In neat rows
On dusty mental shelves.
She was tired of pretending
Tired of smiling
Tired of trying
She wanted to stand
Naked
Reach out and
Shout
 "Hello, this is me"
The one with a tiny, battered heart

The one
With a jumbled up junk shop of a mind
And tears that flow everyday
Causing major floods
And wounds that are bloody
Full of puss
Waiting to be
Healed.
An old friend,
A timid hedgehog,
Just as battered and bloody as she
Crawled up to her and said tentatively,
"Hello, I just got run over by a bus
But I am ok
Come over for tea
And let me put some Dettol on those wounds
They look infected
But with a little care and time
Like a Bonsai Tree
New leaves will grow
You will see,"
The battered hedgehog took her by the hand
Gave her shelter under a bush
Called home
Tickled the naked girl's ear lobe
Farted for the hell of it
And they both laughed until they cried.

CHAPTER 4

A Dissection of Psychosis

In my third essay, I argued that writing a concise mental map of the mind is helpful in understanding the deep-rooted causes of a mental malaise. Plotting the key life events that instigated a shift in the landscape of my own mind enabled the identification of recurrent, life-long patterns. Regarding psychosis, the quick succession of a series of cumulative, stressful events seemed to be the primary cause for the onset of my first episode. Other factors deepened the psychosis; it started with a rupture followed by more ruptures, which my brain rapidly tried to repair. As the stress and ruptures mounted, my mind flipped from the real world into the psychotic one, riddled with fast unfolding narratives that created deep mental lacerations. Just as you wince with pain if a large saucepan falls out of the sky and drops on your foot, the mind will buckle if it is repeatedly bashed. It is the unfolding of the unknown that can be terrifying. Befriending the unique idiosyncrasies of my condition was the first step in taming it.

The purpose of this essay is to demonstrate what happens when your mind suffers too many dents and caves in to psychosis. When you lose touch with what is real and true. Within the essay will be a series of narratives, which attempt to transport you to the time preceding the psychosis, before plunging you in the midst of the psychotic maze, so that you too can experience how easy it is to get ensnared.

Being in the throes of psychosis is something I am determined to avoid again. Equipped with the insights I have attained now, I think it is something I could have deftly dodged when it first came accelerating towards me. When I emerged from the other side, I thought the first episode was an isolated attack, then it struck again and, erroneously, I thought it would never happen another time. As a result of the first prolonged episode, a new code became imprinted on my brain. The times when I am lucid and calm make me hope that psychosis will never return, but it can quickly start up again, given a specific set of circumstances and triggers.

On the occasions when J, my former mental health social worker, came by we often talked about *hot* topics. Once she asked to speak to Fred. He began to speak from deep within, hurling abuse. There he was, the mighty man, standing tall in the pit of my belly, swinging from my ribs, like a crazed monkey, grinning as I tried to suppress him. Becoming more and more manic during the two hours she stayed, by the time she left I was tidying up, fanatically, as I used to as a child, wiping surfaces that didn't need wiping, seeing smears of invisible ever present dirt. Then I played music very loud to drown out Fred's derision. I told my husband upon arrival, "You'd better make everything look spotless, because Fred wants a fight."

Putting my son on the breast calmed me down. Apologising to my son, I explained that today Mummy's brain was red hot. He seemed relieved that I was quiet again. When he was asleep I got up, inspected the kitchen, and Fred leapt out, going for my husband with his clawed tongue. My husband told Fred to leave the room in a stern voice and eventually he did. I watched something easy and mindless on my computer, while the sounds of sirens outside began to encroach. Groaning quietly, I knew it was starting. There was an urge to write but I chose not to, opting to sleep instead. Danger was averted. My husband acted as if nothing had happened, as did I, the next morning.

That evening I said to my husband, "It must be hell for you, some days I am nice and friendly, other days you are the enemy and I am a monster with Fred bleating obscenities through my teeth. Does it make you sad?" He didn't say anything. "I suppose you always said you wanted to take care of someone," I added feebly.

He nodded, looking tired, saying, "Well it's not going to get better is it? I prefer not to dwell."

Is he right? Is it never going to get better, or could it potentially get worse over time? Sir Professor Robin Murray, the esteemed psychiatrist, wrote to me saying my disorder is not a degenerative condition. That's if you avoid further psychotic episodes. Another psychiatrist, whom I saw briefly during my second pregnancy, even proclaimed that it is possible to make a full recovery. Stunned when she said this, it filled me with a naïve hope for the future. Right now, potential future psychoses are sleeping in a padlocked cupboard in my brain waiting to break out if a precise pattern of behaviour plays out. If I had never let psychosis gnaw on big chunks of my brain in the first place, perhaps this wouldn't be the case.

Now that I know it can strike, I am arguing you can circumvent psychosis and this can be achieved without taking daily medication. Apart from the two major episodes, I've had more episodes after giving birth, which were harrowing, but not as intense. Each subsequent episode had all the tell-tale signs of the first two and, after these, I've had a succession of mini episodes, like the one described above, where I've been standing at the door of psychosis, experiencing the first stages, but not plunged into the

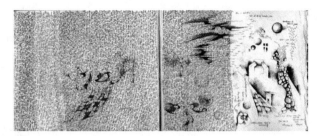

Image 15. *The Ants Are Coming Right At Me* (pen on paper, size A5, 2006). I started writing very small a few years before the psychosis. My handwriting was becoming progressively smaller and I didn't understand what it signified, all I knew was that it felt *safe* to write in miniscule, almost illegible, handwriting.

pit of it. If I had experienced another serious episode, one that lasts for days with accompanying sleep starvation, I don't think I would be sitting here writing coherent sentences. The scrawled notes of numbers, random words and thoughts that became precious and important at the time are, now, a sad reminder of how infirm my mind became as it scrambled for answers to unlock the code.

This approach to dealing with my mind is controversial, something other psychiatrists would not necessarily advocate. Although many mental health care professionals have commended my methods, they have also said, "You are an atypical case" and that I don't represent the norm. [24] There are people who choose not to take medication and live with their condition as I do, implementing strategies to manage their mind, but there is always the danger of a relapse into deep psychosis and eventually the risk of having to go on medication again. Thankfully, this has not been the case for me, apart from the need for emergency sleep medication during times of chronic insomnia.

However remarkable my efforts, mine is a risky strategy. You could argue that it is not possible for everyone to engage in such a life plan, just as it is impossible for many to adhere to a strict diet over a lifetime. It might not be appealing or realistic, you need a certain level of discipline and will power and I have my weaknesses (a propensity to work late, thereby not sleeping enough) and can then rapidly mentally deteriorate. I am also partial to chocolate and cake, my justification being that everything in moderation is ok. Very recently I started baking voraciously. (The last time I baked was at secondary school). Cutting out sugar, butter, dairy and wheat when I bake I've been attempting to make *superhappytreats* that will boost my moods and not leave me sluggish and flat. Baking quinoa and carrot cake packed with berries and chia seeds; fresh buckwheat bread laced with ground linseed; and cacao and beetroot cookies whizzed up from green powder, medjoola dates and coconut oil is satisfying. Each time I eat one of my *happy* cookies I become energised and feel good inside. The downside is that baking is time consuming and, as with most of my pursuits, can become obsessive in nature, yet right now my fridge is packed with *brain food* that is designed to keep me nourished. My baby can also consume some of these creations (in moderation). I will carry on experimenting with carrot, sweet potato and beetroot to create that perfect cake that is so nutritionally charged I will have no excuse to let my blood sugar plummet and perhaps find a sure way to stabilise my moods.

Crucially, will any of the *superfoods* I am feeding my baby fortify his brain mentally? I don't know, but it's worth trying. Foods that increase serotonin levels (pumpkin seeds, for example) or are high in fish oils (salmon and sardines) are easily available; if diet and nutrition from birth and beyond will shield my children, from the dodgy gene, I will carry on providing such foods. I couldn't stop my children inheriting my genes, but I can influence their dietary consumption.

Oddly my weight has roughly stayed the same, around fifty kilos, since I was eighteen, no matter what I consume, even if I am sedentary (I can be working at my desk in the evenings for hours into the early morning) and after two pregnancies. I don't necessarily think it's because of a fast metabolism. My explanation is my mind burns calories like a juggernaut, because it's never off and I don't sit still for long. There is this constant urge to do, to move, to fidget, to paint, to write.

Describing both psychotic episodes will demonstrate how far removed from reality the mind can stretch, like a piece of elastic pulled taut to its absolute limit, until it snaps – the snap is the crash back to life – which can be more traumatic than the psychosis itself. In fact, that is an understatement, a better description would be two hands kneading your brain, pulling and tugging it and planting all kinds of things in it, stirring and tearing it and then mashing it up and stretching it again. There is a huge internal resistance in my brain to recall the details of what happened. Perhaps the brain is scared. As I write, I can hear sounds in the background that seem like angry rumbles emanating from the earth's core, warning me, "Don't go there, you fool". But I have to. If I don't my life will be a truncated one, with half of me in the here and now and the other half hanging about with those dreary, psychotic ghosts.

Shortly after the second episode, I attempted to write about the psychosis in the form of a novel, referencing numbers and the code 3,6,9. Such was the burn in my brain each time I sat down to write that I aborted the effort. Advised to discontinue writing the novel when I fell pregnant in February 2010, for risk of mentally lapsing and jeopardising the heath of the baby, I complied, but there has been an itch to return to that inhospitable mental terrain and several half-hearted attempts after that. This is my final stab at it. You are probably exasperated urging me to, "Just get on with it and stop pontificating." It is not so easy, although I can't forget what happened, it has left behind a muddle in my head, blocking the flow and creation of new memories. I call this *Continuous Psychotic Block* that appear in the form of sounds and flash backs, robbing you of happiness because they wrap you in a cling film of terror. Cling film, because it is flimsy and easy to tear through, but the mind elevates it into something else that seems like barbed wire and impossible to escape from without drawing blood.

Why put my brain through what is clearly going to be onerous? My mind has actually constructed a fairly sturdy wall to deter me from *going back there*. The ghosts of psychosis sometimes walk right through the wall and stand pointing and laughing in my face, reminding me of how they made me dance like a performing animal while dangling mouldy bananas as bait. Granted, there are quite a few detailed accounts of psychosis out there and they all have very similar themes bleeding through them, yet each episode is unique to the mind of that individual. I am more interested in the build-up and root causes than the details of the psychosis itself, which will be impossible to recall in their entirety without tying my brain into tiny knots. If I can write a broad, analytical dissection of the psychotic narrative, then it is worth attempting. If I don't, these ghosts will dog me for years to come; and each second dwelling on what happened is a fatuous waste of life.

2009 – The Year Psychosis Fell Out of the Sky and Infected My Head

Although the first episode occurred in December 2009, it was building up years before, reaching a crescendo in January 2009, the year I would turn thirty-six. My nemesis Fred had made a pact with me. He said, "If you kill yourself then you can join your father in heaven and achieve that stupid peace of mind you long for."

My father never made it to his thirty-sixth birthday; it would be something of a milestone for me, if I could reach it. Fred taunted me, unremittingly, with this death wish. Dreaming about killing myself constantly, in the months leading up to my birthday in April, I bought blades and pills; it was pathetic actually – even risible. I knew it was. The shame of what I was preparing to do didn't stop me telling people about Fred's death wish, I even asked specific individuals if they would be willing to look after my archive of art after I had gone. They all agreed, saying I wouldn't have to worry. Rather than allay my distress it made me more paranoid, thinking they all wanted me dead to get hold of my precious art. Others laughed it off saying, "Don't be ridiculous, you aren't going to do it, just stop talking about it because you are getting boring."

These days I hardly tell anyone I have been diagnosed with schizoaffective disorder. But initially, shortly after the diagnosis, my inhibitions vanished and I would tell people – virtual strangers even – that I was *mentally ill*. It was a catastrophic mistake. Only my innermost trusted circle needed to know. The more people you tell, the more open to abuse you become. I might be setting myself up for vitriolic attack penning this book, but it is a risk worth taking if the questions I raise instigate an open discussion about the stuff of the mind – the stuff that matters.

Just before my birthday, I had an exhibition at LSO; a large converted church on Old Street in London, organised and attended by members of a well-known public arts organisation. I had to install the show in three hours, as well as sit on the panel and read two poems, *Can a Mouse Fall in Love With an Elephant* and *The Suitcase,* to a sea of seemingly stony faces. I recall reciting my poetry and feeling Fred's presence. There was a wall of *Fred paintings* to my left and I sensed him standing there, dressed in black, staring with mocking eyes. There were also three faces in the audience, who appeared as devils. When I spoke I referred to one of my colleagues as *God* and noticed that her forename actually featured in my name in its entirety. She was Bosnian and I was Bangladeshi and then I noticed the B's in Bosnia and Bangladesh and that if I inverted them they became the number 3 and that these B's in my life, which were actually 3's, were everywhere and all these connections were profound and steeped in an allegorical divinity. Associations began to form, pulling all the strands of the *code* together which punctuated my family's history, unravelling in my mind with extraordinary rapidity months later.

The build up to my birthday was excruciating, planning the ending of my life dominated the first four months of that year. Although longing for death, I informed my mental health social worker, Claudia, and a few close friends about my morbid state of mind. The ending that I longed for, ultimately, didn't happen. It was a relief, but strangely I felt like a failure for not going through with it after telling everyone I was going to commit suicide. These were just Fred's games, which continue today. Before my son was born, Fred was forever telling me to chop my head off or stick my face on the hob or drink bleach, now his malice was transferring to the children. Choosing to ignore Fred these days, I understand the rules of the game he's playing. Sometimes I shudder when I experience intense visualisations of his vile instructions. Playing out like short films they leave deep scratches to the brain, making it sore and bleed.

These hallucinations, riddled with complex narratives, peak during psychosis, where the brain is working in overdrive and descends into fight or flight mode, thinking that the danger is imminent. It is the adrenaline and dopamine rush, which makes you talk without breathing or pausing. Your life speeds up by three hundred per cent and you are running a race you have to win, or risk losing everything.

My birthday party took place at Shoreditch House in London, two days earlier than the actual date.

I remember setting up the party on my own in the bowling ally, blowing up balloons, feeling subdued and slightly morose. People came and had a good time and then I decided to read a poem, just before I was about to cut the cake.

36

Sometimes it gets very fuzzy in my head
And I can't see the clouds anymore
I grow sad and give up
Curl into a tiny ball and Fred clings onto my toes and won't let go
The last birthday I had, when I felt truly happy
And free was when I was nine-years-old
My mum had made me this awful dress out of curtain material
It was turquoise and pink
All I wanted was to be the prettiest girl in the room
My fringe was wonky
My teeth were crooked
And my legs were dangly
I was a sorry sight
All my friends came
There was a big cake that was a bit squashed
But even then
I sort of felt alone and thought who are all these little girls
They are not my mates, yet it was my happiest birthday, in a fucked up sort
    of way
Cling to this notion that I am alone
That I have to conquer my demons
Even when I would like to reach out and hold someone's hand
Presume that the skin is clammy and I might catch something awful
So off I go, when perhaps I should reach out.
A lot has happened since I am about to turn 36
Was supposed to kill myself on my birthday

Had it all meticulously worked out
Was going to lock myself in my room
Stare at some blades and a bunch of pills
And will my life away
I thought no one's going to notice
Life will carry on and everyone will go about his or her business.
This is bollocks, I realise that now
Last November I lost a friend of mine. I loved him dearly
He snorted the white worm and his infected heart
Stopped pumping
I think about him, try to reach out and talk to him
But I can't hear his voice anymore
Life is precious, my late father died before his prime
I never knew him
He was a handsome man with style,
I have his eyebrows and nails apparently
He was a popular man, too, and used to sing and drive a VW white beetle
Actually, my father was the 5th member of the Beetles in another life
He used to say, when my mother became trapped in a morbid web,
"Why wish for death when death comes to all of us?"
And so I say to my Daddy, sitting up in heaven, that I am not about to join
    you just yet
I am going to try and be strong even when
I am flagging, weak and lonely
Will try and reach out to good souls and feed myself
When I am starving
Will try to be kind to myself and give without wanting or clawing
Will try to smile when I feel like crying because it is painful and too much
    effort to frown
My dad never made it to his 36th birthday, but I, bloody well, will
Thanks for being here
I love you all in my own warped, twisted, sweet eccentric way.

After I finished reading the poem, there was silence. My friend Dani told me, with a grin on her face, "Dude, why the fuck did you read that shit man? It was so embarrassing."

Someone arrived late; someone I had been trying to extricate myself from for years, someone who had become a toxic and negative influence. If I didn't leave London and cut myself off from the people I had become embroiled with, I might lose my husband and the prospect of having a child and family of my own. The stable existence my mind craved would also be in jeopardy. The chaotic life I had led for eight years had become normal.

My life was dysfunctional, reasserting stability was something I mentally, staunchly resisted. Artists were supposed to pursue an unconventional, bohemian, left field path with a lick of hedonism and debauchery. I was fulfilling the role, that's for sure, but my soul was dying a slow death.

Finally breaking away from London and all those that had kept me there, created a massive rupture in my brain. The other dominant influence was my closest friend and confidante, the philosopher: an astute, charismatic and canny businessman who was, openly, without much moral compunction in the conventional sense. Our conversations were like no other, endlessly interesting. During lavish suppers and all night dancing we conversed for hours about everything and nothing; some might call it pseudo, philosophical nonsense. My husband dismissively referred to our discourse as intellectual masturbation. Now I can't properly recall what we ever discussed – at the time, though, it was completely engrossing. I saw him as my metaphorical male twin separated from birth. Severing contact with him was, equally, very hard.

All these people were creating dents in my brain. There was a consistent stream of them all jabbing and gouging. It was impossible to achieve extrication from them without some mental fallout, because they had been the glue keeping the plate of my life together – a plate that had been smashed multiple times cracking into 3,699 tiny pieces, which I had tried to piece back together painstakingly. As my stepfather wisely told me, "It's time to throw away the old plate, you need to get a new one."

After the last guests left I cleared up. Making my way down in the lift I saw the philosopher with his then girlfriend. He'd completely forgotten my birthday, even though he knew about Fred's death wish. It felt like a callous betrayal. It seems inconsequential now, but this oversight rendered our friendship hollow in that instant. We'd known one another for over a decade; now I began to question the substance of the union. The people in my life were not nourishing, they left me eviscerated; in fact I let them chew on my flesh. Physically I was gaunt, emaciated even. I needed the metaphorical food of stability, consistency and a trusted network – not dressing up, going out, cavorting, posturing and preening in towering heels. The philosopher went on his way and as the lift opened, two famous artists, Peter Doig and Dinos Chapman, walked out. Living in the East End I had collided with most of the *big name* artists of the day. I had the gall to start talking to these two and persuaded them to come for tea, recalling the time we had met before in a pub in Kings Cross when I was twenty-three-years-old. It was the early hours of the morning and a completely incongruous thing to do, but it was Mia who was in charge now, she'd taped my mouth shut. Inviting relative strangers to my home had become commonplace behaviour.

Dinos said, "She's mad, you read about women like her, she will chop us up into small pieces and we'll be discovered in plastic bags the next day." Peter seemed to be more obsessed about my age and insisted, "Take off that silly hat."

Hoisting up my long dress, folding it into my red belt, I cycled to my flat off Brick Lane. We had tea; they sat and stared at all my artwork, not quite expecting what they saw.

"This is a lot of work," said Peter. I stared at these famous artists and they seemed like the most ordinary people, refusing to talk much about themselves, asking me all the questions. As they left, I showed Peter a tiny book of sketches of landscapes drawn in Thailand with microscopic photographic detail.

"You really are very good aren't you?" Peter said. I didn't say anything. After they left I felt ridiculous, stupid and empty.

Fred was laughing his head off, "You fucking sad idiot" he said, "do you really think you are in their league, do me a favour and go kill yourself."

In the months that followed, trying to steer clear of certain people and marijuana proved futile as long as I was in London. Due to move to Brussels, where my husband was based, I kept on returning to London. It wasn't hard to find the people that I needed to avoid, getting hold of weed to have a smoke, mounting my bike late at night. I often told myself that, "Fred and Mia are making me do all this bad stuff, stuff that is harmful to me." It was a lame excuse.

During this time I wrote a novella entitled *A Short, Sharp Adventure in New York Followed by a Sly, Sudden Descent into Hell*, three further

Image 16. *Honeymoon Sketch of Some Place in Thailand* (pencil on paper, size A6, 1999)

volumes of poetry: *Can a Mouse Fall in Love With an Elephant? Dented* and *A Further Dent*, several short stories and essays. A project that consumed my time over several years was a novel: *Is it – 369* comprising sixty fragments about the adventures of Sophie, Mia and Fred during the years 2001 and 2009, from the ages of 29 to 36. The pattern of 3, 6, 9 appears again, this coincidence perturbed me no end during the psychosis. The sixty fragments depict a life unravelling at a speed that leads to the unavoidable mighty implosion of the brain. I was also making paintings, working hard on my scroll, and generally being disturbingly prolific. Words seemed to gush out of me, sleep came patchily, and my life was still on hold. Cooped up with Fred ranting nonsense that reverberated in my head, most days, it was not healthy. While Mia also ensured that I constructed an elaborate and glamorous veneer to hide behind, which dazzled and entertained any willing audience. I was acting, every day, while getting increasingly knackered.

One night I cycled from High Street Kensington at around 4 or 5am, filming the whole journey with one hand on my mobile phone, while screaming out to unsuspecting pedestrians, "I'm making a movie." When I finally arrived back home, dawn was breaking and I danced outside under an umbrella of pink light, before collapsing indoors.

I fast forward to November 2009, it is raining, cold and dark; the dreariness of London is interminable. In Brussels, I am able to work for hours, eat and sleep well. Life is ostensibly good. Each time I return to London I revert to old ways. Despite my earnest efforts to keep abreast of certain dodgy characters, I can't.

Naively, I think periodic interaction with certain people is possible without any repercussions. On a sanguine note, I did move to Brussels, after eight years of vacillating and roaming the wilderness like some half-starved, crazed animal. Settling in, after an awkward and reluctant start, I have forged a new life and yet you can't create a new life while still clinging onto the old one with its *rabid* ways.

In the weeks leading up to the psychosis, a series of events happened in quick succession. I was working on a number of murals for an upmarket restaurant, *Hix* in Soho. I'd met Mark Hix at the Rivington restaurant, which he formerly owned. At the time I was writing in microscopic handwriting while seated at the bar. Not knowing who he was, I persuaded him to come to my exhibition *Schizophrenia Part 1* at the Truman Brewery in 2007. Seeming to like my dildo drawings he asked to purchase one, as well as asking me to doodle in the toilets of his Farringdon restaurant. Pleased with the art I created, we struck up a good working relationship. Telling me that either I could get paid or have a tab, I asked for the tab, and was astonished when I received a contract stating the tab was valued at twelve

Image 17. *Doodle 5 for Mark Hix* (acrylic ink, acrylic paint, gold leaf and pen on painted wood) I completed this painting in Mark Hix's Soho restaurant in 2009 working directly on the walls of the men's toilets. Making this work was intense and taxing, especially executing the tiny writing.

thousand pounds. It was staggeringly generous. Swiftly learning that Mark was a well-respected chef and an avid art collector, he seemed to like my work; I valued his support and respected him too.

I built up a reputation, of sorts, for doodling in upmarket toilets, having created artwork in the toilets of Shoreditch House, too, in 2008. My husband told me, "Your work is too good for the toilets, it is demeaning for you to do this."

Perhaps he was right; at the time I never thought of it like that. On the contrary, I believed when people urinated or defecated, they should have something visually arresting to look at. Inseparable during our first ten years together, my husband was my protector, guiding and advising me, but after he moved to Brussels I didn't do such a good job of this on my own in London. Incapable of saying "no", incapable of being discerning, every opportunity was a "great" opportunity and not to be missed. There was something very desperate about my manner and perhaps people could see this and took slight advantage because I let them.

As soon as I arrived back in London from Brussels, I would cycle over to the Brewer Street restaurant and paint for hours, writing in my miniscule hand in the toilets, as people came and went. Before I could hide in the cubicles and work discreetly, but in these toilets I was working directly on the walls instead. Working in the women's toilets was fine, apart from the occasional inane comment. Trying to work while men were urinating and clearly finding my presence titillating, was stressful. And yet, I wanted to make beautiful art and felt grateful for the opportunity. Mark also asked if I wanted to create a mobile, I said, "Yes" almost immediately. At first Mark and his business partner said they would put my mobile in the toilets, because I was thinking of incorporating the dildo motif. After I protested, Mark kindly agreed to put mine next to Damien Hirst's of fish in formaldehyde. Looking at all the mobiles in the restaurant how could I possibly compete? The challenge was a daunting one, and yet I was not able to say, "I don't think I can do this".

I'd come to London, not to paint in the toilets, but specifically to participate in an exhibition in which I was showing *A Soul on a Scroll*. Cycling from east London to south Kensington, dripping with sweat when I arrived, starving and manic I locked up my bike, removing my coat and helmet, knowing that people were watching from inside their cars. London was my stage and life was one big performance. I was always performing, not knowing who I was anymore. Disorientated, I tried to regain my composure. During my poetry recitation my gangly arms were flailing, I spoke very fast and people stared, with complete fascination, as if I was an alien creature.

Seated at a table, unrolling my scroll, I sat down to work as part of a performance piece. Actually, just as people become less nervous after a

Image 18. Mia performing at the opening night of a group show in London, 2009 – a few weeks prior to the first psychotic episode.

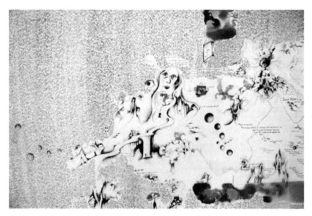

Image 19. Detail 4 from *A Soul on a Scroll*, (mixed media on 30-foot scroll of paper, 2012)

drink, I felt better with a pen in my hand. It allowed me to avoid eye contact and remain productive instead of engaging in idle chatter. As people came over they placed their wine glasses on the paper skin of the scroll, which had taken years to create. I became totally incensed.

People wanted to take my photo, were coming by to chat, and all the while my brain was getting hotter and I was talking faster. Deciding to leave, even then people watched, as I got ready to mount my bike in my red stilettos. Tossing my head back I laughed, living up to Mia's flamboyant persona. Cycling back into town, eating an apple with one hand (I was hungry) and not wanting to dine alone, I invited my friend the philosopher for dinner. When I locked my bike a man followed me into the restaurant and became abusive, saying he would call the police if I didn't park it

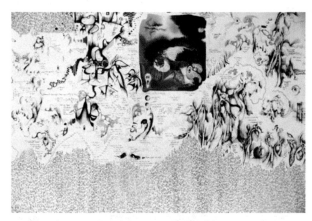

Image 20 Detail 5 from *A Soul on a Scroll*.

Image 21. Detail 6 from *A Soul on a Scroll,* (mixed media on 30-foot scroll of paper, 2012). Starting the work in 2007, I completed a little every day or when I could. I recall writing the first line of the scroll and groaning at the prospect of beginning the journey, knowing it was going to be a feat of endurance. By the end, my hand was aching and swollen. There was an addictive quality to working on the scroll plunging you into a meditative state and being transported to other worlds.

elsewhere. He was shouting and I thought, *this happens to me a lot*, so after being polite, initially, I yelled right back, "Go have a wank and die you fucking bastard," before obliging and parking the bike in another spot.

One of my standard lines of abuse, I would never say such a thing to an angry man today in case he might kick the shit out of me. Audaciously unafraid in those days, I swore at strangers on a daily basis, especially when I was cycling very fast and people *dared* to get in my way. Arriving

Image 22. Portrait of Mia (oil on canvas, size 10x10 inches, 2011). When I look at this portrait of Mia, she looks fake and manufactured. I understand her allure, but I resent Mia, she got me into repeated trouble because I didn't know how to handle her power, I still don't, but it helps that I am getting older. Mia is unimportant these days and almost, peripheral.

at the restaurant, the layers of winter clothes came off as a performance, revealing the skimpy, orange, backless silk dress I was wearing, people ogled, and I felt all their eyes on my body. Mia was parading as a sexual object. Now, such a scenario makes me cringe. Mia was outlandish in everything she did. Certain items, such as my large, felt purple hat, became part of the elaborate costume she donned to face society. It was something that the philosopher nurtured, he always wanted Mia to come out and play.

The philosopher frequently told Fred to "fuck off" and although he found me interesting, it was Mia he was seeking, consistently encouraging her to dress in a risqué fashion, "The sluttier the better", he would say. Preferring chic and elegant, I was often in conflict with Mia's outlandish sartorial proclivities. She always seemed to win though. Mia revelled in all the attention; I did not and found it, decidedly, unnerving.

The philosopher arrived; he was late. Sitting down to eat, the conversation quickly descended into something unpleasant. Our friendship had changed after I became artist in resident on his pet art project. Not used to

Image 23. Series of self-portrait sketches, begun when I was eleven to present day, (pencil on paper, size A3, 1998). I have completed numerous self-portraits over the decades, but this one reflects how I see myself. A girl who is searching for answers, scraping for a way out, a little haunted, often melancholic, overly sensitive, fragile yet fierce who, despite it all, could still muster a smile and a giggle. But be warned those bony shoulders could poke your eyes out if you get too close.

operating within a company hierarchy and acquiescing, I found the process stultifying. The friendship became tenuous, no longer the passive passenger on the philosopher's train, I had hopped off and preferred to cycle instead. He was losing his protégé. My husband later said somewhat disparagingly "Don't worry he will find his next willing victim."

More specifically, the internal landscape of my own mind changed dramatically in 2006, after an evening at *Synergy*, a club night in SE1. While I was there with the philosopher, I came upon a diminutive bearded chap selling cookies for a pound. At the time I was ravenous and paid my pound willingly. He told me openly that the cookies were laced with skunk – the smell was pungent. Nonetheless, I gobbled up my cookie without much thought. Very soon I was laughing hysterically, then I became acutely paranoid and my mind seemed to be flowing like the waves of the sea, back and forth. Unable to sleep that same night, I called up the philosopher and it soon mutated into a *perverse* conversation. He found it all very *interesting*,

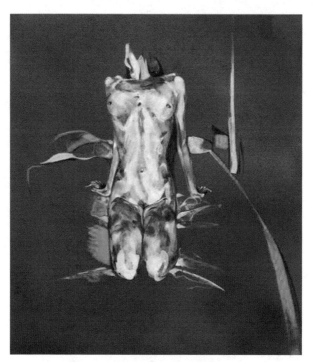

Image 24. *Painting of Mia on a Red Bed,* (acrylic on MDF block, 16x16 inches, 2000). I have painted a series of nudes of Mia, usually headless or faceless, playing with notions of being just a body, woman as a sexual object, in control or existing to be controlled, in charge of her body or inhabiting a body that has become fodder? I see beauty in the naked form, but I find it repellent too. This painting is almost a cliché, an arresting one though.

but I was completely off my head. Unable to sleep for three days, I called up people I hadn't spoken to in years declaring my love for them all, as well as writing hoards of emails. People were either very amused or didn't respond to my outpourings. The mental consequences were catastrophic. The philosopher wanted to meet up on the third day, Mia was having a ball and wanted to go out and have fun. Trying to rein Mia in, I called another friend, he came round and told me to go to sleep and get some rest.

Finally, emerging from the skunk *trip*, I felt as if something had changed inside my head for good. It was the most intense thing I'd ever experienced. Never managing to live down that episode, nothing was ever the same afterwards.

That night at Synergy, I'd eaten a piece of the devil and now he was inside me, sitting with Fred plotting their next move, at least that's what it felt like. Would I go the way of Peter Green, The guitarist from the band Fleetwood Mac who went on an ill-fated acid trip in Germany?

Were they trying to steal my brain? Cut off my fingers and pluck out my eyes. There were *metaphorical* devils everywhere, and I was cavorting with them, in my head and in the playground that was London. When I speak of devils, I am referring to the dissonant energy and people that everyone encounters. If a shop assistant is churlish, I often believe that Fred has infected that person. If a cab driver is abusive, I will see Fred in his eyes. If I read about an unscrupulous dictator, I will say he has made a pact with Fred. If something bad happens that I find intolerable, it will be Fred up to his tricks. Now, disturbingly I see the face of Fred in Jihadi John, brandishing his knife menacingly as Fred does, telling me to slit my throat as John slits the throats of innocent, good men who don't deserve such a despicable, gruesome, undignified death. I struggle to grapple with what is happening in the world, as Fred seems to be taking hold of the reins of power.

Fred's presence is pervasive, but it is easy to blame everything on Fred and allow him to contaminate my perception of people and the world obliterating all that is inherently good within it.

Even though I wanted to go home, Mia yearned for the old times and agreed to go elsewhere to talk and waste away the night. As I walked towards my bike, I saw it lying on the ground. It looked as if it had been raped and kicked to death on a side street – I was distraught. I know it was just a bike but, painstakingly hand painted, to me it had been a trusty companion, my psychedelic spaceship and loyal protector. The philosopher dropped me off at my flat, helped to deposit my beleaguered bike, and invited himself in for tea making lascivious comments with a wry grin. Throughout our friendship, he'd never been that scrupulous about personal hygiene, often reeking of stale body odour, with blackened fingernails. He always seemed oblivious and I tolerated it, even though his physical presence polluted the air I breathed.

During the psychosis I penned a passage where I came up with an elaborate theory. It was an erroneous one, but at the time I thought it was entirely plausible. The reason why he didn't notice his body odour was because his soul was rotten and the rot permeated the very core of his being, contaminating all those he came into contact with. If I kept him in my life, at that specific juncture, when I was mentally weak, I might have fallen the way of Oscar Wilde's *Dorian Gray*, ending up with a soul that was riddled with worms and gnawed away by maggots. Sometimes I thought I saw maggots in the philosopher's eyes that twitched, it could have been Fred's tricks. Was it the philosopher or Fred who had already planted maggots in my brain, years ago? They were copulating and feasting gleefully. Asking him to leave politely, he advanced towards me, placing his hot hands on the flesh of my back; my body recoiled and stiffened like wood. Wanting to scream, "Get your hands the fuck off me", I knew that this would be the last occasion I saw him for a very long time.

Several years after the psychosis we met up in 2013. Years had passed and maybe I thought, as a new parent himself, his lust for hedonism would have abated. Perhaps I wanted him to see my mid-career retrospective at Rich Mix in London and show him that I had not crumpled into a mess, but built a whole new life, a better one than the life I'd led before. When I tried to tell him about the psychosis, he appeared bemused, disinterested at times, insensitive, and more concerned about my sex life. He also dealt me the blow saying if I had not initiated contact, he never would have bothered. This admission stung somewhat, although unsurprising. I said, "But I was very ill." It fell on deaf ears. Since then our contact has been infrequent, and this was after, literally, baring our souls to each other for years. At the time he was the closest thing I had to a sincere and enduring friend, and I miss those carefree times, slightly rose-tinted perhaps, but stuffed with fond memories aplenty. I have even invited him to Brussels to visit the Magritte museum, a painter he much admires, and share my favourite haunts with him. Although he says he would love to come, it has yet to happen. In a recent email to him I wrote:

... I do miss London, especially cycling on a balmy summer's evening, miss our never ending chats, our late gluttonous feasts and delirious dancing, but motherhood offers something else, something deeper, and that was then and this is now and when my baby gazes at me with those impenetrable blue eyes I can see the universe in its entirety and almost understand what life is about, if not for a second. The coruscating clarity is gone, the fog returns, there is a storm, it is dark, the baby blinks, the light shines and I can see again and fumble on. We must fumble and stumble and simply carry on mustn't we?

He didn't respond to my words (not intentionally, he's "madly" busy and emails can get lost in his spam box, or so he has professed). Words are my way of reaching out and often these sentences written deep in the night never receive a response that could be described as meaningful. In Bangla he would be dismissed as a "ha ha, hee hee, hoo hoo" friend, a good times only friend, or a party friend. These days I am overly cautious in my interaction with others and, due to my predilection for *Fred* types, find it difficult to make new and lasting connections with people.

The next day, after the ignominy of the bike fiasco, the arts organisation called to tell me that my show, which had been scheduled off Brick Lane, had to be cancelled. After devoting months of careful planning to the project, the officer in question was effusively apologetic.

"But why?" I asked, trying not to blubber down the phone.

"We can't take the risk. Certain 'people'[25] have threatened to boycott the show because they think you are a bad role model."

"What?" I retorted. I couldn't quite believe what I was hearing.

He was referring to a *Time Out* interview in which I had spoken about a taboo subject that was a ticking time bomb in the community. I had gleaned this information, inadvertently when discussing general community issues, from a lady who worked for Tower Hamlets Council specialising in sexual health.

At the time of the *Time Out* interview I was unwell and uninhibited. As soon as I divulged the statements, I immediately wanted to retract what I said, knowing the details could be misconstrued and were, potentially, inflammatory. Telling the journalist at the time that it was, strictly "off the record" she included my comments anyway. The article has since been removed from the internet at my request. My words were taken out of context. But I will stand by the fact that many men have accosted me. I saw an Asian man being given a blowjob by a working prostitute near the bins outside my flat, as I cycled home one evening. Another man, donning religious garb, exposed his erect penis with a grin as I walked through the park. I'd been groped by a group of Asian boys in their car as I cycled. Pursuing them on my bike, I got the registration number and reported it to the police, but to no avail. An Asian youth assaulted me on Brick Lane, while I bent down to unlock my bike. Chasing him, swearing in a gut-wrenching voice, I lost him. The sound of his cackles continues to rile.

While walking though the corridor of Mile End Hospital, I saw an Asian man staring at me with glazed eyes, then he hit me. Distraught I sought help; no one came to my aid. The security man became angry when I asked him to check the CCTV footage, threatening to call the police to have me removed. When I finally left the hospital, still shaken, he was standing there, with blazing eyes, hurling disgusting expletives at me. I was in my local bike shop, next to my studio, when a bunch of Asian boys came in and surrounded me like a pack of hungry hyenas and the staff looked on and went quiet. As I tried to escape by cycling out of the shop, two boys groped me. Once when I was sitting at the bus stop on Bethnal Green Road, a car pulled up, and an Asian man tried to talk to me. When I said, "I'm married," he was scathing implying that I dressed to deliberately court attention. To clarify I was wearing a long black coat with fake fur trim and elegant heels. Irrespective of how I was dressed there was no justification for speaking to me like that.

To say that these experiences didn't impact on my mental health would be an understatement.[26]

Below is a poem I wrote recounting some of these assaults.

The Assault

What is the definition of an assault?
Rape,
Mutilation
A black eye
A severed leg
Do you have to be violated
Slashed and scarred
For it to be real?
Does there have
To be blood and entrails for it
To be worthy of empathy?

She was locking up her bike
Talking to her mother
On her mobile phone
About her deceased father
And the fact that, although their relationship was brief,
She had loved him as the father of
Her three precious girls
It was a poignant moment
For mother and daughter to share
Until
A slap hard and sharp
Made her start and jump
She looked up
A boy in a hooded grey top
Ran off in hysterics
Capturing her reaction on his mobile phone
Laughing as he sauntered off with his mate
An anger rose within her
And she yelled,
"You fucking coward"
No one batted an eyelid
No one came to her rescue
No one gave a shit
She took chase down an alley way
Her voice echoing
Her cries reverberating
She lost him
Saw two police officers sitting on a wall

Chatting amiably
She was hollering, "Get the bastard"
Sick of men who thought they could touch her
Prod her
Hit her
When she would never, willingly, hurt a soul
The police officers began to jog
As she raced down the street
Still screaming, "Why does this bullshit always happen to me?"

The other night three drunken men
Knocked her over on her bike
Could have been killed,
But they were laughing
As if it was all a joke

"Don't dress like you want it"
Words hissed four years ago
As she sat at the bus stop
Sketching trees and moons
Absentmindedly

He was Bengali, this lad
The one who slapped her like she deserved it
Same blood as her
She imagined what would have happened
If she caught up with him

Punched him first
Then spat, three times, in his face
Followed by a deft
Kick in the balls
That brought him to his knees
Then daintily stamped both his eyes out with her red stiletto heels
Cut off his dick with a blunt knife
And stuffed it down his throat
Until he squealed like a pig for his last breath.

He was nowhere to be seen now
Melted into the coppery tower blocks
As if by magic

This life
This world is so
Sick and twisted
Where untold numbers of mothers and daughters
Are kidnapped
Sold into slavery
Raped repeatedly
And no one flinches

Memories of her first assault returned
Just seventeen, studying in a public library
Dreaming of a future that was almost within her grasp
Wearing jeans and a cream shirt
All covered up,
No flesh on show
Head bent over *Hamlet*
Then creeping fingers, from thin air, began to
Touch her,
She screamed at him and in response
He called her a "bitch" and fled without rebuke.

When she walked down Brick Lane
Unable to return home
In search of comfort
Justice
Anything
Something
Dejected
Still stinging from the pain
She saw familiar faces
Told them, "I've been assaulted"
They looked at her with blank faces
The black bouncer just dismissed her with a nod and
A grunt
She said, "They persecute men like you and women like me
For simply being who we are, we need to stand together
And confront these bastards, fight back..."
He didn't want to know
Her friend arrived, sat her down
She began to rant and the tears kept on coming
"Calm down, don't cry in public, otherwise people will think you are mad."
She got up to leave

Head stooped low
She cycled home
Although there were people around
To see and hear
She didn't care
Unashamedly
Cursing the thin air
Threatened to snip off all the
Rancid cocks and burn them on a sorry heap
No one stirred, no one opened a window
As a child bawls without fear
So did she
Hoping the night,
That was her only friend on this sorry street
Called home,
Might find that wretched boy

Image 25. *Her Body* (oil on canvas, size 10x10 inches, 2012) This oil painting seemingly depicts the classic, idealised nude with buffed luminous skin in the tradition of the French neoclassical painter Ingres, except this is the naked body of a Bangladeshi woman who has been assaulted multiple times, her skin, painted so carefully, is sullied by unwanted fingers. Belying the surface there is dirt and hurt conveyed in the poem written in tiny scrawl on the upper left-hand-side of the painting.

With his wretched smirk
And smother him
Silently
Gently
In his sleep
Until he choked.

Why am I telling you all of this? Because when the show got cancelled and these men cited me as the *bad one* spreading "lies" about the community, I became livid. Then I even questioned my own integrity. This is not the place to debate who is right or wrong, but everything that happened to me did happen and at that moment my mind cracked open some more.

At the same time, I had learnt that the arts organisation had rejected my application, the one I'd been working on for nearly two years. It was a thirty thousand-word proposal, emails had been going back and forth and I was told to make this change and that. No concessions were made, even though the officers in question knew I had a mental health problem, classed as a disability. Actually, this was used against me when it came to the final assessment regarding my ability to deliver the project. For years, I had kept my mental health issues a secret, delivering project after project, within budget and on time, now that people knew about it, I felt I was being stereotyped as someone incapable and impaired. This was the next crack. I could literally feel the strain upon my brain. The rain kept pouring, and London seemed as black as tar.

It was 23rd November 2009. Later, during the psychosis, the number 3 and the 9 in this date loomed large in my consciousness. I'd just completed a fashion shoot for a glove shop on Cheshire Street as a favour, not slept the previous night and found myself at 33 Portland Place, where my friend Laurence lived, a former male model. 33 Portland Place had something of a reputation, where regular orgies used to be held (although these have since ceased). Again, I noted the number 33, only for it to resurface during my psychosis, like a computer spewing out reams and reams of numerical code.

A party was happening at the house after I finished the shoot. I decided to meet with a certain individual. My nickname for him was the "Nazi" (not very politically correct but the name stuck) and I was planning to break all contact, indefinitely. We met at *Hix*, where I was painting. Again I endured people urinating and making lewd remarks as I worked. Deciding to be civilised, I bought the Nazi dinner. It was excruciatingly awkward, with the same old tired conversations, long pauses, silences and averted eyes. Whenever I saw the Nazi I always vowed "never again" sensing the growing antipathy between us, where once there had been geniality and fondness.

Image 26. Photo of Mia on *The Spaceship*, November 2009, during the modelling shoot, a few weeks before the psychosis. When I physically move my mind is as empty as air, when I stop it fills up with shit. Cycling is (and remains) an effective way of expelling all the *hot stuff* inside, in London I would cycle so fast it used to scare me.

Perhaps going to the party was a release, an escape from the mess in my head and my life. I should have gone home to sleep, but I didn't. I returned to Portland Place. An all-out orgy was underway; a mass of writhing bodies was heaped on a table with people watching hungrily. It's strange how anodyne such a scene can become. Changing clothes six times during the night, becoming more and more manic, Mia was in complete charge, while I wanted to sleep. At one point I was wearing Superman hot pants with matching top and heels and then I changed into a swimming costume. It was beyond exhibitionism, I was out of control. My speech was speeding up, I couldn't keep up with the words firing out of my mouth; finally I changed into something appropriate, unable to stomach the party, the people or the scene. I hurriedly got on my bike, heading back east in the early hours, carrying a huge bag of clothes from the shoot on my shoulder.

The following night, despondent about my cancelled show, I wrapped up my scroll, cycled to Shoreditch House and deliberated whether or not I should burn it. I saw the artist, Dinos Chapman.

"How are you?" he said cautiously, as if I was a dog that might bite him very hard.

"Not good." I told him about the boycott and that I was going to burn the scroll. He said that the Bangladeshi community didn't know anything about art and tried to dissuade me, then we parted. I reflected on his words thinking *I'm Bangladeshi and I'm an artist, does that mean I know nothing about art?*

Image 27. Photo of Mia from the glove shoot at 33 Portland Place. A few hours later I would be disturbingly manic and unfettered. The artificiality of this airbrushed image coupled with the fact that I can see Mia and Fred smeared all over my face, even down to the red painted toenails, is very unsettling.

I sat down at a table and wrote a poem called 10p directly onto the scroll.

10p

There was a little girl
She was forlorn
With muddy splash marks on her white socks
She was waiting for the bus home

Image 28. Painting of *Fred with a Gun*, (oil on canvas, 10x10 inches, 2010). This painting serves as a visually stark reminder that Fred is part of me. The giant dildo belonged to my friend Laurence (otherwise known as Jake the Phantom). The painting is based on an iPhoto he took of me at 33 Portland place when I was 36 in 2009.

She'd been waiting for at least
Four days, six hours and eighteen minutes
Her mother had left her there
Told her, "I don't have enough bus fare for you, I'm afraid you will have to
   walk home"
But as her mother boarded the bus leaving her behind
The little girl, suddenly, realised
She couldn't remember how to get home
Instead she dreamt of a shiny 10 pence piece
A 10p that would miraculously appear
10p that would save her and help her to get home
But no 10p came
So the little girl waited
For the bus that never came
And it grew dark
The cars sped by like big shiny monsters with gleaming white eyes
And still no bus came
She was cold

The pavement was no substitute for her bed
Then the dark, black blanket of night turned into dawn
The little girl shivered
Her belly rumbled and she squinted as the sun shone bright
She saw this blast of colour
Coming at her in the distance
It was a butterfly
With wings painted in every shade imaginable and the butterfly flew
    towards her
And pulled her up
Hoisting the little girl on her back
And she held on for dear life as they soared and dipped,
Travelling through vistas in seconds that tasted like precious drops of gold
"Don't worry little girl I have come to rescue you," said the butterfly
"Do you have 10p, I need it to pay for my bus fare?" the little girl asked
    meekly
"No I have more than that I have the whole world in a secret pocket tucked
    under my wings
Climb in there and you will be safe and snug
You will never need 10p or ever stand at bus stops in the rain waiting for a
    bus that will never come."
The little girl climbed into that pocket and warmth filled up her tiny frame
What she saw was beyond golden
She touched it with her own hands
Closed her eyes and never opened them again.

Writing 10p ameliorated the pain. These arrangements of words pour, thick and fast, out of me and are much easier to write then awkwardly constructed fat sentences where words frequently obstruct what I am trying to convey. Writing poems mops up the horse manure that Fred relentlessly pumped into my mind.

The next night, my mood somewhat improved, I returned to Shoreditch House with my scroll and a friend who was broke. Becoming my new walking stick, the scroll propped me up. If anyone tried to undermine me I could bash them over the head with it and, internally, say, "Look what this mind has produced, I dare you to do any better you cretins." There was a mild belligerence that I carried within for years. It was as if preparing for battle and all the battles I had fought – and lost mostly – were nothing compared to what I was about to face. We sat down, my friend drank an espresso, and as she talked I drew. Then Damien Hirst, the artist, walked in with a group of people. I'd seen him several times before, once I was

Image 29. *"Do you like my art or my arse?"* (pencil on paper, A3, 2006). I really can't stand looking at this image. Mia arranges her body provocatively, yet it appears stilted and contrived. Is it empowering or degrading? I don't know. Why do I even have to pose the question?

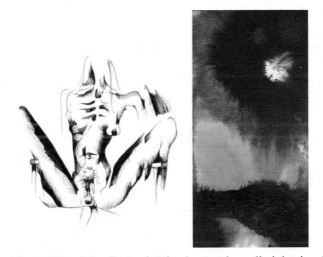

Image 30. *This is What I Really Look Like,* (pen and acrylic ink, size A4, 1994–2014) I did the drawing when I was studying at the LSE, the painting came later in 2008 and I put the two together a few nights ago, the abstract colours mirror what is going on in my head, in the top right corner you can see a face screaming, a white hole of a mouth and two blazing red eyes. I have done hundreds of these abstract paintings and I always see harrowing faces and images of terror within them. As they evolve it's like watching a wild alchemy unfurl.

formally introduced to him at a White Cube dinner, when he was with Jay Joplin, the founder of White Cube Gallery. That was in 2006. Mentally on edge the night we were introduced, I tried to keep my cool. A reputable art collector, Guido, had invited me after attending the private view at the Serpentine Gallery of Damien Hirst's personal art collection.

Guido had once told me rather bluntly, "I have seen three thousand bodies like yours; it is your mind that interests me." Despite the cutting arrogance of the statement, (believing he had probably seen all those bodies), maybe he was interested in my mind, although I would have preferred it if my art had been his sole focus. Naively, I tried to play the game. My interaction with him inspired a piece of art called, *'Do you like my art or my arse?' Mia asks*. Printing the provocative image on T-shirts, I wore them in defiance.

A year later, I saw Damien Hirst again on the 6th floor of Shoreditch House, this time I was less deferential.

"Oi Damien, I'll give you 50p and a mouldy carrot for that diamond skull of yours." I yelled.

He said, "Done."

Then I showed him my sketchbook and he asked, somewhat incredulously, "Did you draw that?"

I replied, "Yes, I did" and then he said, "you're mad."

What was it about me that constituted being mad? It was perplexing and belittling to be dismissed like this by my contemporaries.

I am just as good as the bloody lot of you, I shouted inside, when actually I felt smaller than a dissected, stamped on pea.

Throughout my life, I've bumped into a litany of famous (or soon to be famous) people – too time consuming and tedious to list here. All these collisions have been completely random, such as an early modelling assignment with Led Zeppelin, who at the time I had vaguely heard of. During the photo shoot I fainted on Robert Plant, who seemed to enjoy the experience and encouraged me to call him, which I never did. More collisions ensued. Finding celebrity culture intoxicatingly repellent, it would irk me that I kept on encountering these people. It might be the subject of another book: *The random collisions of a skinny Bangladeshi girl with a random bunch of famous people.* [27] I also found these collisions stressful, as if these were potentially big opportunities that I was failing to convert into something tangible and meaningful. My mind attached significance to all of these encounters and during my psychosis, they took on a mythic importance, as if I was the underdog being continually repressed. Somehow I was supposed to champion all the globally oppressed hidden talents, fight their corner, and usurp a culture that lauded the mediocre. I was frequenting circles, which made such interaction more likely. These people seemed to be drawn to the flamboyantly painted image I presented as Mia. Problems arose when I spoke – as if the words that were coming out of my mouth disturbed and alienated rather than engaged and illuminated. Maybe they were right and I was actually mad?

On this final occasion when Damien Hirst saw me, I was amiable and relaxed. As soon as he saw the scroll he came over, inviting his friends to take a look, they all seemed dazzled by the work and then I read out the poem 10p. They listened and midway through my rendition I wished I had just shut up. Afterwards, Damien asked for my number and his companion, a famous Hollywood actor, asked for it, too. Hollywood actor man, who I shall refer to as HAM, politely enquired how long it had taken me to create the scroll.

"I did it all in one night" Mia lied to his face blatantly, with a wry smile, then she wrote my number on two scraps of paper leaving me thinking: *This life of mine is bonkers.*

All these incidents were happening too quickly. It felt like stuffing too much food in your mouth without giving yourself adequate time to masticate. My brain was being crammed with one thing after the other, bang, bang, bang, like shots being fired, leaving a myriad of holes that were growing bigger.

The next day, I got a call, "Hi, is that Pigment Explosion?"

"Yes, is that Damien?" I said nervously knowing it wasn't because of the distinct American accent.

"No, it's HAM, listen I would like to come by to the Pigment Explosion Gallery, could I come between 7 and 10pm?" he said in his quiet, easy LA drawl.

Inside, I thought, *I am not staying in for three hours waiting for you and if you want to come you should have the courtesy to visit during working hours.*

Instead, I replied, "I'm due to see a play in the West End, but I could cycle back."

"Ok that could work. Listen did you really do that scroll in one night?"

"Oh no, I was joking," I said, getting more and more nervous. Then Mia interjected, "By the way, if you could describe your mind as a visual image, what would it look like?"

HAM was taken aback, perhaps he thought it was a ruse, "We can discuss that later when we hang out."

"Ok" and then I continued talking very fast when I should have stopped. "Why are you in town?" I asked abruptly.

"I have some stuff to do in London," he said. Afterwards I surmised he was here to promote his latest big budget Hollywood film.

My sentences were disconnected; I was incoherent and beginning to ramble.

"My show just got cancelled," I blurted out '

"Why?" he asked, getting agitated now.

"Because certain people in the community wanted to boycott it."

"Why?" he said again, and it sounded as if he was regretting ever calling me.

"Because I am dangerous."

There was silence, then a pause followed by, "Oh, ok, right, well I'll call you later and we can hang out then."

I knew what that meant and he unceremoniously hung up. There would be no later. Of course not, time and time again this had happened. People would be enticed by something, a spark, a burst of fresh energy, delightful eccentricity, the quick leaps and somersaults of my mind, or Mia's glossy surface, they'd request my number, even suggest meeting and then they would just retreat, perhaps because, as an acquaintance astutely observed, "The problem with you, is that you are too much." I didn't mind being snubbed, it was Mia who was courting the attention of these people, not me, but Fred reveled in the humiliation and would try to bring me low.

My husband once said, "It's because of your 'illness' that you haven't done as well as you could have." The political journalist, Andrew Neil has often said to me, "Why aren't you more known?" And Baroness Kennedy, the barrister, once wrote:

It is clear that when you enter the room you are one of the brightest people in it, you need to confound people with your beauty and dazzle with your talent.

The problem was, Mia conspired to create mischief, Fred alienated those who were allies, Sophie would escape to her ethereal landscape in the sky dithering with the clouds, while I cowered in panic under the table. Whatever talent I had was being smothered and I was sinking in the boiling excrement that Fred was stirring, while Mia danced in the fire, naked in high heels, egging him on.

It was still raining and bitterly cold. I didn't want to get on the bike or see the play because it was with the Nazi. Abysmally, I had failed to cut out him out from my life like a recurring verruca. Each time we met, it ended up in unpleasantness. Addicted to rejection, I returned for more. This *friend* was the personification of Fred. Most of the negative people in my life were a manifestation of Fred – this was why it was so difficult to walk away, because it was like gouging out parts of myself.

That same evening I met with an officer from the arts organisation to discuss my failed application. Arriving late, drenched, freezing and wolfing down food while trying to conduct the meeting, I rang the Nazi. Becoming irate when I explained that I was still in a meeting, he also seemed annoyed that I had eaten something without him and was going to be late by a few minutes. Sensing his ever-darkening, mood, I was afraid, but I didn't cancel, I went to see him. He'd already gone inside while I was standing in the crowded theatre, with my bike lights flashing, in my red PVC raincoat, partially drenched, while he stood looking immaculate and very perturbed. His nostrils flared imperiously. Almost appearing taller, he stared down at me as if I was a snotty tissue on the ground. Hurriedly walking to our seats, he didn't offer to assist with my two bike bags and then launched into his diatribe, for everyone in the theatre to hear.

"Stop sending me emails. That poem, *10p* was pathetic. Don't you realise that Damien Hirst and all these people are not interested in you? You are such an idiot." Trying to defend myself, inside I was emotionally deflated.

"If you talk to me like this I am just walking out, listen I am sorry I was late, I had to eat something. And I had to have this emergency meeting, it was important." It all fell on deaf ears.

I had been looking forward to watching *Breakfast at Tiffany's,* but the play washed over as my sadness became overwhelming. How could I allow someone to speak to me in such a derogatory manner? It was this night that I knew I had to kill off the last remnants of this attachment – whatever it was – for good. During the intermission, he laid into me again, in that booming voice of his, not caring whoever heard, and I shrank further into my seat. Appearing to enjoy my humiliation so did Fred.

The play ended and I was trying to be *friendly* like someone with battered wife's syndrome who could not sink any lower. It was very reminiscent of my relationship with my middle sister, still pining to be close when she wanted to get the hell away from me most of our childhood. I was reliving tired old childhood patterns of behavior – seeking out the human *Freds* of this world.

Telling him, "I need to go to the loo," he walked off, not waiting, and I scuttled after him. Pointing to a random bar I said, "Shall we go in here for a drink and a chat?"

"No, you go inside and use the toilet, I'll wait here," he said. By now I was fuming, took my time, tried to take a few deep breaths, "Just be nice, it always pays to be nice," I said out loud, staring at the tired, gaunt face in the mirror.

As I walked part of the way with him he said, "Let's just say goodbye here."

I continued to plead and speak softly, "But I am leaving tomorrow."

"I want to be on my own," he said coldly.

I followed him pathetically, "What is it?" I asked.

Then he raised his voice, people were looking, I became deathly silent, watching as his face turned a different shade and saw complete revulsion in those dark eyes of his.

He spat out his last words, "I don't know how to be with you anymore" then he walked away. Watching forlornly, I partially followed him, but he escaped in a cab and was gone. That was the last time I saw him. Although it was never spoken, he knew I was going to Brussels. He'd always been against it, thinking it was the cowardly easy option. But it was nothing to do with him or anyone, this was my life and I was going to reclaim it.

My husband told me that it would be impossible to be friends with such a person and that it would be better to just cut off all ties. He believed that my condition impaired my judgement, meaning I continued to be attracted to *Fred types* and always would be. Such interaction only fuelled my disorder. In London very few people ever made any concessions for my mental health issues. Something I have learnt the hard way, it is absolutely imperative to surround yourself with kind and compassionate people, which I try to do now, although such people are in short supply.

The next morning, after twenty-four hours of abject numbness, an incandescent rage returned – a red-hot, irrational, inflated anger that burns down forests. I wanted to make the Nazi pay and suffer just like he'd tormented me over the years with his sneering taunts about Bangladeshis being "inferior, smelly and hairy". Why had I put up with it? Because I was ailing. Citing the condition as the cause of my impaired judgement has been one way of explaining an extremely uncertain time in my life. Not perceiving myself as the maliciously vindictive type, ever since I became mentally unwell these impetuous rages have become all too frequent, when I suddenly lash out and write and say things that are best left unsaid. Desperately wanting the Nazi out of my life, I penned a letter that I knew, if sent, would emancipate me, but potentially destroy him.

My husband didn't approve of my actions, he said, "It is never good to try and be God, whatever he did to you nothing can justify your actions, silence is always better." Of course, with a rational mind, I wouldn't have bothered. Instead I would have walked away, shrouded in a dignified silence. With a rational mind I would never have spent five minutes with such a person. With a rational mind I would have been in a completely different place. Mia was encouraging me to send the letter. Fred was

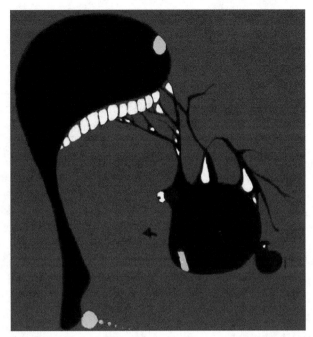

Image 31. Painting of *Fred Is Trying To Eat Me*, (acrylic on MDF block, size 10x10 inches, 2006). It often does seem that Fred is literally trying to eat me and now my children, too.

screaming at me, "Make the bastard pay, make him pay, go on– do it." My husband's sage words grated somewhat because I knew he was right.

Cycling in the rain yet again, standing with my hand poised in the mouth of the post box, Sophie, the Cloud Catcher, said softly, "Don't do it, your mind won't be able to take it."

Mia's voice, which was louder, just kept on screaming, "Do it, do it, do it, punish the Nazi, look how he humiliated you in front of all those people at the theatre, he's done it over and over again, now you can kick back, go on kick him, kick him in the balls and make him cry."

"But Mia," I said, "If I do it then I will never see him again, he will hate me, and we will never be friends."

"He already hates you, stop being a pussy and do it, he was never your friend."

Then Fred joined in, "Do it you fucking pussy."

My hand was poised in the mouth of the letterbox before snatching the letter from my fingers, swallowing it up in a gulp.

When I got home, I was shaking. My train back to Brussels was in a few hours. Popping into a shop on Bethnal Green Road where three girls in hijabs were standing by the counter, they all started laughing in unison. My bike lights were flashing in my pockets, my silver cycling helmet was still on my head, and I wanted to cry. As I sat on the Eurostar I thought what have you done? My husband picked me up and said, "Everyone is staring; you look like a clown in those pants."

They were PVC leggings with purple trim, designed by my friend, Dani (a budding fashion designer and artist). Fred began to join in, "Yeah the whole world is laughing at you and now is the beginning of the end."

Three days after I sent the letter I was in New York for six days to show my artwork at SPin. Those six days inspired my novella. During the exhibition I was manic, garrulous and felt as if I was crashing. Susan Sarandon, the actress attended, as did the best-selling writer Hari Kunzro (whom I had met years before in 1999, before he had found success). Finding their presence distracting, I was unable to deal or interact with them. Perhaps sending the letter was the final spark that created the fire in my brain. The letter led to a barrage of abusive emails from the Nazi, and it all had a devastating finality about it. Rather than solve my problems, these violent and abrupt severing of ties began to sever something inside. At one point I was in my friend's New York apartment, standing on his balcony with the overwhelming urge to jump. He became scared and told me to step away. Later he told me he really thought I was going to take a leap, and I think he was right. Needing to destroy all that I had known, I was trying to contain the complex range of emotions I was experiencing, which wanted to tear right through me.

Then I went to London on December 23rd (I only returned to see the Turner Prize exhibition at Tate Britain and then planned to go back to Brussels as soon as possible – I knew then, already, that trip was misconceived). As soon as I arrived in London and stepped into a black cab, it felt as if the whole city was a revolver pointing at my head and I was about to pull the trigger and watch my brain splatter to smithereens. Spending those few days living life at a frenetic pace, I got to my flat, was back on my bike, cycling to Tate Britain with, unbeknownst to me, a flat tyre. Then I cycled to Hix, to complete the artwork. Later I noted that Hix rhymed with the number 6 and crucifix, which I believed was another augury during my psychosis. Not eating properly and hardly sleeping that first night, each time I mounted my bike I was cycling too fast. Interacting with too many people in a very short space of time, I even did an impromptu photo shoot with a stranger I met on Brick Lane and bought him a hot chocolate at Shoreditch House. I was manic, paranoid, verbose, emotive, volatile, impulsive and utterly unable to make safe decisions. I travelled in 3 different cabs and 3 different Asian cab drivers each gave me their personal mobile number. I met up with 3 acquaintances and they hardly spoke as I talked and entertained them the whole night, then I took them back to my place and they trashed my flat. The night before the psychosis, I smoked dope for the last time in my life.

My first psychotic episode began on December 23rd 2009 lasting three days and nights until

$$3 \qquad 9$$

(9-3) 6

Dec 26th 2009

$$6 \qquad 9 \qquad (9\text{-}6)\, 3$$

$$> 3, 6, 9$$

The fact that the numbers 3, 6, 9 featured in the specific date (in multiple variations) on which the psychosis occurred has continued to confound me, or maybe it was just another bizarre coincidence. Or maybe I was simply looking for patterns and connections.

What is that expression? There are only "6 degrees of separation."

This last paragraph might seem like a jumbled up assemblage of facts. However hard I try to recall the details with any precision, they always end up in a disarray of tiny fragments of memory, like a mirror that has been smashed into shards. This is just a piecemeal recollection of what happened – a jumble shop of splintered memories sewn together with the flimsiest of thread.

The next morning, my flat looked as if a bomb had exploded in the living room: there were empty beer bottles and cigarette ends. I was disgusted and angry that I had let these people into my lovely, pristine home and allowed them to debase it. I began to write to one of the girls, expressing my disdain. At some point I was crying and hyperventilating. Calling my neighbor, she came by at once, I grabbed her arm and began to sob into her lap. Naturally she was very disturbed by my behavior. She left, I tried to sleep, but couldn't breathe, I thought I was having a heart attack. Calling my Bosnian friend and begging her to come, she agreed to take the day off work and came to see me. Outside, east London was concealed under a thick blanket of white snow. Standing in front of the window, partially clothed, I stared at the silently falling snow, totally mesmerised. For a second I felt compelled to remove my clothes and go out bare foot. I didn't, thankfully, despite Fred urging me to do so.

My Bosnian friend came and that's when the ranting began with gusto. Talking rapidly and fluidly, the words meshed together as I fired off names and numbers that were visually gigantic – in my head. They were standing in front of me in my bedroom – all charging at once like a row of pent up horses. My Bosnian friend just sat and listened as I gesticulated and said, "Wait, wait, oh my God, don't you see, don't you see the patterns with the names and the numbers...?"

She never once said, "You are talking complete shite," she just sat and listened, enduring it for hours, unable to say one word without me cutting in to stop her.

Here is an example to illustrate the randomness of the mental pattern making. For three months, in 2007, I had some interaction with the actor Jude Law, whom I had bumped into, off Brick Lane. I asked him rather cheekily, "What are you doing on my turf?" and the dialogue, ensued from there. During the psychosis, his name appeared as Judas. Guido, the Italian art collector, had a daughter called Eva, which was close enough to Eve and my friend Adam, who had tragically died, prematurely, in 2008, also appeared in the narrative. Judas, Eve, Adam... all these names had some biblical association and within the name of Guido was God U and I. What did all these curious associations signify? Why was my last exhibition in a church and why had I called my Bosnian friend *God* in front of all her colleagues. Why was her husband's name Christian and why did my own name have an overtly religious connotation? Why had Christian and I both done drugs and become so sick? This is just one example of the word association game that my mind began to indulge in. It was just that – a sad game playing out with ferocity in my head.

Scrawling down all these names and numbers I thought they were packed with some momentous significance. Now I understood why I felt persecuted and why I was special because, clearly, I was the chosen one. This was the code that my mind was going to crack to give me the answers, abort my pain and feelings of failure. I would be reborn – clean, shiny and successful. I have kept all the notes and the scribbles, as a visual reminder of what a carved up pile of string my mind was. At the time, the psychotic revelations appeared magical and unadulterated but now they just read like a warbled scramble. If you look for patterns hard enough you can discover them in everything and everywhere.

Forced to fly, because the snow had disrupted all services on the Eurostar, for six days after I managed to get home to Brussels, I was ensnared in a psychotic state, believing that my husband was the enemy, that his flat was bugged, and that I was the messiah. I lay on the bed, arranging my body in the shape of the cross, experiencing strange taste sensations on my tongue and in my throat. I heard recalcitrant voices in my head and thought I saw Jesus Christ flash past. A black crow appeared on the terrace, which I believed was the devil incarnate. Three birds flew in the distance, that I was certain signified something and when the curtains moved, I thought it was because I had special powers. Every sound was a sign that the flat was being monitored and I was convinced we were being watched. My husband remained calm throughout. His response was to ensure that I slept and that's exactly what I did, sleeping for at least two weeks, and it was after the psychosis that my relationship with my husband changed beyond recognition.

For years, I had been experiencing symptoms individually, but psychosis meshes together all the individual strands – the wayward voices, the associations/patterns and the hallucinations – playing them out in a parallel, seductive psychotic universe.

In terms of a dissection of psychosis, I have tried to show how my ongoing mental scuffles, which commenced in childhood, culminated in a succession of events that unfolded rapidly in 2009, creating the perfect conditions for psychosis to strike. Perhaps it could have happened sooner or later, but it was always going to happen, it was only a matter of time and had a pathetic inevitability about it.

I have attempted, to the best of my ability, to dissect the key factors that created these so called *perfect conditions* and you could argue, as Sir Professor Robin Murray does, that psychosis can strike anyone, sane or insane, given a specific set of circumstances.

For me it was:

1. The pressure of Fred's death wish that I kill myself before I turned 36 in 2009 and hence die the same age that my father died, at 35.
2. The isolation from my family and, most significantly, from my husband, meant I lost my protective buffer.
3. The continued smoking of marijuana/skunk.
4. The build-up of stress.
5. The poor diet and sleep patterns and various behaviors such as dangerous cycling, reckless behavior, embarrassing peccadilloes, and getting into altercations with relative strangers.
6. The alignment with people that acted as triggers and became human manifestations of Fred.
7. The rupture caused by the sudden wrench from certain discordant and potent influences that had been precariously holding me together.

At this stage I hadn't been attuned to my behavior patterns, nor did I accept that my occasional weed habit was sabotaging my mental rehabilitation. Believing that moving to Brussels and slicing out certain people in my life would solve everything, when I returned to London in December, I crashed – spectacularly.

Throughout this essay I wanted to show the broad-brush strokes and paint a clear outline, in primary colours, of the mental picture in my head. Clinging onto the bizarre minutiae of psychosis, I am better off throwing these details away because they only impede me from moving forward completely. The details remained strewn, like burnt confetti, on the cracked floor of my mind and I continue to hoard them, as if they are precious jewels.

More details related to the psychosis appear in my next essay: *Do Psychiatrists Have All the Answers?* I wish I could write about it all succinctly and coherently. However hard I try, it is just impossible: psychosis isn't neat and tidy, so you have to tolerate the convoluted style of writing and try to piece it all together, just as I have.

I only managed to write about the second psychotic episode, which occurred in 2010, relatively recently in April 2013; the psychosis was a brutal way of rebooting and reprogramming a brain deeply rooted in destructive patterns that left me woefully stuck. Admittedly I do miss parts of my old life, I don't miss the gravitation towards flakey, bullying types. Unfortunately, part of me is naturally drawn to the Freds of this world; I also seem to attract them, too.

I often perceive my mind as a lump of stone, with life unfolding like trickling water that flows into violent rivers: these rivers form grooves in the stone. However hard we try to chip away at these grooves with our fingertips they become ineffaceable, which is why it is nigh impossible to change a mind carved over decades by forces that are often beyond our control. This doesn't imply that you should stop trying to change them.

Months after I had recovered from the psychosis and discovered I was pregnant with my first child, I wrote scores of letters of apology, after firing off emails when I had been unwell, believing that what I was writing at the time was the definitive truth. Such is the compulsion to expose what is true, it's very difficult to exercise restraint, despite knowing that the consequences will be bitter tasting. I now say to myself, "Even if what you write is not a lie, some things are better off left unsaid".

The only people who have unconditionally forgiven me are my family, a mere handful of trusted friends, and my husband. This counts for something because how can anyone understand the twists and turns of this condition with its myriad of triggers, the long history of mental decline, the patterns, the rituals and the obsessions? It all creates revulsion in most people and the fundamental fear of a mind unravelling in a mush. Keeping my mind tied together with safety pins, when the flimsy protection was finally blown away by the hurricane of psychosis, there was a skinny, scared little girl sitting there, alone on a hill, under a leafless tress, shivering in the cold, waiting to be rescued and saved from Fred's gaping gob. Fred not only wants to *eat me*, more specifically he is trying to devour my mind.

Below is the poem I wrote about the second psychotic episode. It remains the most coherent account that I have mentally been able to write about psychosis, maybe similar such poems will naturally emerge in the future. Hugely cathartic to write, it imbued the whole experience with some dignity at last. I continue to write poems – words assuage the mind. The wounds inflicted by the psychosis remain raw though.

Naively I thought the first psychosis was a one-off when it struck, I never believed it could ever happen again, but it did.

Psychosis Recalled Part 2.1369

London,
I love you, but how you kill me
With the heat
This night
My brain was bursting
Poems were coming at me
Perfectly formed
With sculpted lean limbs
And I had to let them sprint past
Because my son was sleeping and another
Life was growing inside
Don't do it
They are just words
No one is really listening
Too busy scrutinising Victoria Beckham's handbags
And Catherine Middleton's beige bland shoes
Sick
Society is sick
Or am I sick?
This stuff is making me sick
Don't read it
Don't look at it
The Internet is breeding worms in the cracks of my
Tired, battered brain
It's starting again isn't it?
Rewind to 2009
I don't want to
Don't want to go back
It was the spliff,
Too many people
Too much talking
Not enough sleeping or eating and don't forget the threats
The brain
It was slowly starting to fragment

Into a million shards
With sharp pointy ends that
Began to prick the insides of her skin
And stuff oozed out
Slugs, ants and their gelatinous spawn
Feeding off whatever was left
3, 6, 9
Those numbers
They are just numbers,
They don't mean anything
Brick Lane
"You know if you invert the B it becomes 3" she said
You are talking *crap*
"But don't you see the same goes for the B in Bangladesh
It's actually a 3
It's a pattern
A code
3,6,9
I'm 36
And the year is 2009
Can't you see it?
The numbers"
"No, I can't
Shut up"
"But what about the colours
Red
White and Black
And Mia
Sophie and Fred
It's there in your work
There for everyone to see
They rule you
There is no you anymore"
"Shut up,
It's nonsense"
She was clutching her head,
There was nothing there,

Just mushed up maggots singing in a green stew
The flat became a church basking in painted iridescent light
She was the chosen one
The art – sacred symbols

Part of the story
About her past
The true history
That has never been written about why her family came here
From a distant, lush land
Because no one cares
Too preoccupied with Harper Beckham's clothes
Or Kardashian's burgeoning bump
That's what's important
Don't you forget it?
Someone had to make sense
Of the horror of what had happened
To her family
She kneeled and spoke to her paintings
Adorning the walls
The art spoke back, each and every one of them
That night she talked to Rothko
He told her why he ended it and shared a glass of verdant Absinthe
With Van Gogh
The dolphins, they came up through the floorboards
And Coco's eyes,
That beautiful, melancholic greyhound
Her eyes flashed blue
She knew
She got it
"I get it," she howled "but why were they so cruel to you, to me, to us?"
She was standing by the window
Paranoid and jittery
Heart had slowed to a pace near death
A policeman ran past glancing up at her before running off
What's going on?
The lights went out
Then she counted 1, 2, 3
Clapped her hands
And they were back on
She sang at the top of her voice
Her neighbours were scared and worried
"Is she going to come back?"
Under the cloak of night
She ran naked and didn't care
Who saw her
She wasn't ashamed

That's how we all came out of the womb
"I am a warrior," she roared
And her husband
He grabbed his wife
All skin and bone
"Please" he begged,
"If you don't calm down, they'll put you inside
and our dreams of a family and children will be destroyed."
All she kept on saying was
"Avatar"
Pointing to a man who sat in the window not moving
"If I do everything Fred says the world will be pure again, but if I fail then
    all the evil that was ever committed will be inflicted on me. The holo-
    caust 6 million times over,
Stonings, beheadings, torture and rape
My limbs won't be able to take it"
She almost collapsed at the sheer terror
By now the police were there
They wanted to cuff her
This naked, ranting woman
They didn't let her put on any clothes or shoes
Even though she was a step away from the safety of home
Her husband covered his wife and she was led away
Like some criminal
Not looking at anyone
Thinking the council flats were cloned
And the East End was full of brown zombies
By the time they'd reached the hospital
The voices were getting louder
Staring brown faces were closing in
Sounds were coming through the walls and punching her in the face
She lay on her husband's lap
Her feet looking like they had grown claws
Black varnished with scum
The brain had shut down
3,6,9
Sophie, Mia and Fred
Red, white and black
"Stop it"
Turn your brain off
And she did
Her husband did all the talking in those soft, dulcet Swedish tones

Those doctors they didn't care
Soporific bunch of morons
Another mad cow they might have thought,
"Moooo," she said silently
They handed over a very round pill and the men in white coats said,
"You are free to leave"
He let her wear his shoes
And he walked in his socks, slightly on tiptoe, afraid of being sullied by all
    that East End grime
They entered the gaping mouth of night and there, waiting for them, was a
    cab, it looked like a shining red light
The driver didn't say anything
He seemed strange,
Edgy
Like a cartoon character ready to break out and shoot up into the sky
London was, suddenly, glowing orange
When they got home
He put the giant pill on his wife's tongue and felt it melt
Into nothingness
She didn't argue and obeyed
With child-like compliance
Slowly the brain began to repair and renew
New branches and tiny leaves
Lined with fur
That uncurled amidst the rusty, sharp nails
She woke up to silence
After the storm or a brutal kill
Thought her husband had gone for good
How could she blame him?
And then he appeared
"I thought you'd locked me in and left me to starve"
"No, I went to get some bagels, eat something and try to sleep now, love."
    He said
"Will it be ok?" she said
"Of course it will, I knew you'd come back."
"Fred is here, in the room," she whispered
"No he's not, he's gone now, I got rid of him."
He stroked her hair, her eyelids closed
It wasn't over,
Psychosis recalled
Part 2.1369

CHAPTER 5

Do Psychiatrists Have All the Answers?

It has been some time since I wrote about matters of the mind. Stumbling to overcome a tyranny of mental blocks with my last essay, I believe that all my attempts to understand why I succumbed to psychosis have been warbled, incoherent, confused and inadequate. Having said this, psychosis creates knots of confusion. Each time I try to revisit both episodes, my mind clamps up as if warning me not to dare go there. Experiencing the mental burn almost immediately I sensibly retreat. Just now I returned to pick over the carcasses of my psychotic memories – what can I do with dried up bones? My inability to recreate that fluid mercurial train of thought has left me defeated. I accept that I won't be able to fully accurately document what happened to my mind during psychosis. The prickly psychotic fog won't completely lift, and I will not be rid of the piecemeal memories that linger and taunt just as vividly, like a tune that blasts loudly with no off button. Time doesn't make these ineffectual memories fade; they simply cut deeper. For now, though, I have to settle with what I have tried to assemble and hope it makes sense to the reader.

This morning, wrestling in the dark with Fred (in my head), he was sitting on a pile of furry pus and ranting. Fred wants me to stop writing and creating indefinitely; he makes very convincing arguments. If I listened and stopped working, it would mark the beginning of the death of my mind. Without the taxing daily exercise that constructing art and writing provides, my brain would lose its elasticity becoming a bloated, dribbling blob. Some days Fred wins and even if I have a good day and manage to scribble down something or make a mark with my brush, he spits something out that lands in my eye and makes me squint. Will anything make Fred go away for good? A sweet, magic tiny pill perhaps. I could ignore or even befriend him to mollify that acerbic tongue of his.

During these last weeks I began to ask why I was actually writing these essays. After an application rejection by the Wellcome Trust, to complete a mental health related project, I began to question whether I was equipped to write about mind issues. The rejection is a small setback – a necessary failure – that everyone faces. Of course Fred enjoyed my rejection and taunted me viciously. After weeks of shying away from words, here I am, trying to make sense of stuff. How do I manage to carry on, when a voice is screaming at me to stop and drink some turpentine instead? Not only that – Fred makes me visualise the outcomes of my actions in gruesome detail. He is a fiend. One who is forever by my side, especially when I am alone. Continuing is the only option – a way of fighting back and keeping Fred in his box – which seems to be getting bigger and consuming more space in my head. His hand is poised on the self-destruct button; he wants me to keep on failing. For this reason I tease the words out with tweezers, as he tries to keep them buried.

Although I have seen numerous people over the years – doctors, psychiatrists, psychotherapists and psychologists – none have provided a viable solution to the intractable problem that is my mind, nor have they come up with any strategies to kill, numb, silence, or turn Fred into a friend. My friend the philosopher said I should, "Just tell Fred to fuck off." This has never really worked. Rather than devising my own ad hoc methods, I wish the experts had come up with something sensational, except they never have done. People working in mental health are stumbling around in the dark just as much as I am. If this is the case, treating the mentally ill must be rather difficult. The effort made to treat *us mad folk* is something tantamount to containment and support rather than cure. Am I being ungenerous in my assessment? I might even back track and contradict myself in the essay, it will not be an easy one to write; it will attempt, at least, to ask if people working in the area of mental health could ever have the answers and solutions that can fix a broken mind. Fundamentally, why do we assume that everything can be fixed? What if some minds can't be and no one wants to openly make this admission? Some of us may just have to learn to live with the mind we end up with and understand its mechanisms, as best we can. This is a realistic conclusion; more realistic than believing mental afflictions could ever be permanently eradicated or that there is a miracle cure.

Historically, proponents of eugenics believed eliminating the mentally ill was the answer, during Hitler's Nazi era. Mandatory or voluntary sterilisation, if you suffer from mental health issues, has been enforced in various countries, including the USA, Switzerland, Japan and even Sweden (until the law was abolished in 1976), to name just some of the nation states advocating the policy. What did our hunter and gatherer ancestors do when confronted with the mad? They consulted the wise shaman in the tribe, the closest thing to a doctor or therapist. Later the mad were burnt at the stake, deemed as witches and Satan worshippers. Born in another time then, I might not have been here and the *dubious gene* that has surfaced in my lineage would have been killed off. Even writing this last sentence leaves me sickened. It's the great, mad, dented minds that have left such a rich legacy of art, music, philosophy, mathematics and literature. Unfortunately, some of those minds succumbed to suicide. There is no need to list them here, they've been immortalised, their stories somewhat romanticised and yet their torment remains real. My own daily torment, however visceral, imagined or inflated, is a familiar and irritating part of who I am. I turned to the doctors to lift me out of a mind that was:

A knife
A thick sea of mush,
A bed of fire,
A claustrophobic prison
Without a small "tent of blue"

More parasites than blooms grow in this mind. Once blooms were abundant and lilac, now you can barely see them for the blood stained thorns.

Is the fight lost then?'

In my essay about mental mapping I explained why I have the mind that I do. Despite having a detailed mental map and rational explanation for all that has transpired, there remains a secret wish for someone to produce a panacea. For years, I thought discussing anything mentally-related to anyone, let alone doctors, would be the beginning of the end. An open admission meant that people would never perceive you as normal, even though a normal being does not exist. After struggling for years on my own, I remember the first time I turned to a doctor with my secret. I was twenty-six and on the verge of getting married to my long-term partner. We'd met at the London School of Economics (LSE) when we were nineteen. Before my wedding day I was not excited or thrilled at the prospect of spending a potential lifetime with my husband to be. Instead my head was burdened with dark thoughts and a gushing sense of panic. Not pre-wedding jitters, just a realisation that after years of trying to dodge the darkness, I was confronted with it – Fred had been stalking me for years and now he was staring me straight in the eye. Finally I used the mental health services provided at the LSE. Although I was no longer eligible for care they kindly made an exception. I found myself sitting in the familiar doctor's surgery opposite a bald gentleman with a low lull of a voice. His name was Adam. In that short hour I vomited years of self-loathing, the sense of being infinitesimal, alone, a failure, a loser, a very bad girlfriend, most probably an appalling wife to be and – as Fred, succinctly, described me – "A bag of shit." It all sounds trite; women the world over have self-esteem the size of half a squashed grain of rice.

Adam thought he could fix me. He said, "Whatever you've done, it doesn't matter and I'm sure if I called up all the people you know you'd discover that many of them, do in fact, like you."

I went along with the wedding, with a glum face; my mother even commented, "You looked like the saddest bride in the universe."

My unhappiness was not related to my husband, it was just the shade of my mood that clouded everything. Continuing to see Adam until, one day, I had nothing left to say, I was embarrassed, as if I couldn't wait to get out of his office. He was quietly triumphant, "I knew that you would find a way out, you just needed some guidance."

Adam never said I was depressed or mentally ill, maybe just mentally stuck, that's all. Settling into married life, dare I say I was happy, living in Covent Garden, building up my practise as an artist, exhibiting, creating, writing, working hard and very driven – clearly I was cured. Then it started up again, within the year, and I contacted Adam. He was now in Bosnia, aiding people with real problems who'd been raped, lost everything, and were grieving for a country that was no more. I told myself: "My problems are imaginary; you don't need help. You don't deserve to be helped, snap out of it you solipsistic twat!" Trudging on, I didn't realise that what was happening in my mind was impacting on everything, especially my ability to interact with others. Relying on the multitude of masks I had to wear in order to function effectively was exhausting.

When my husband moved to Brussels in 2000, just one year after we got married, I was now alone in London for long stretches of time and subsequently the blocks of blackness, the need to sleep more, the inability to wake up, the lack of appetite, and the constant state of wretchedness intensified.

Deciding to stay put to build up my artistic practice was a disastrous decision. Aligning myself with a coterie of the wrong sort, my stable life was dismantling, my mind continued to crumble, and I had started smoking marijuana. Rather than apportion blame, I was the architect of my own collapse.

One thing happened after the other in quick succession, culminating in my realisation that I needed to confide in a professional about what was happening in my head. I recall running through the back streets of Covent Garden, my heart pounding, half mumbling, then waiting, sweaty and nervous, at the LSE doctors' surgery. I sat there looking at the cherubic faces of the other students – where had ten years gone? I ruminated on the hundreds of wasted hours consumed with brawls in the dark with Fred spitting, venomously, in my face. All the multiple, carefully constructed masks had shattered and the complex tapestry that was my life was on the floor, the bright threads a forlorn and convoluted mess. My gravely careless behaviour was putting everything in jeopardy – my ability to work, my interactions with people, my family, and my recent marriage. When I sat in the GP's surgery, facing a doctor that I barely knew, he smiled and asked, "So what can I do for you?"

Bursting into tears, it all came tumbling out, starting with, "I'm depressed." I'd never said those words before and saying them didn't create a release, only a thick block of shame. The doctor didn't know what to say or do, he looked shocked because I was so distressed and for a long while he stayed mute. That day, he wrote something new in my medical files. My brief encounter with the amiable psychotherapist, Adam was not going to be a one-off. This really did mark my plunge into the world of mental health. Should I have opened up or struggled on in stubborn, proud silence? Did my subsequent interaction with mental health professionals ameliorate or exacerbate an illness that was mutating into another beast?

The ineluctable dark, sticky goo in my head gets stickier
People ride on the fluffy cloud of life.
They laugh and I can't move
"I'm being robbed," I shout
"Robbed of life"
No one comes to my aid
Only the sharp studs come closer
Slashing at my heels
How I bleed
But I can still see a fleck of light
Buried in the shadows
I stoop down to pick one up
And stash it safely in my pocket.

Medication for the Mind – Is it a Trap or a Way Out, Towards the Light?

I have to ask myself why I am inherently sceptical about medication. Since I've never been a long-term user of meds, maybe I am denying myself a potentially attainable mental peace and a happier existence. This illness, affliction, disorder – whatever it is – has eaten up chunks of life, ruined friendships, impacted catastrophically on relationships with people, destroyed professional alliances, and fundamentally stolen my dignity. I have good reason to try and seek a cure.

Knowing people who swear by anti-depressants, one friend told me she would literally not be able to function without them, in fact she believes her life would fall apart. My friend experienced the Bosnian war and saw unspeakable horrors. She moved to the UK speaking barely a word of English and found a job as a cleaner. She is now working at a senior level in a respected public organisation, married, with a mortgage. She is the main breadwinner and supports her family in Bosnia, including her sister, brother-in-law, niece, elderly father, and chronically sick husband. She has to be an invulnerable tower amidst the rubble of her mind and find a way to carry on. Growing vegetables on her allotment has been a powerful source of substitute therapy. The medication eases her off to sleep, to get up in the morning, to shower, dress, eat, get on the tube and do her job, which is stressful. No one is going to look after her, she has to look after everyone else, be strong and keep going, even if she'd rather curl up and sleep forever. When depression hits her like a hammer to the head, she goes scarily quiet, you cannot reach her, the pills don't work, and she has to sit it out in the bunker she's constructed in her head until the nails stop falling. Then she re-emerges, gripping her spade and gets on with the business of clearing up the unwanted weeds.

Never really going into detail regarding the causes of these devastating, black lows, she doesn't have to, you can see it in her eyes. I understand and wish I could obliterate it. She says seeing me and the time we spend together, laughing and taking the piss out of life, makes her feel better. Always feeling better after seeing her, too, I wish there were more people like her who *get it* without having to explain, but there aren't enough Bosnian warriors. Often we are both left stranded, holding onto some rot-infested tree in the middle of a raging ocean that won't stop raging. For my friend, the medication is an anchor to get back to shore. It is a form of fuel that magically starts the process of transforming the rubble of her mind into a provisionally workable structure with normal pathways.[28] Admiring her courage, I understand why she takes the medication. There are plausible arguments why I should, yet the resistance within me is stronger than the will to try. Even if these pills could miraculously change my life, I believe that they are not the answer. The answers lie in my mind, although my mind is smashed with rusty pins holding it together.

Incontestably, we know very little about the intricate workings of the brain. How then can doctors prescribe medication to ensure that the mind functions, as it should, in a balanced way, without violent oscillations and tyrannical twists and turns? Medication can thump the brain into submission when it refuses to switch off for days. Medication numbs the mind, castrates the violent wagging, uncontrollable tongue, and inhibits behaviour that could be deemed perilous to oneself and others. Medication can cool down an overheated brain and step on the brakes as you accelerate towards psychosis. Medication is a palatable strait jacket for unpalatable behaviour that emanates from minds that have grown unkempt. Medication can induce weight gain, unwanted tremors and awful side effects. Medication is prescribed for people with mild depression, clinical depression, schizoaffective disorder, bipolar disorder and schizophrenia. There's a plethora of pills, from a mild anti- depressant at a low dosage, to stronger anti psychotics – a carefully prescribed cocktail to keep the mind properly balanced, or sleep medication – vital when your own natural mechanisms to fall asleep fail. When I tried *long term* medication each foray left my mind and body worse making me question their efficacy. I experienced pain in the joints, an inability to work, physically walk, or even talk because of a locked jaw. So-called mild anti-depressants have induced psychosis or made me soporific. After all these disappointing experiences, my confidence in the competence of the *professionals* has plummeted to the point where I am stubbornly resistant to taking any form of medication on a daily basis apart from omega 3 and vitamins.

Over the years, I've been told a variety of things – that I should have sought assistance years ago to nip it in the bud, that if I didn't take medication I would be more likely to commit suicide, and most recently that mothers with my condition have, in specific cases, had their children taken away. I've also been told that it would be unsafe for me to have a second child. The risk of psychosis is great and the risk to my mental health potentially devastating. I trusted the person who told me this – my old mental health social worker, J – who added that it was just her professional opinion and that I should also seek the advice of another two psychiatrists. When she said this, I groaned painfully inside because I didn't want to talk to psychiatrists about the impact another child might have on my mind. Vehemently disinclined to let them in, I didn't want to divulge anything that was deeply personal. I've poured my guts out on numerous occasions to one mental health professional after the other. They sit laconically, nodding occasionally, scribbling stuff down that I never get to see or read. They seem fascinated or bored, but if I ask myself whether they have really helped me I have to say, emphatically, no. Why? Because I've often felt as if I'm sitting naked in the room being scrutinised as I vomit my mental shit, which I swiftly re-consume before being forced back out in the world. My regurgitated mental vomit continues to swirl in the belly of my mind, while they have, dispassionately, written details of my life on random pieces of paper or in their books. They take and give little back. Their subdued, monosyllabic offerings leave me bereft; stripped of the armour that everyone needs to protect themselves against the daggers that fly daily in the form of actions and words.

For many people, doctors prescribe medication and it enables them to function again. I envy them, but I'm not one of these people. I've almost lost count of the number of doctors I have seen since *coming out mentally* with my brain condition. When I write this list, I will try to be as objective and dispassionate as possible. Just as it is important to write a mental map, it is crucial to evaluate the care of mental health practitioners. With most of these people I have no further contact, yet they have intimate mental truths stored on file somewhere – and that is disconcerting.

A Comprehensive List of Each Mental Health Practitioner I've seen From 2001-2013

1999 September – number 1

I first saw Adam at the LSE doctors' surgery for a few weeks. It was pleasant, even cathartic, chatting with him. He never said that I suffered from depression or that I was mentally ill.

2001 June – number 2

Speaking to my GP, for the first time, I used the word to describe what was occurring in my mind. I told him, "I think I am severely depressed." Alarmed and not sure what to do, he was extremely concerned, I was crying violently and was referred to the LSE mental health services.

2001 July- number 3

My next psychotherapist was a portly, spotty man, wearing socks and sandals. With a strange way of talking, he said "hmm" rather condescendingly after each revelation. At one point he leapt up, reiterating something I said right up close in my face. Finding him intimidating and rather scary I decided not to see him again.

2002 August – number 4

My BUPA health insurance guaranteed eligibility for four sessions with a psychiatrist and I was sent to see one who practised in St Albans. I'd written a ten thousand-word essay detailing the undoing of my mind. Upon arrival I saw it was a private residence. The elderly psychiatrist spent half the session reading my essay, "Did your father rape you?" he asked rather bluntly. "Have you been sexually abused?" He continued to ask questions without looking up. "If you find yourself so repulsive why on earth did you go into modelling?" His tone was verging on derisive.

At the end of the session he said, "You'll be alright, you're intelligent, so you'll work it out."

This didn't reassure me. He referred me to another psychiatrist in central London who he thought would be better equipped to deal with my case. He kept the essay.

2002 August – number 5

Seeing the private doctor near Harley Street, he made a point of mentioning that, at the National Health Service (NHS), I wouldn't get bottled sparkling water. Accidentally missing my first appointment because of a miscommunication, he charged me anyway. Very soon he was asking if I wanted long term therapy. He tried to sell me self-help books and after each sentence he said, "Do you get me?"

He told me, "It is very unlikely that you will get help from the NHS for a long time – there's a waiting list – and you need help now. If you go to A&E that is one way to get seen quicker."

"So, I have to be desperately suicidal for anyone to see me?"

"Yes, I'm afraid so, unless you pay to see me. Do you want more sessions?"

We parted company soon after that. I was almost queasy at the prospect of seeing another doctor.

2002 September – number 6

A trainee plastic surgeon acquaintance of mine said he knew someone who might be able to help. Sending my confessional essay, in an envelope, to the doctor he suggested, I made an appointment. The lady sat me down in one of those clinical hospital rooms with shiny floors.

"I read your essay with real interest" she said, "but I specialise in eating disorders, anorexia and bulimia. You are very thin, do you have an issue with food?"

I said, "No, but sometimes I have no appetite, it all depends on my mood."

We parted, she didn't give back my essay; no one did. What became of those very private thoughts and words?

2002 October – number 7

Remaining in London while my husband was working abroad, I was smoking marijuana when I could get hold of it and engaging in behaviour that was emotionally draining and hollow. At some point I had stood on the bridge over the Thames, called my stepfather and told him that I was going to jump. He said, in exasperation, "Go on then, jump" and hung up.

I looked at the water for a long time, transfixed by the intoxicating, yet violent dance of the waves. It was dark and death by drowning seemed an awful way to go. Walking to the nearest newsagents, I bought ten boxes of

Aspirin. The man behind the counter didn't flinch, just happily took my money. Then I sat in my flat and made neat towers of pills and wondered if I'd bought enough to snuff out the light that grew dim inside. A *friend* came to the flat, threw all the pills away and refused to leave me that night. The comfort he gave was short lived. A few weeks later, I walked into Accident and Emergency (A&E) off Tottenham Court Road and waited to be seen, along with drunks and people with bloody wounds inflicted on faces and limbs. Sitting amongst these people, looking down at the floor most of the time, I wondered how much lower I could sink. Eventually, a relatively fresh-faced Chinese doctor saw me. Seated, with a file on her lap, she noted my age, gender and name, writing that I was well presented, as if that mattered, "The clothes are just a mask," I wanted to say. Commenting on how thin I was, she seemed genuinely concerned. What did I tell her? The same story I told the other doctors. It was never easy to repeatedly launch into the details. She said I could stay in the hospital and that's what they could offer. Calling my husband, he said it wasn't a good idea. Arguing with the doctor, he questioned her treatment suggestion. Eventually, two mental health workers took me home, they were awkwardly convivial and kept their distance.

October 2002 – number 8

Referred to see a psychiatrist based in Kings Cross, she was from Mexico with a face as round as the moon and a smile that made me feel safe. Sometimes she would come and visit me, "You are working," she would say, clasping her hands like a delighted parent when she saw me concentrated at my desk. We talked, often for more than an hour.

"Do you want to be with your husband?" she asked.

"Yes, I think so, but there are all these people in London who are against it. It's as if they want a piece of me, tearing off great big hunks, and munching happily. I want to leave London, but I just can't seem to get to Brussels. Maybe it's too late, I don't know."

"This is because your marriage is over, you know that getting a divorce is the right thing to do." She sat there with an affected expression of sympathy, which made me feel even more pathetic.

Actually, she would often tell me to leave my husband. I didn't know what the right thing was to do, nor was I sure that psychiatrists were supposed to tell their patients to get a divorce. She barely knew me, I was at my lowest point and yet she was trying to exert a great deal of influence on my life, when I wasn't in the right frame of mind to make such decisions. I didn't want a divorce, I loved my husband; he was a good man. It was Fred who wanted to destroy all that was positive and it was Fred that I wanted to expel out of my life. After a few weeks she announced that our sessions were finished. I was referred to someone else, a psychologist based in Russell Square.

Jan 2003 – number 9

My new doctor was Spanish, diminutive with a matter of fact way about her. Her office was spacious with a large window and I liked sitting in it. Referring to what we were about to do as *work* she made it clear that I could only have a limited number of sessions. Having moved out of the rented Covent Garden flat, my home for the past eight years, I bought a flat in east London, with a hefty mortgage, in 2003. Although successful with my grant applications and commissions, I was under enormous financial pressure, which only intensified my mental health problems.

For psychotherapy to be effective, you need to trust your therapist. While professional and listening carefully to what I said, there was a persistently vacant look in her eyes. Arriving soaking wet for one session and asking, politely, if I could remove my wet shoes to let my feet dry, she obliged, but with such a begrudging look. Often late, citing my need to leave the flat absolutely perfect as my reason, maybe my tardiness was because I dreaded seeing her. At the end of the sessions I would leave her office like a small, shivering, naked child; no one gave the child some clothes as she walked in the street – everyone ignored her.

The Spanish doctor wrote assiduously as I watched, getting angrier and angrier. Bumping into her again, months later, at the Curzon Soho cinema, such was my shock at seeing her in a public place that I literally ran away. Never connecting from the outset, I was not given the option to choose my therapist. You had to accept the person allocated by the NHS, even if they were not the right match. If you declined the offer of treatment you went back on the waiting list and there was no guarantee that the next person would be any better either.

February 2003 – number 10

Referred to Mile End Hospital, I had my first appointment there with a Welsh psychotherapist. He had a large office with dull decor. There was a sizeable distance between us, as if we were sitting at two ends of a muddy field. Barely audible, he came out with that, now, very familiar "hmmm" sound. Deliberately terse, the calculated pauses between each chunk of life uttered, were long enough to make me splurge out more. These were pauses contrived to make you reveal. Revealing my life, yet again, to another stranger was damaging in itself, after years of being, very carefully, extremely private. At the end of my consultation he said I would be eligible for treatment, but that it would take some time before they could arrange for someone to see me.

May 2003 – number 11

Eventually, assigned with a trainee psychotherapist, I had a finite number of sessions on a set day and specific time. The fledgling therapist addressed me formally by my surname. Requesting politely that she simply used my first name, she refused. Was it a deliberate measure to keep a professional distance between patient and therapist? It seemed mildly inhumane. The sessions were hopeless. Firstly she had a set way of talking which was very vexing, beginning each sentence with, "It seems to me that..." and although she listened intently, with wide eyes, and nodded enthusiastically, nothing that she came up with was useful. What were these people trained to do? At the end of our sessions I gave her a present, a framed photo of an orphan I had worked with in Bangladesh (looking back it was a rather incongruous thing to do) and thanked her. Although I was being disingenuous, she needed encouragement; maybe with time she'd improve. I decided that I was through with all these mental health aficionados, seeing them was making my head hurt.

July 2003 – number 12 and 13

After turning off my mobile and disconnecting my landline, I was lighting up a second joint when I heard my intercom buzz. I didn't answer. It buzzed again and I ignored the loud intrusion. Then there was a fierce bang on the door. The banging was so violent that I ran downstairs. When I peered through the window I saw it was the police. In fact, six burly police officers.

"Good job you answered because I was just about to knock the door down," one policeman said, half-jokingly.

Striding in, with their clomping, black, shiny shoes, I thought about the dirt on the souls of their lumbering policemen's shoes. They saw my Tesco's shopping strewn over the floor, which I started, hurriedly, to put away. I was quite stoned and trying to gather the shopping proved rather difficult when the apples were rolling amidst twelve giant feet.

I asked them, "Why are you here?"

"Your husband called, he was worried because he couldn't reach you."

"Yes, my phone was off, I wanted to be alone that's all, everyone was doing my head in, I'm fine now, honestly."

Refusing to listen, I was escorted into their van. A couple of neighbours watched with interest, speculating if I was a clandestine criminal being arrested for some minor misdemeanour. As I sat in the van I put my feet on the seat in front, out of nervousness.

"Please put your feet down," said one officer curtly.

"Yes, sorry, of course" I replied, somewhat, sheepishly.

Taking me to The Royal London Hospital on Whitechapel Road, I was left sitting with the drunks and hapless wounded. One suspect character filed in after the other. Maybe they weren't miscreants, just unlucky souls who'd taken a few wrong turns and ended up smashed up on the pavement. A tramp vomited violently on the floor. The neon glare of the hospital light imbued everything with a nasty green hue. After one hour of waiting, an Afro Caribbean nurse escorted me to a small box shaped room. I saw a man leering at me through the window, making lewd eye gestures. Shooing him away, she then looked at me as if I was scum.

"Are you anorexic?" she asked.

"No," I replied.

"You are, aren't you? Look at you, you are skin and bone," she said, almost angrily.

"No, I am definitely not anorexic, listen, I want to go home, I don't like it here, there's been a mistake." I said.

"You are not going anywhere and I can keep you here against your will if I want to." The nurse was getting more and more aggressive.

"What? You're scaring me, I want to see someone else." I said, panicking inside. Her eyes seemed to get bigger and bigger until they were bulging out of her sockets. Desperate to flee, I was confined in this poky room in a neon green hospital, flooded by a thick river of lumpy puke.

Another doctor came, he was also Afro Caribbean, but he didn't glare at me, he had a gentle face and was softly spoken. He was instantly reassuring. I told him about the nurse, and he assured me that she would apologise. He asked questions, I answered all of them truthfully. Then the nurse re-entered and said sorry, although her eyes were blazing, and her modulated tone was clearly forced. A few minutes later they let me go. It was the early hours of the morning, first light in fact, and I was expected to walk home alone. Several cars stopped, asking "How much?" thinking I was a prostitute, even though I was wearing casual sportswear. Breaking into a run, I got through my front door and collapsed onto bed. Frantically relaying what happened to my husband he said, "Next time pick up your phone."

August 2003 – number 14 and 15

Shortly afterwards two male mental health officers visited me. When they arrived, my home was spotless and they stared at the walls visibly shocked.

"Is this all your work?" they asked.

"Yes, it's all mine." I said.

Something compelled me to produce art like a factory; it was all I could do and it was the only thing that made me human. Giving the men a rudimentary outline of my life, telling them I had no contact with my family either and was very much alone in east London, they gave their input and left. It was yet another exposure to strangers. Unable to hold back, anyone purporting to be a mental health expert was entitled to ask me intimate details about my life and I was obliged to tell all. Would I become an anecdote down at the pub that evening?

August 2003 – number 16 and 17

A few weeks later I was referred to see a trainee psychiatrist. Why were hospitals such gloomy and wretched places when they were supposed to be sanctuaries of healing and recuperation? Whenever I walked into one I felt decidedly worse. This youthful trainee psychiatrist asked me a series of questions and I answered them all as objectively as possible. I was then told that I would have to see another psychiatrist. The one psychiatrist whose name I still remember. His name was Dr Bass. Dr Bass told me that he'd been practising for over twenty years and had a great deal of experience in this field.

"My colleague diagnosed you with bipolar disorder, but I think you have schizoaffective disorder. If you don't go on medication and carry on the way you are, there is a strong possibility that you could be dead," he said.

I do remember the *dead* part very explicitly. It went very quiet in that cell like room, then I almost started laughing, such was my shock. Yes, I'd told him about Sophie, Mia and Fred. Yes, I'd told him about my suicidal ideations that had begun as a teenager. The highs, the lows, the extreme behaviour, the possible *mad* gene in my family, but to be handed this diagnosis was, paradoxically, a huge blow and relief. It wasn't chimerical, self-indulgent bleating. I could call what was going on – in the warren of my mind – a name. It was a disease – not my fault – and potentially treatable. What Dr Bass didn't tell me was that it was advisable to only tell a very select few about the condition. In my experience, once divulging you have an infirm mind, the life you once knew and the doors that once opened with ease abruptly close.

September 2003 – number 18 and 19

I would see Dr Bass every three months for a review at Pritchards Road, a shabby, neglected place for people with mental health problems to hang out. Always conspicuous because of my glamorous and elaborately painted mask, hiding behind Mia most of the time, Dr Bass would often say, "What do you want me to do?" I usually wasn't sure how to answer this question. Suggesting various medications, which I dutifully tried, I only recall the name of one: *Abilify*. The name suggested that if you consumed these pills somehow you would become, miraculously, able and sane. Most of the pills I tried made me drowsy, phlegmatic or impacted painfully on my joints and legs. My venture into medication was short-lived. On two occasions he asked if I would mind if a trainee psychiatrist sat in on our session. I did mind, two more strangers hearing my business, but I passively complied while seething inside. In their company I shut down becoming reticent and withdrawn. Often, I found that as soon as I entered Pritchard's Road I felt worse than before – there was a smell of rotting minds in the air that infected my own. Asking if someone could visit me at home to check how I was doing, Dr Bass assigned me a mental health social worker, the first of several.

Dr Bass was the first psychiatrist that I trusted and believed might, actually, be able to help.

October 2003 – number 20 and 21

My life was in limbo; I was travelling abroad extensively for work, donning elaborate masks, dealing with Fred, smoking the occasional joint and being pulled in different directions by insalubrious people. I was jammed in mental concrete, with flailing arms and a mouth that screamed silently in the dark. The first mental health social worker I saw was an Afro Caribbean lady, she was exuberant and amiable. Trying in earnest to instil some positivity in the mud of negativity that I preferred to wade in, she once even bought me some lunch when she learnt I hadn't eaten one day.

For some reason, I can't remember why, I was assigned to a new psychiatrist – a female and heavily pregnant one. Upon arrival for my appointment I became inexplicably mute. Increasingly annoyed, the psychiatrist began to talk over me, "Look if she doesn't want to be here then just let her go," were her words and I promptly left.

My mental health social worker showed no leniency, "I'm very disappointed in you." Disappointed about what? That I wasn't able to spill my guts to yet another stranger? How many people had I seen now? Twenty-odd, in total, and I was continuing to decline mentally. Yet I felt a close connection to this particular social worker, she became more like a friend each time I saw her. One day, she announced I would be assigned someone else because she was leaving. Disappointed, I began to reflect on the mental health care I was receiving. It wasn't the psychiatrists who had helped; it was talking to someone heartfelt in my home and making them a cup of tea that soothed my mind. Unsure whether this apparent closeness was a good or bad thing, it was an issue I would struggle with later – establishing professional boundaries with my mental health care providers.

January 2004 – number 22

My new mental health social worker had an earnest, Northern manner that put me instantly at ease. Soon making habitual cups of tea, she would sit and listen to my woes while looking at my art, often interjecting with an, "Oh my word" when I told her funny stories about my encounters with yet another random, famous person that I had bumped into. Often sabotaging these encounters, my perpetual blunders made amusing chat. I didn't see her as a mental health social worker; rather, she became someone to talk to openly, without shame or judgement.

April 2006 – number 23

I received a letter from Mile End Hospital, informing me that they could offer one year of psychotherapy with a fully trained psychologist. On first meeting Ms A, I remember her dark eyes and thick accent. There was also a solemnity about her. Addressing me formally, she led me to one of those dull, carpeted treatment rooms with the smallest window imaginable. Whatever the weather, the light was coated in dusty grey and, from the very beginning, I caught her slyly looking at the clock, or staring into space. Ms A didn't exude the warm charm of my mental health social workers. Paid to listen, she did just that; barely interjecting and waiting for the moment she could say, "It's time." Do psychotherapists really listen, or are they groaning inside and wishing to God they could be somewhere else? I enjoyed the cycle ride to and from the hospital more than the sessions. Because sitting in the waiting room made me uneasy, I would stand in the corridor. Ms A told me not to do that. Asking "Why not?" she couldn't give a proper answer. She also refused to call me by my first name, despite my frequent requests. How can you realistically establish any rapport with someone who addresses you that formally?

I told the head of the department, the Welsh psychotherapist, that I was ill at ease with Ms A. He just replied with his, now annoyingly familiar, "hmmm". I had no choice but to continue because I was sinking by the day. Any help was better than none, I thought. We are all masters of own destinies and only I could break the concrete in my mind with a hammer. Sometimes it seemed as if Ms A was pouring more concrete in there.

After I told her about being sexually assaulted by four Asian men in a car she said, "Well, you do dress sexily?" That statement was incursive and at that juncture, Ms A became the enemy in my mind.

When I spoke of leaving London to be with my husband, she would say glibly, "If you go, it won't solve your problems". This was not helpful or constructive input.

At our final session, when I inexplicably handed over a present, thanking her, she told me, "You know the therapy is finished now, that's all we can offer you, I'm afraid. This really is it."

Reading her final report and the description of my extreme emotional difficulties, she concluded that my psychological problems stemmed from an inability to bond with my mother. This was due to never receiving my mother's milk as a baby, hence my failure to emotionally form an attachment properly. Scoffing when I read her theories, afterwards I thought there might have been a kernel of truth about the reason for the lack of maternal closeness. To sum up my time at Mile End Hospital, I was once leaving Ms A's office, wearing my sunglasses to hide my red, tear stained eyes, when an Asian man hit me for no reason. No one assisted. Eventually leaving the hospital, I saw the assailant waiting for me. He was swearing and I was shaking, afraid and helpless. This was a hospital, a place I was supposed to get better, not assaulted, yet my time spent there felt like one protracted mental assault.

2007 September – number 24

My mental health social worker told me one day that she was leaving to do further training. "Not again", I thought.

"I won't find anyone like you," I said sadly.

She assured me that her replacement was very good. For a few months in September, although spiralling towards a dark place, I thought I didn't need anyone. Claudia, my new mental health worker, was insistent on visiting me. I'd just done an interview for the *London Evening Standard*, at the request of my publishers Chipmunka Press. They said it would be good exposure for me. The caption for the article was "I suffer from the Amy Winehouse syndrome?". The only difference being that I didn't drink or do hard drugs. My naiveté was astounding and agreeing to do such an interview is further proof that my mind was not an ally. The journalist asked deeply personal questions and, like a naïve twit, I answered them honestly. I believed the focus of the article would be on my art and writing, instead she promptly twisted my words and the final article was horrifying, yet I'd handed it all to her on a plate without being under the slightest duress. Within days I demanded that the article was removed from the internet and vowed never to do another press interview again. (This was in 2007, I only felt confident to do interviews again in April 2013, to promote my exhibition in London and even then I was overly cautious.) Over-simplified segments of my life were left dangling and exposed, as if anyone cared. Realising I did need to confide and talk freely to someone, I agreed to see Claudia; she was the last mental health social worker I saw in London.

Claudia was German and maintained a certain detachment, while remaining concerned about my mental state. She came to my exhibition in 2008 – *Schizophrenia Part 1,* where I exhibited as Sophie, Mia and Fred. She also took a keen interest in my work. On occasion Dr Bass cancelled our appointments, or was late and/or, for whatever reason – and I am sure it was a valid one – sometimes didn't even show up. Claudia was never late and always reliable. Again, I felt I could trust my mental health social worker more than my doctor. There was a closeness that was unattainable with a doctor, simply by virtue of the time constraints imposed on them. Dr Bass often looked exhausted and drained. It was easier to have home visits. Claudia even persuaded Dr Bass to visit me at home once and he appeared to be entranced by the artwork. It was a mental boost for him to see me as the working artist, rather than the debilitated, mentally ill patient.

Dr Bass often told me to stop smoking marijuana. Asking him why it was so damaging, he said it was, "Like trying to cycle with the brakes on." I believe it was the skunk that I had inadvertently smoked, that transformed what was a depressive condition into one with auditory and visual hallucinations and extreme highs and lows. Despite my awareness of the dangers, I found it difficult to resist a joint if one was being passed around. Dr Bass only offered medication as a way out, which I was deeply sceptical about. Claudia was a good listener and told me to be more positive. Neither of them offered practical strategies to deal with the condition. When I mentioned my desire to go and live with my husband, Dr Bass was quite brutal when he said, "If you leave London you will have to find new mental health provision." The thought of finding new people sent me into a panic.

Garnering the impression that I was a unique case, I recall reading Dr Bass's report regarding my mental health. He wrote that he found my case perplexing and that he wasn't quite sure what to make of my case or how to treat me either since I was a high functioning, prolific artist and *atypical*. He once asked if I was making a living and if I needed to go on disability benefits. My pride took offence at this: working was my way to escape the inveterate mental torment, irrespective of what I was earning. Working was the only thing that was keeping me motivated to stick around a little longer.

2008-9 – Leaving London – The Year Psychosis Struck

Finally, after years of procrastination and vacillation on both sides, I moved to Brussels to be with my husband, only coming to London for work or meetings. Seeing Claudia and Dr Bass intermittently, fundamentally, nothing had changed – Fred and Mia continued to play havoc with my life. For years I'd been leading a complex dual existence and an innate refusal to relinquish that way of being put tremendous pressure on my brain. In my previous essay, *A Dissection of Psychosis* I go into more detail, explaining the circumstances that were ripe for mental collapse. In short, 2009 was a stressful year personally and work wise. I had also begun the process of severing ties from certain people in my life. Any break was going to be psychologically violent – and it was. I smoked my last joint in November 2009 and psychosis struck in December 2009, like frenzied daggers attacking my brain, each slash causing something alien to seep and infect my consciousness. During the episode I had little recourse to mental health services, just my friend from Bosnia who saw me through it and listened for hours to my ranting while giving me food and making tea that I didn't drink, which sat instead like cups of tar by the bed.

January 2010

Returning to London, shaky but stable, I decided to see Dr Bass and Claudia and get advice regarding medication. My husband and Bosnian friend said I should, at least, give it a shot. After what had happened in December, I thought it was time. A few days after I was in London the symptoms began very quickly: mania, not sleeping, loss of appetite. I was heading for another crash and sensed it coming. When I went to Pritchards Road. I was at my tipping point, Claudia was not there, nor was Dr Bass. People stared, when I went outside and I couldn't breathe because of the cigarette smoke. Big clouds of it engulfed me and were getting bigger and thicker. Becoming more and more stressed, I demanded to see Claudia and she appeared with her blue eyes blazing. Starting to scream at her, I asked why she had kept me waiting. She told me I could leave if I wanted to. Shocked – surely she was the only person who could help? – Now I didn't trust her anymore. Raging at the other patients, they ignored me or were too drugged-up to respond. Calling up my musician friend, Saskia, I asked her to sing down the phone to calm me down. Then Dr Bass arrived and I shouted at him, asking why he was late. He apologised and they led me to a room. As I continued to rant, he asked me if I had taken cocaine.

At this stage, I was incensed and said, "No, I'm not on cocaine, I haven't slept that's all. I was here on time, where were you? How do you expect people to get better in a place like this? Can you not smell the stench of sickness in the air? Look at you, you both look ill, you need more help than me and I'm deemed the mad one. I came here because I need meds, I want to go on anti-depressants – now."

Dr Bass told me that anti-depressants could make me psychotic and then, I don't recall why he came up, I mentioned Stephen Fry and his wise words that: "Mood is like the weather."

Dr Bass asked me how I'd met Stephen Fry and I told him that I was in the lift at Shoreditch House, planning on going for a swim, when the doors opened and Jude Law stepped in. Wearing an enormous hat, with my head stooped down, he stood directly opposite me. Looking up and seeing who it was I said, "What happened in New York?" He was rather speechless at first, then we chatted, he bought me a Virgin Mary at the roof-top bar, gave his *explanation* and invited me to a party being held by the owner of the Groucho club on the fourth floor. Tagging along, the first person I saw was Stephen Fry. Going up to him, I introduced myself, even interrupting the conversation he was having. Mr Fry was so tall he resembled a noble tree. Within seconds I told him I had schizoaffective disorder and asked for his email address. He politely, if surprisingly, obliged. Dr Bass listened intently, it did sound as if I was fabricating the whole story and I was speaking so fast I could barely breathe. I watched Dr Bass as he frantically tried to write everything that I said down and it looked pathetic, because it was impossible to keep up.

Dr Bass said, "You are experiencing flight of ideas." Yes, they were coming at me very fast and I tried to fire them off as they entered my head and tumbled out of my mouth. Dr Bass then told me the session was over and Claudia escorted me out, urging me to sleep. I didn't sleep, I went out shopping, entertained strangers and made people scream at the tops of their voices in Agent Provocateur. I was singing and ranting with my friend Saskia. Later I went out, accompanied with my Bosnian friend, to the restaurant Hix, on Brewer Street in Soho, to meet my old LSE tutor Dr Chun Lin. On my way there, I vociferously berated the taxi driver, rang my parents, and told them to call the police because I thought my nephew was in imminent danger. Swearing at the cab driver, he was scared, but repelled at the same time. As soon as I entered the restaurant, I couldn't stop ranting. People were staring, so I told them to stop. They didn't. People who worked at the restaurant, who I thought were my friends, now looked at me with frightened eyes. My husband turned up, having flown in from Brussels. I was telling everyone how to behave and that if they didn't do what I said Fred was going to "get me", while scribbling notes, barely able to eat, and didn't touch the 16 oysters on the plate. Dr Chun Lin, my husband and Bosnian friend didn't want to leave my side. Taking charge, my husband and I left. Mark Hix and his business partner acted as if I didn't exist. Prior to that night, after completing three paintings on the walls of the restaurant male toilets, when I excitedly showed Mark the completed work, he was so pleased he over enthusiastically kissed me several times on the face. The work had taken many hours to render in trying circumstances, as men stared, pissed, and made disgusting remarks. I sought recognition, not sloppy kisses. Afterwards he said he had only tried to give me a hug to say thank you for all my hard work, and this was probably true. His semi-inebriated attempt to *hug* me pressed a button in my head, releasing all the memories of the previous sexual assaults and negative encounters with men. It was too much for my mind to compute, as I was dealing with one incursive mental wave after the other and each one left me flattened. I was also struggling to create the mobile Mark had requested me to make, to hang next to Damien Hirst's, and now Fred was saying, "Why should you sweat blood for them?" Fred wanted me to smash the restaurant to pieces there and then. I didn't, instead I vowed (rather dramatically) to never set foot in the place again, which was a shame because I used to enjoy dining there.

I didn't see Claudia or Dr Bass again until March 2012, when I requested a meeting to achieve the closure I needed. The manager of the restaurant wrote an email saying that they were happy with the artwork and that the owners wanted to say thank you but that it was "probably enough" and to stop working. In the next sentence I was reprimanded for my behaviour. They never asked how I was, or if I had been ill, I do recall the use of the word "disappointment" and the last sentence of the email read:

> *I hope that I am not speaking out of turn here and you understand the position I am in when saying that it's unacceptable that some of our guests were threatened and we as a restaurant were compromised, as you are a "friend" of ours. I hope that when you do come back, you take note of this and behave accordingly.*

Mortified to receive such a mail, hurt and incensed, I wanted to scream, "But I was deep in the throes of psychosis. If I was a *friend*, then why are you kicking me?" The wounds and humiliation of the evening are still sore and palpable, even though the incident is probably long forgotten.

As we enter 2014 and I reflect on that night, I can see how the psychosis smudged out the reality of the situation, heightening emotions, distorting the truth and turning people who were once allies into the enemy. I can imagine how alarming it must have been for all those around me. Yes, I was an eccentric, colourful artist. Sometimes I hammed it up, but I always tried to be amiable, polite and professional. Acting this role was a strain at times, but for the act to collapse and be suspended in a psychotic stupor, for everyone to witness, was distressing. I don't blame those people who ostracised me. I don't blame the restaurant for issuing a warning; and I don't blame Dr Bass or Claudia. I only wish that I had known I might be vulnerable to psychosis and what to do if I found myself in that position. My Bosnian friend had begged me not to go out that evening, she knew I was not well. She couldn't stop me. Now, of course, I know that the key would have been to sleep. I believe that the majority of the general public don't actually have any conception of what psychosis is and it is only by experiencing it that I have finally understood the beast that lives in my head and learnt how to, not necessarily tame or befriend it, but walk away when it rages.

January 2010 – number 25 and 26

The psychosis lasted a few days, I was sleep deprived, ranting and singing – it was all blurred fragments with torn edges. The final straw was when I believed I had to obey Fred's demands, however compromising,

within a set time frame and, if I did so, all the global ills would be eradicated and we would live in a utopia.

One of these demands was to run naked down Brick Lane towards
Shoreditch House. Stripping off, I slipped out the door and ran. My husband
took chase, he was pleading with me not to. Defiant, as I stood naked in the
black of night in some alleyway where dogs pissed and prostitutes skulked,
now my toes wriggled amidst a mosaic of broken glass. My husband was
forced to call the police. Enmeshed in the psychotic narrative, I had a black
out. I do remember refusing to look the police in the eye and standing naked
outside my flat door and it being eerily quiet, even though I was being very
loud. They could have had the decency to let me put on some clothes and
shoes before they led me away and drove me to the hospital. Or, at least they
could have allowed my husband to retrieve a few garments and footwear.
Later my husband told me they had wanted to handcuff me. The above is a
lamentably truncated version of events. One day, when I am able, I will
revisit that night properly, even if my brain leaks with pain to do so. All I
have managed so far is a poem and this rather rambled version of events. It
will have to do and it is the best version that I can write for now.

I sat in a hospital room with my husband afraid to speak, scared of
what might happen. Eventually two psychiatrists came and I didn't dare
look at them. My husband did all the talking and eventually they released
us. Wrapping me in his coat and letting me wear his shoes, he walked in his
socks to the taxi. It was then that I realised that, "Despite the nightmare that
Fred has put him through this man must love me unconditionally." None of
the people in London I'd shamelessly devoted my life to came to my aid.
They were all gone now, apart from a pitiable handful.

One of the psychiatrists gave me some anti-psychotic medication and,
although I was able to sleep, it took a few days for the strands of the psychotic narrative to melt away. How vivid that parallel world was. It was a
world in which I counted and had spoken to artistic giants and – no longer
a puny being – I was imbued with a divinity. When I finally came out of the
psychosis, I was very angry with Claudia and Dr Bass and felt completely
let down by them at the time. Assuming they had witnessed psychosis
before, how could they let someone go home in that state? They'd known
me for years and yet it seemed they didn't know me at all. Although they
both wrote that they were sorry I cut off communication. Dr Bass had
agreed to meet after I returned home from my brief hospital admission. My
husband cancelled the meeting, thinking it was time to leave London and
create a brand new mental health care plan in Brussels.

In 2012 I felt able to make contact with Claudia and Dr Bass again.
Happy to hear from me, they agreed to the meeting I requested. It was an
intrinsic part of my recovery process. On a suitably sunny day, I cycled to

the hospital on a Boris bike. Looking forward to seeing them I recalled walking into their office. They were both sitting there and we all smiled. It was a big relief to see them and to know that they were not angry or disappointed. They listened as I talked nervously (wishing I'd been less voluble) and at the end of the session I felt mentally lighter. Dr Bass asked me for a sample of my blood, saying they would study it to see if they could identify the gene that had blighted my family and could perhaps impact on future generations. I obliged and am still in contact with them. When I visit London and start to ail I can call Claudia for support. They both attended my mid-career retrospective in London in April 2013 and I read out my poem that partially recounted the psychosis; it was cathartic, difficult and necessary. Both Dr Bass and Claudia offered the best care they could at the time and I have since stopped being angry, I also think it's important that I remain in touch. They are part of my mental health journey, they know intimate truths about my past, they have my life on file, this is why I can't quite disconnect from them – and keeping contact is something I value. For risk of sounding sycophantic, I believe that out of all the people I saw in London, they remain two of the most committed people who work in mental health. I think the respect is mutual.

Feb 2010 – number 27

After I left London, my husband tried to find me a new doctor in Brussels almost immediately. When I first sat in Dr R's office I noticed the view of trees out her window. Seeing the constant sway of leaves was soothing. Her office was bright, strewn with toys for the children that came with her patients. Calling me by my first name, she shook my hand with a beaming smile. She was Spanish and the first time we met I wore my purple hat. At our initial meeting I didn't say a word, but then it all came out, like a ball of string unravelling very fast. With each subsequent session I became calmer; she saw me throughout my first pregnancy, too. Believing she was against the idea of me becoming a mother, she said that was not the case at all. I talked about London and the people I had aligned with and how I went crawling towards them for the mouldy crumbs they tossed. They were out of my life, but not out of my head. Like ants they refused to leave. I talked about my unborn child. I talked about difficult and awkward things. She never once interrupted, as I rabbited on, to say that I could plausibly be at risk of postpartum psychosis. She never told me that at all during the nine months of my pregnancy.

October 2010 – number 28 – 34

Going into labour in the early hours of the morning and giving birth quickly and relatively easily, rather than allow me to sleep, a flood of midwives, student doctors and an array of other people came filing in, constantly disturbing me. Even when I was asleep they woke me up. After three days of continually disrupted sleep, psychosis struck just when I was due to be released from hospital. This time I was acutely aware of the patterns and understood what was going on. When I opened my mouth, I was loquacious, emotional, indefatigable, disorientated, and facing a torrent of constant and deeply disturbing hallucinations. I confided in one midwife revealing that, "Fred is telling me to pour boiling water onto my baby's head." Horrified, she notified the relevant doctors.

I'd told my obstetrician about my condition at the beginning of my pregnancy but the hospital psychiatrist said there was no need to see me. No one was informed that I was potentially at risk of postpartum psychosis. It is surprising that such an experienced ward would be so ill equipped to deal with the condition.

If I'd known that telling the midwife about Fred and what he was ordering me to do to my newly born son would result in being kept in hospital for one month, maybe I would not have been so open. If I had also known that six different psychiatrists and psychologists (all with varying degrees of spoken English) would have descended upon me in a swarm, I would have remained mute. And if I had known that being placed in the mother and baby unit at St Jean would actually have made me worse, I would have kept my mouth shut.

My husband told me that it was better that I stayed quiet and I complied. The psychiatric mother and baby unit was a place in which I was supposed to recuperate, but the focus was purely on the baby, not the mental recovery of the mother. Exposed and vulnerable, they knew everything about me and yet they did nothing apart from poke and ask questions.

The last two weeks of my one-month hospital stay were horrendous.

One particular psychiatrist visited me when I was working on my scroll and my baby was sleeping. I asked if he wanted to see what I was working on. He declined and his refusal left me incensed. These people asked all the questions; I was supposed to answer truthfully, revealing my mind and soul and he couldn't even look at the very thing – the only thing – that was keeping me calm, coherent and focused. All these doctors, examining and scrutinising me like a specimen, created resentment. He did, however, remind me that I was a mother now and that perhaps it was time to make contact with my family. I listened to him and wondered if I needed a doctor who was tough. Telling Dr R about his no-nonsense approach, she seemed offended that I was questioning her methodology and became standoffish. It turned out that this new doctor was too busy and not that keen to take on any new patients. I saw Dr R a few times after that, because she was a genuine and temperate person, but in my eyes she'd lost credibility. The final straw came when she prescribed something that was supposed to aid my sleep and instead it augmented the symptoms of psychosis.

During the last two psychotic episodes, my husband and I developed strategies to deal with the psychosis. Often in the presence of the doctors we spoke in a code that only we understood. Our objective was to get out of the hospital, because the longer I stayed the more likely I was to relapse. In the end I *acted* my way out of the hospital, even though I remained unwell. It worked, but I battled with recurring hallucinations from thereon that involved *harming my baby* in the most gruesome of ways for at least the first year and a half of my son's life and I had to deal with that alone. There was no follow up, no monitoring and no support.

October 2010 – August 2012 – number 35 and 36

Experiencing recurrent mini psychotic episodes, without the psychosis ever becoming full blown and protracted, my husband and I continued to implement our strategies. When my husband said that I was getting worse not better, most likely because of the sleep deprivation, I saw my local GP and she referred me to a therapist, who worked on my very street. The therapist told me she was not a doctor and ill-equipped to deal with my condition. I told her that I was looking for a special kind of treatment, but I didn't know if it existed, that I was not on medication, and didn't see it as a way forward, and that I wanted to share what I had learnt about my condition to assist other sufferers. I told her that I used art to calm down my *hot* brain and that this was crucial for my stability. Specifically, I was looking for an innovative approach to mental health, tailored to my needs. She listened with interest, saying that she would try and find what I was looking for. Discovering a place called TrActor she found a new doctor; his name was Dr Thys.

Number 37 (plus his team of 6)

During my initial encounter with Dr Thys, I wasn't sure what to make of him. Recalling his firm handshake and the homely atmosphere of his practise – set in a house, which was newly refurbished, with old wooden floors – I soon ascertained that he was different from all the previous doctors I had met. At our first meeting I brought my scroll and explained that I needed mental health support, but in turn wanted to collaborate with his organisation. It quickly became apparent that we were on the same page. He, too, believed in the positive impact of creativity on the mind, he also made music and was an avid doodler.

Although TrActor was, in effect, a hospital, it was set in a majestic, converted church. It had an atelier where they held workshops and they had recently started organising exhibitions that revolved around the subject of mental health. These were organised via their sister organisation KAOS. Dr Thys introduced me to his whole team, which was quite exhausting (and I actually thought, "Oh no, here we go again, a bunch of strangers asking me awkward personal questions."), but it was unavoidable protocol. I told him that I would like a mental health social worker, someone to visit and check on how I was doing, because I was very isolated. With no close friends in Brussels and, at that time, minimal contact with my family, the mental health social worker was going to be a lifeline during these initial lonely years in Brussels.

Number 38

When I first met my new mental health social worker, J, my son was a year-and-a-half old. I can't remember what he was doing, as I overwhelmed her with my art and the words that fell out of my mouth in a mess. She sat down on the sofa, trying to take it all in as I bombarded her with sketchbooks. She was slight and delicate; she'd lived previous interesting lives and her eyes held deep wounds within them. Taking some time to find a rhythm, often I would be exhausted after her visits becoming rapidly manic. In short she could trigger me, simply because we often engaged in *hot topics*. By *hot* I am referring to subjects that were personal and expended lots of energy when discussed. She could sense this and see when I was getting unwell, her advice was always, "Try to breathe, to relax and – crucially – to sleep."

Gradually, she understood how my mind worked, becoming aware when Fred was around. Observing the swift transformation she knew what to do and genuinely cared, telling me that when she visited my home it was as therapeutic for her as it was for me.

"You are the only person who offers me something to drink and asks how I am," she said.

Often engaging in deep discussions about art, philosophy, motherhood, family, childhood and relationships, she told me how she spoke about me with her friends and described my work, saying, "It gives me goose bumps to look at your art – it really is unbelievable." Hearing these words gave me a modicum of hope to carry on and ignore Fred's taunts.

J assured me that whatever she said was not designed to flatter and that she genuinely believed in what I was trying to do with my art and writing. What was I trying to do? Scratch at some truth and move people – I don't know. Compelled to make marks and mess around with colour and shove words on the page, I just hoped they made sense. She frequently had to repeat the same constructive affirmations because I couldn't hold onto them, like water through a sieve. Nothing stuck. Fred's dissonant narratives were too powerful. I could not let go of them and was unable to catch the food that J doggedly tried to feed me. When I embarked on the scroll with my son, J took photos of the process and became excited with each new section that I unravelled. Her visits spurred me on, just like an over enthusiastic child eager to please her teacher.

Was this level of care inappropriate and too close? Did boundaries need to be set? Professionally, those that work in mental health must maintain a distance; simultaneously I needed someone to talk to, someone I could trust – someone who would come to my home – and to be able to open up without being deemed pathetic. A level of closeness, to get to the heart of the problem, is essential.

J's generous doses of praise and these weekly visits became part of my substitute for medication. Often she would stay for two hours. During this time she moved freely in my space and I would end up sitting at my desk, painting or drawing, while we talked, went out on errands or took my son to the park. Sometimes she even revealed parts of her *self* to me, which I appreciated, but other times it was incongruous. We were not friends, she was my mental health social worker, boundaries needed to be established. Sharing gave a false sense of closeness. Although it was refreshing not to be scrutinised, analysed and pitied.

Subsequently, we had a few clashes –the reasons for these conflicts have never been straightforward, but the key factor here is that we could be open, have it out and say what aggrieved us quite candidly. There have been times when I haven't seen J for a long while, like now for instance. Then I write an email and she usually calls back. I can pour everything out and we pick up from where we left off. I might retreat for longer periods, then she texts or gets in touch. She has usually left the door open and it's been up to me if I wanted to resume contact or not. I never surmised that one day maybe that door would remain shut.

In 2011, Dr Thys published sections of my scroll in the Flemish psychological journal *Psyche*. It was exciting to see my art in print. However, I told him that Fred made me doubt his integrity because he didn't publish my essay like he said he would. Dr Thys looked at me earnestly and said quietly, "It was too long, that's the only reason why we didn't publish it."

I laughed and said, "Perhaps I should submit a short poem instead."

When doubts have surfaced, for whatever reason, J has assured me that Dr Thys is an ally and these are hard to find. I should have faith. How do you grow faith in a mental landscape of arid nothingness? You keep on working, trying to create something magical and never give up.

When I proposed an art project, Dr Thys's colleague, Mike, obtained the funds to realise it. In the summer of 2012, I created a scroll with patients with mental health problems who were based at TrActor. By inviting people to participate in a series of intense workshops, we became a family for a few short hours, working collectively, in harmony and unison. All our creative energy was poured into the scroll, as a form of pure, undiluted expression without the pressure of producing something perfect. By planting these initial seeds, at the end of the workshop sessions we created a visual *Forest of Minds*. There were times when I became sucked in by the scroll and worked too intensely, but it was worth it. During the final session we all sat together, eating Mike's homemade cake and drinking tea, plucking key words from our heads and throwing them back into the scroll where they could find new roots. These workshops were an opportunity for people to observe, comment and discuss. It was a chance to forget about mental infirmity, to be liberated artists, and to revel in what our hands and minds had produced.

Not just the teacher, I am also the pupil during my workshops. It is a process of exchange, an open ended dialogue, and can continue long after the session has ended. It is the long-term conversation that I am interested in. Dr Thys thanked me for what I had achieved with the patients and KAOS has asked me to produce a second scroll in the autumn of 2014. This time I will be working with a patient, Lieven, a sufferer of schizophrenia.

Lieven has become a new ally who *gets* what I am trying to achieve through art and words. He can also relate to my daily struggle to keep sane. Recently, I wrote to him saying how excited I was about the prospect of working together. His striking photography needs a greater audience and it is photography that ensures he stays well. Lieven, promptly, wrote back saying:

... I really do feel the difference compared to the years before photography... sometimes I experience stuff that has been left over from the times

Image 32. Detail from *A Forest of Minds* created with patients at TrActor (ink, pen, acrylic paint, gouache and tempera on a 30-foot scroll of paper, 2012).

I must have been psychotic... about being a mystic and that I could walk down paths that others don't get to walk on. Jim Morrison once said, "Life is an experiment". I have a lot of forces in me but if I start to talk to you about those things I'm afraid I can't stop, because it would be nice to talk to someone else who, maybe, can relate to my psychotic episodes... and thank you for admiring my photographic work.

A few minutes after sending this email, he wrote again saying he was sorry, *I did not want to say these things,* as if he was ashamed.

This was my reply to Lieven.

... Keep on taking photos, I always recognise your work when I see it... like you, I experiment... I always feel better after I have written or been creative, this is why I think working with you could be interesting. We could both learn from the process and produce something phenomenal...

Once you have had psychosis it haunts you, it still haunts me – that's why I keep on creating, it's my way of fighting to keep well.

I like that "Life is an experiment"...

Sometimes I think I am obsessed by psychosis, I think about it all the time, because I know it could strike again...

This psychosis has ravaged us; we have to do something useful with it, at least this is what I think...

I am not on meds, it's hard to keep well, I go to bed early and keep waking up and then I work, write, paint etc. but I have two small children to think about and I would like a third, so this dream of completing my family is going to motivate me to stay on track...

It will be great if I can help you in some small way, to get your work shown in London, you deserve that recognition...

I understand what you are going through... I have been there. It's not your fault. Psychosis strips you to the bone, if anything it is comforting when you share, because then I feel I'm part of an exclusive club. Not everyone has had psychosis and comes out the other side, we are lucky so, please, don't apologise.

Lieven is the first *schizophrenic* that I have connected and identified with, someone else who has been through psychosis. I remember when he first attended my scroll workshop, with a camera hanging around his neck. He was so afraid to make that first mark on the scroll.

"Just make circles," I said, "don't be scared." He was, at first, anxious to make a mistake on the mighty scroll, but then he said,

"I think I can make circles..." and he did, lots of lyrical, perfectly formed circles.

Lieven had never properly drawn before; the experience changed something in him. It was a revelation for me, too. There was a connection, a bridge formed by the fragments of psychosis that created a trust and ease. This collaboration will be mutually beneficial creatively and make us both more robust mentally; maybe it will melt away some of those psychotic memories still welded to parts of our brain. Together, we will create photographic portraits of the participants and document the creation of the scroll from start to finish, learning and bouncing off ideas. We are planning an exhibition of this work in the atelier in May 2015 and also, in London, at Rich Mix in June 2015. There will be a debate about art and psychosis and finally, I will create a play/performance/lyrical narrative (still trying to work it out actually) that addresses the themes of art, madness and motherhood. It will be intense and I am, admittedly, nervous about revealing intimate parts of my soul on a stage without the aid of my usual prompts.

The show will also consist of new artwork related to motherhood and psychosis. Since the birth of my second child I have embarked on a project: *1,000 Postcards*. So far I have created 150 postcards and a new scroll with my three-year-old son. The postcard idea stemmed from Dr Thys. He asked me to produce one for a show, *Return to Sender*, they were organising consisting of thirty postcards created by thirty artists. Attending the private view two days after giving birth to my second baby, this is where the idea took root in my brain, to do 100 and see where these postcards lead me. Mike provides them in batches of fifty at a time. Thus far it has been a merry dance of squiggles with dinosaurs, monsters, trees, landscapes and butterflies.

Image 33. *Silly Monster and Two Angry Dinosaurs* (pen and pencil on postcard, 2013)

Image 34. *Some Ancient and Lost Land in China* (pen, acrylic ink and pencil on postcard, 2014)

Image 35. *Piggy At the End of the Rainbow* (pen, acrylic ink and pencil on postcard, 2014)

Each postcard, each mark on the scroll, each sketch of my baby, each new poem penned – all this amounts to the creative strategies that keep me balanced and protect my children from Fred's malice. Fred spits out venomous nonsense, he is not real, but the marks on the paper are. I can look at them, deriving great satisfaction that I am working, fighting, creating – and leaving something behind for my children to scrutinise, to help them understand my daily war and unerring belief in the beauty of the fluid dance on the page that the marks can make with a simple pen or a brush dipped in ink. Watching my son create his squiggles and transforming them into something that will make him smile with wonder and curiosity the next morning, is all I need to empty out my brain at the end of the night to start afresh the next day. My son and I have become addicted to making squiggles, needing our daily fix, and the squiggles keep our bond intact, however hard Fred tries to cut us with that sharp scissor of a tongue of his.

The key, then, does not lie solely with psychiatrists or talking therapy or pills; it's embedded in having an outlet and a *reliable consistent* support structure. Art has helped to maintain a balanced mind. Sharing this work with like-minded people is just as important as making the work. With an over-abundance of stimuli, people can find ways to escape it by engaging in art or writing. Art enables me to offload the noise and disquiet that rumbles continuously in the mind. Concealed within the scrolls are these crucial spaces that have become a refuge and a place for mental rehabilitation and healing.

Mental health remains an area of acute interest, precisely because I have been deemed *mentally* different from others. My work tries to address questions of *what does it mean to be normal, to be allowed into the room and to fit?* Being labelled schizophrenic, for example, is immediately stigmatising, often an unfortunate consequence that comes from any open admission of being mentally ill. It was fitting that my first exhibition in Brussels was organised by TrActor in 2012, providing something different from a pill – it rebuilt my confidence, obliterated during the psychosis. Recalling how good I felt at the opening, I listened to Dr Thys's speech in Flemish, none of which I understood. While organising the show, J reminded me to rest. Sleep is vitally important for a *hot* brain and having people around reiterating this basic truth was a reminder not to let my slumber slide. Mike, the curator, treated my work with the utmost care, and Dr Thys popped in during the installation to commend what we were doing.

This exhibition, the animated meetings, the long discussions, the meticulous planning – all of this is a better substitute for medication, because it is about *doing* something with your brain, not being inert and dependent. My mind seemed to be getting stronger and Fred's presence faded in 2012. Having the right people in your life can make life more tolerable, if the commentary in your head is ripping you apart.

What Constitutes the Right Type of Mental Health Care?

Getting the right type of care is crucial then? I had an appointment at TrActor. J picked me up and we got the metro together. I told her about my trip to New York, my show at Soho House and the screening of my film, *White Wall* at SPin. We bought some lunch and she sat in on my meeting with Mike, then she took me to see Dr Thys.

I told him that, "If I see myself as very small, I can cope and if I set myself tasks that are small enough to put in my mouth and chew slowly, than I can carry on."

Doing the show was a method of getting mentally stronger. Being less alone and surrounding myself with people who believed in my work and supported my artistic endeavours was part of my recovery.

"I see this project as a step in the right direction. I am inching towards a small and safe place where small and perfectly realised dreams can be born in the form of paintings, poems and books," Dr Thys listened carefully as I paused to doodle in my sketchbook.

During my consultation I also asked Dr Thys about the potential impact of having a second child on my mental health. He said he knew of a woman who had my condition. "She has two children, been through a divorce, had cancer and she's ok – it is doable," he said.

Despite the risks, and the risks were great – hanging over me like a swarm of mosquitoes intent on pricking my skin with the poisoned needle of psychosis – his words made me smile inside.

Then I said, out of the blue, "Perhaps these essays, along with my artwork and poems, might enlighten people – that would make me less useless, you see this disorder has stolen great big chunks of my life. It's trying to stop me from having a second child. It's trying to stop me from reaching out. It wants me to shut down and stop doing anything meaningful."

Dr Thys said, "It is all possible, no one is going to deny you the right to expand your family."

To which I replied, "I understand my condition, I have strategies, as long as I have the structures in place I can do it."

Dr Thys told me, "You have a special gift, remember that, we will support you."

Leaving with a little spring in my step, I was glad to be away from the sweaty, hot, noisy mouth of New York that I had been immersed in only days ago. There had been no mental episodes in New York, just the closure I was seeking by proving to myself that I could show my work there again, even after I cancelled the exhibition in 2009 because of the psychosis. Fred was not going to steal any more of my life; each time he tried I would steal every part of it back.

Conclusion

At the beginning of the essay, I was adamant my conclusion would be that psychiatrists do not have all the answers. A complex question, the answer is not at all straightforward. Dr Thys told me that, with much of the new medication, they do not know the long-term effects of taking such pills. For some people, taking pills allows them to function and work, but many live in secrecy, knowing that if they told their boss they were mentally of unsound mind they might get the sack or be discriminated against. The pressure of performing at work means that taking the pills becomes mandatory rather than a choice.

Being told that I had schizoaffective disorder made my life worse, not better. It was easier not knowing, easier pretending and trying to fit than exposing myself to a lack of empathy and, often, cruel derision because of my condition. There is a threadbare residue of tolerance towards the chronically mentally ill. People don't want to be near the mad. And that includes me, even though I am a member of the club.

When I have been in close proximity to people with mental health problems, I can sniff out the Freds, see him in their moribund eyes, distorted posture and infected demeanour. Something has died in them. Fred has killed off part of their soul. Those bits can be revitalised, not by being institutionalised or pumped with pills that are sapping, but by *doing stuff* with the life we are all trying to live and understanding the mechanisms of the illness. Everyone needs to work, especially the mentally ill, because work provides vital exercise for the brain.

Despite all the time lavished on psychiatrists and psychotherapists, no one told me some home truths about living with my condition and dealing with it. That it was better to keep my diagnosis private, that certain factors such as stress, sleep deprivation, and smoking skunk – in particular – could lead to psychosis. Crucially, I was not warned that I could be at risk of postpartum psychosis. The wisdom that I have attained, over many years, helps me to mentally self-regulate and arrange my mind and I will pass everything I have learnt to my offspring. I would, even, argue that families with a history of mental health problems have an obligation to educate their children about the affliction.

Surprisingly, no one informed me of the impact my condition would have on my ability to parent. In January 2014 I, found myself in the unfortunate position where I had to tell my three-year-old son about Fred. Finding a language to describe what was happening, I told him that Fred likes to climb into my brain through my ear and sets my brain on fire and that the only way to make Fred go away was by talking softly. If we shouted at him he would grow bigger and try to eat us, conversely if we were calm and quiet he would shrink and go away.

Needless to say my son doesn't much like Frederick and said, "Mummy, I don't want Fred to come." I am still not sure if telling him was the right thing to do, but I would rather tell the truth than be mendacious.

I wouldn't say that I have been entirely failed by the mental health services, but it was seeing so many different people that caused more damage than good, leaving me exposed rather than supported. Is my experience unusual or the norm? Therapy was not an opportunity to dislodge the mental turds wedged in the bum crack of my brain and flush them away; therapy generated more turds that left me wading in a sea of mental shit (excuse the scatological metaphors). Disagreement and a break down in trust can impede the efficacy of psychiatric care. There have been times when my trust in psychiatrists has totally collapsed, leaving me desolate. At the same time, mental health services are under incredible strain, with not enough resources to provide the intensive, one-to-one care, that patients often need. Imagine fifty patients, firing off emails with demands and questions to the relatively small mental health team allocated to them. It is not feasible to reply immediately. Although this *lack of immediate* response can create a false state of abandonment, patients need to recognise that, typically, this silence is not personal. Inundated with scores of emails, perhaps those working in mental health are overwhelmed. They lose track, do not have the time to respond in detail and are simply doing the best that they can within incredible time constraints and an ever-increasing workload, as more patients come into the system without adequate resources to treat everyone – another essential reason why I want to be mentally more self-reliant.

A few months ago I discovered the anonymous English speaking mental health helpline in Belgium run by the Community Health Service (CHS). I can call them in the middle of the night, or whenever I need to. It has now become one of the key strategies I employ to ease me to sleep. After picking up the phone, talking, offloading, drawing and painting at the same time, I can then go to bed, usually sleeping quite soundly. The other person has been trained just to *listen* and has the generic name of Pat. After calling numerous times over months and months I recognise the plethora of Pats who answer. I have even established my favourite top five Pats whom I refer to as the *Pat elite*.

There is *Posh Pat, Engaging Northern Pat, Insouciant Pat, Monosyllabic Pat, Somali Positive Pat, Softly spoken Irish Pat, Bagpuss Pat, Geordie Pat, Sensible Flemish Pat, Gentle Korean Pat, Eastenders Pat*[29], and *Northern Irish No-nonsense Pat* to name a few. *Eastenders* Pat sounds just like Fred. I once asked her why she was volunteering and she replied curtly, "Someone has to do it." I told her that when she had spoken to me in the past her words were like stabs, she told me, "That doesn't sound good," but she seemed nonplussed.

Actually, what she said is not correct, she didn't have to man the phone because it is a voluntary service. Mentally, I am quite robust, but what if someone had called who was in real trouble, when faced with such indifference from a person who is purporting to help? Another Pat said some of them had been doing it for a long time and this particular Pat had probably burnt out. Usually, when I hear the voice of Pat who sounds like Fred, I promptly hang up, however much I need to talk, since after speaking to her I can often feel worse, which defeats the purpose of the helpline[30]. On the whole, when other sources of mental health assistance are not available and I have an irrepressible compulsion to talk in the middle of the night, it is better to talk to someone rather than battling with oppressive thoughts. At night, Fred is strong and I am weak, talking temporarily banishes him from my head.

The problem with trying to treat brain issues is that everyone's mind is different. Despite all the labels, each condition has its own specific idiosyncrasies. People working in mental health perhaps have identified the main colours, yet they certainly don't understand the complexities within the infinite shades. No one could ever profess to have such insights. I probably have a better understanding of the inner workings of my mind than any mental health care professional ever could.

Understanding the type of care and support I need, it is the mental health social workers that have listened beyond the rather restrictive one-hour time slot. It is the mental health helpline that I can usually call at any hour, rather than the psychiatrists and psychotherapists. They have been my main guide through the dark and testing times. Yet, my staunchest ally, unequivocally, is art, not, people.

When writing this essay, I heard about a schizophrenic who died while in police custody. An image of a group of policemen restraining the prostrate individual made me shudder. Granted, if the individual was experiencing psychosis then perhaps he was behaving in an aggressive, erratic and disturbing manner. When I was psychotic this was certainly the case, but every human being deserves to be treated with dignity. This man, who is now dead, was alone when he fell into a thorny psychotic state and found himself surrounded by people who perceived him as a *dangerous* threat. They didn't know what to do or how to handle him. The treatment of this man was an egregious mistake with a fatal outcome. If I had been on my own during the psychosis, I don't want to think about how I could have been treated, if apprehended by strangers or the police.

After identifying a problem in my head and actively seeking support it is only now, over a decade later, that I think I have possibly found the right team of people I can not only talk to, but also work with such as Mike who is involved in the art projects and organises/curates exhibitions through KAOS. TrActor assisted with practical things such as accompanying me to hospital appointments, when they could, which was a massive help. Currently, I am not seeing my mental health social worker, J. The reasons why are complex, but in this instance important to identify.

I'd called J, sleep deprived, unable to cope with the two children shortly after my husband had left for Asia. She came immediately and wanted to be there for me. We called my husband via Facetime to try to work out what to do, but I was unable to speak to him because when I opened my mouth I would just start ranting. Not wanting the children to witness me ranting I asked J to speak to him on my behalf. It was a strained situation, perhaps too much for her to cope with. Shortly after this I received an email from her delineating what she was able and not able to do as prescribed by her colleagues. It was a conversation we should have had face to face. When she wrote, "(I am not a relation(ship) therapist)" that was the tipping point. Extremely unwell, I had sought her assistance to communicate with my husband because I was not able to. She wrote that she was not trained to mediate between couples, but I wasn't asking for mediation; I couldn't speak because my mind was breaking down. Writing that "you are very well supported", I couldn't fathom what she meant by that. Inappropriate support is ineffectual. If a mentally ill person has carers who are making their condition worse doesn't that person have the right to express their concerns, or should they simply put up and shut up and conclude some help is better than none? I would prefer none.

It was at this juncture that I requested to stop her home visits.

This has been the longest period I haven't seen or spoken to her. Nor was it a decision I made lightly and it's regrettable – sometimes you need a break, to reclaim your privacy, re-establish boundaries and avoid triggers. This was my problem: J, unfortunately, had become a trigger and, since I am alone with two small children while my husband is abroad for three weeks of each month, I cannot afford to get unwell.

In time, I hope to resume contact because I would like to see her just once, to clear the air and make sure that things end amicably between us. It's important for us talk in person because I want to acknowledge all she has done for me and discuss the reasons for my decision to stop seeing her. The situation I find myself with J is reminiscent of when my relationship with Claudia and Dr Bass broke down, the difference being they agreed to meet when I was ready to resume contact to achieve closure. Recently, I emailed and texted her enquiring how she was after a recent operation. Her continued silence is unsettling, but I would like to give her the benefit of the doubt. It would be strange for her to refuse a meeting, other than for health reasons.

Ambivalent about starting a relationship with a new mental health social worker, I am trying to manage alone. On occasion, I have turned to Jean Pierre (a mental health social worker who has assisted in times of emergency), or I have written to Dr Thys, although he can be frustratingly elusive. Mental health is a sensitive area, there are no hard and fast rules; dealing with mini crises that life hurls at you is testing. With the birth of my second child I am mentally more challenged and isolated than ever. I was contemplating cognitive behavioural therapy (CBT), although have not progressed very far in terms of finding anyone. Hearing about a support group, via my midwife, for people who *hear voices* I signed up for it. This was some time ago and it looks like it is not happening. All these forays have been independent of TrActor. Patients shouldn't feel obliged to stick to the same people; it's natural to explore other options and perspectives, even if they don't come to anything. Embarking on psychotherapy again is not something I wish to re-engage with – the very idea makes me exhausted to even think about it.

When Dr Thys agreed to publish my essays in the form of a bespoke book, I envisaged the words, colours and images conspiring together to create an alchemy that would melt away that heavy mental rust. Waiting for the book to come to fruition has been frustrating and a seed of malignant doubt was planted during this protracted process. I have tried to be patient and not lose faith in Dr Thys and his colleagues. Knowing that Fred is waiting in the wings to destroy any meaningful opportunities I have generated, it's easier to believe Fred's invective bile than to have faith in people. When Dr Thys has promised something, I have clung onto that promise to fight Fred's inveterate negativity. Fred wants me to doubt, to retreat, to write accusatory emails, and destroy the relationships I have painstakingly tried to construct out of the rubble. A sign of a good doctor is one who understands this and never takes what you write or say too personally – especially emails written at some ridiculous hour in the morning when emotive and mentally weak. Dr Thys displays sincere humility and despite a delay in reply to my emails, when he does eventually write back, he writes in a quiet, methodical way that, inadvertently, tries to build bricks of mental trust in a mind that is just dust.

Dr Bass assisted in finding a UK partner to publish the English language version of this book. I emailed his contact, Dr Tim Read and was overwhelmed when he agreed to publish my work after reading the first essay I sent him. Having amassed a small tribe of allies in the field of psychiatry, we are all working to improve mental health and global awareness.

Dr Thys and his mental health team have not only come to my aid during times of real crisis, they are also, crucially, my colleagues. You could argue it is not possible for a doctor to observe their duty of care and work together with patients – and is certainly an unusual set up. To become an integrated member of society who can function and make a contribution, whatever your handicap, is vital. The glimmer of self-belief that was ravaged during psychosis (although fragile and easily trampled upon) is slowly being reignited.

It is
Not solely pills
That a mind needs
But
Time
An eager ear
A sympathetic tongue
Truth
A clean and serene home
A future
And the possibility of
Living again even when psychosis has
Snapped you in two.

CHAPTER 6

Should You Tell People About Your *Mad, Hot, Wonky, Unpredictable Mind*?

Recently there have been a slew of programmes about the impact of mental health issues on young minds. I watched one of them, but couldn't manage to sit through the next episode in the series. The filming style was voyeuristic, the participants were specimens trapped in a TV freak show, for us to scrutinise rather than gain any real insight into what was really going on for them. It is incredibly hard to get inside anyone's head – how can you feasibly do it in a one-hour documentary? Did participating and opening up actually help them in a meaningful and rehabilitating way? More fascinating and disconcerting, were the private meetings with the staff, the psychiatrists and mental health workers, discussing each case and deciding the fate of the respective patient. I questioned the approach of the staff towards the patients, which was coercive at times. One anorexic patient refused to eat; the food they wanted her to consume was unhealthy stodge. Although, not professing to understand the complexities of an eating disorder, offering her a piece of fruit, some nuts, a salad, grilled fish – food that didn't equal fat in her eyes – seemed more appropriate. It also appeared that the patients had very little opportunity to exercise physically. From personal experience, I might wake up feeling dreadful but, weather permitting, if I get on my bike and go for a ride, my mood is much improved. My brain feeds off the endorphins for an hour or two, no longer consumed with stale thoughts and futile memories – my mind is clear just for a short while – and that gives some respite. The kids seemed like rats confined in a clinical space (although attempts had been made to make it homely), with nowhere to go apart from roam the corridors and punch holes in the walls. Staff patrolled the corridors, clutching enormous bunches of keys, transforming it into a modern day setting for *One Flew Over the Cuckoo's Nest*. The mental health unit in question was a specialist one in Manchester, a place for patients to mentally recuperate, eventually leave, and go on to lead a meaningful existence. My original hometown is Manchester and, although my problems began in my mid-teens, perhaps even earlier, I would never have wanted to end up in a place like that. I know I would deteriorate very quickly if confined to such an environment.

Why should you tell people and be open about your *mad, hot, wonky, unpredictable* mind? The corollary of confessing is terrifying – being medicated, institutionalised, sectioned or ostracised, even. Having people's expression of incredulity, bafflement, even paradoxical amusement etched onto your brain, after confiding, is beyond difficult. Alternatively, is it preferable to confide in a very select few trusted parties, or just remain stoically silent and seek other, self-generated strategies to cope with your mind issues?

Being Open About Madness

For some years now, since 2008, I have been in correspondence with Stephen Fry, the broadcaster, writer, actor, performer and all round polymath. He is a face I grew up with as a child, who made me laugh, riotously, in *Blackadder*. When he first broached the subject, years ago on the cult Channel 4 programme *Network 7*, that all was not well in his mind, I warmed to him even more. Never did I envisage that I would manage to sustain a meaningful correspondence with him for all these years. Having sent him my books, essays, poems, artwork – even a film, perhaps – he usually replies with warmth and encouraging feedback, despite being chronically busy. Valuing this exchange, sometimes I ask myself why he bothers to stay in touch, when most of the high profile people I have met, by accident rather than design, soon lose interest, once they sniff that something is awry upstairs. His recent admission that he was close to suicide in a hotel room compelled me to reach out to him. At the time I was very low; it could have been pregnancy hormones, or just one of those agonising, prolonged dank periods. Possibly it was due to the injury to my left hand that was preventing me from working, or the feeling of nothingness after the end of my exhibition in London. Knowing what the real cause was, even now, I can't write it down. All I recall was that it was dark outside and dark in my head and a noose of dark thoughts were gripping me tighter around the neck. This is what I wrote to Stephen Fry that summer:

Dear Stephen,
    I should be sleeping because I have to be up at 6am and my husband is abroad, so it is naughty writing at this late hour. I just wanted to say how brave you are to talk about your bid to end your life last year, as someone in the public eye, with the incessant pressure to appear perpetually erudite, charming and witty it must be a real strain at times. I find it taxing to wear a mask in public, which I do, out of necessity; it

is exhausting. When people ask, "How are you?" I wish I could say, "Bloody crap!" but we don't do we? If we expose ourselves, it's tantamount to flashing our bits, which people really don't want to see, so they often recoil and run. You are fortunate that people respect you too much to ever do that, and yet you must be very conflicted within, carrying this heaviness that never seems to dissipate and lighten.

*Since my exhibition I've been ill, on and off and, because of excruciating pain in my left hand, not able to work very much, apart from writing. This creative lull is killing me, since I am convinced that art is keeping my heart pumping. My mid-career retrospective was also a bit of an anti-climax leaving me with the "what now?" question. Whatever I do, Fred says I'm a big failure and your reference to the "genital wart" did make me laugh out loud. A wart is exactly what it is. Now, with the second baby due, I've been having visions to make a "quick exit" after the birth, thinking the children would be better off without a mad mother. I also had some other news, which brought me down like a mountain whacked over my head, I am too ashamed to divulge it, since it's another mental conspiracy. My husband, who has that typical dark Nordic humour, said, "If you really want to kill yourself, I'll help you" – he was joking, that's his coping mechanism, not to give my **dark** bouts much credence and to laugh in the face of them – it seems to work.*

I was thinking I prefer my ranting phases to the depressive ones; they just linger like a very bad smell contaminating all the air around you. Oh yes of course, you just try to get on with it, go for a bike ride, water the plants, read a book, anything to get out of the hole, but I know what it's like to be stuck there and unable to see the light at all. At least you feel something inside when manic; the depression is heavy, all-consuming and murky. It taints everything, even the good stuff. It just saps you of life, time and energy.

I've started a new scroll. It will take forever to complete it and now I am trying to finish writing my book, but the desire to gravitate towards that "exit" is stronger than ever.

I told my husband that I might jump off the terrace. He told me to call him before I do so; I think he was joking again.

I might use these five weeks alone with my son to just set myself very tiny goals and do things that make me feel good, although it's hard. I become guilty whenever I do anything nice. It's such a strange world we live in, where people in Syria are being massacred while the media is getting hysterical over the imminent arrival of Kate Middleton's child, although the birth of a child is something to rejoice, isn't it?

My new scroll will be a juxtaposition of the superficially grotesque and the horror of war that the world has heaped upon itself over the centuries. I hope making it will keep me going. It's certainly going to take years and years to finish, better to make a scroll than not, and hopefully it will motivate me to cling to life rather than discard it.

So Stephen, what I am trying to say is that I value you, I value this exchange, I value your existence, and if you were no longer alive it would be a poorer world for it. You are brave and stronger than you think and you are kind and polite. You've stayed in touch and not run away and, as a fellow creative person who also suffers from a wonky, hot brain I would be really devastated if you died...

...Regarding my own fantasies about suicide, I just think no one would notice or care much if I did snuff it...maybe you think the same about yourself, but that's just Fred weaving his sly narrative of insidious nonsense.

Tomorrow, I will work on my scroll, even if I grimace with pain as I do so. Perhaps I will draw a dragon, no matter, I will continue with my insignificant art projects and try and be a patient and engaging Mummy to my little boy.

Your openness has helped me nudge a bit closer towards the light. I attach a short video of my son singing – this is a happy, carefree time for him, I wish I had memories of that time – watching it might make you smile.

Xx

Preferring to keep his response to my email private, I will say this though, that Mr Fry's reply made me think I had done something good that evening. Ejected out of my morbid solipsism by his startling openness, the revelation that someone could say, "Yes, I wanted to kill myself" with candour, was emancipating. Such thoughts, if openly expressed, discombobulate people (not always, but often this is the case). They usually don't want to know or go to the dark place that everyone has in their head. Being around depressed people is draining; their negativity can infectiously *rub off*. People generally can't deal with it, nor want to for that matter. "Go away" you see their eyes scream out at you, and you become this black force, a profound irritation. Instead you repress it all, very deep inside, and opt for a socially acceptable façade. I often think that, because Mr Fry is the consummate professional, because he acts the way people expect him to, makes us laugh with his razor wit and mental zeal, hides his moods stealthily, in deep mental pockets so that the public seldom see it, Mr Fry is embraced, respected and accepted. If he, however, he had an outburst while presenting the BAFTAs, began ranting and acting very strange, his career might meet an abrupt, untimely end. Mr Fry seems to have got the balance between openness and acting normal in public just right. That doesn't diminish the pressure he must feel at times, when he's not well and behaves as if everything is just dandy upstairs when his mind is, in fact, collapsing.

As part of my personal rehabilitation post-psychosis (and it is a torturously protracted process) I have extended the olive branch to people who were in the firing line of my psychotic fervour. Some former friends and good acquaintances preferred to break off contact indefinitely. Although painfully humiliating, I had to accept it; you can't force people to absolve or understand, although you can certainly try. There is a shame factor to breaking down in public, it's as if you have been traversing the streets naked and everyone has seen your private parts dangling. Sometimes I do have to question my motivation for reaching out. Do I really want these people in my life? If they can't make the distinction between the pleasant person they had known for years and the blatantly ill person I had temporarily become then good riddance. It is more complicated. They might not want to know you anymore, yet there is this innate need to explain yourself in the hope that they might show empathy.

What is more ironic, is six years before the psychosis, in 2003 when I was working in Dhaka, Bangladesh, I saw something that I will never forget, a sight so stark that I penned this poem after witnessing it.

The Naked Woman

It was another day
Dhaka was waking up
To brilliant light that made you squint and sweat
My legs were folded neatly in a bright green CNG taxi
We chugged along
My aunt and I, at a steady pace
Along the teeming streets
Then I saw her
Bathed in iridescent, liquid gold
Skin jet black, as if painted with tar
Flanked either side by scores of people
In a hurry to get to work
She walked tall
And slow
With a shaven head
And yet she was
Totally

Naked
Like Jesus being reborn in Bangladesh
And floating to heaven
On a golden cloud
Except she was ranting nonsense
She began to shake her head
Uncontrollably
Didn't seem to know
Where she was going
No one batted an eyelid,
Not even worth a second glance, she was.
My head arched forward
My mouth dropped open
Couldn't believe what I was seeing
As another misfit of society
Crawled on all fours like a
Hungry dog
With matted hair
And a ravaged face.
I nudged my Phu Phu,
"Did you see that?"
"What?"
"That woman"
"Don't pay any attention, she's a *pagul*"
Which means mad, in *Bangla*
Just a naked, mad woman
Roaming the streets of
Dhaka city
Nothing to register
Nothing to be concerned about
At all
I sat back and closed my eyes, for a second
To try and contain my emotion and frustration.
That women roamed naked
And men crawled on all fours
In this country of my mother's birth
What could I do?
Photograph
Document
Pen a poem to remember
To never let my conscious forget
And then what?

This woman I had witnessed in Dhaka was now part of my consciousness and part of me. I had become that woman. I remember thinking how pathetic she looked; how no one cared; maybe this was why I wanted people to care, to understand why a mind disintegrated. Even if people really just didn't want to know – I was driven to try.

Recently in London, I had arranged to meet an acquaintance; someone I'd chosen not to see in three years. At the time of the psychosis, his unflinching conclusion was that I was a mentally ill miscreant. His hysterical response reflected his utter alarm and revulsion towards the out of control person I had mutated into. His words were scathing, as if I was culpable, and his conclusion was that I had finally revealed my true self and that I was a social pariah. When I recovered from the psychosis, the damage was done; the person that I had presented to society was a fake, masking the mad, psychotic monster that I was beneath. Often I imagined people talking about me behind my back, laughing about that dark episode in my life, dismissing me as severely unhinged. The mask was off and I couldn't escape the ghost of psychosis. Being psychotic was almost tantamount to committing a crime; my reputation was tarnished, the damage enduring.

Now pregnant with my second child and three years on, perhaps enough time had passed for the dust to settle. After exchanging superficial niceties and greeting one another warmly, we eventually spoke about my mental health condition and to my surprise, he said, "Oh you are not ill, there's nothing wrong with you. You were just playing it up. You loved all the attention."

Steadfast in my response I said, "No, really, I was very unwell, I was actually severely psychotic."

Refusing to accept what I was saying his response left me confused. At the time he had dismissed me as mad and now he believed I had fabricated the whole thing, as if that was the more digestible truth. Not even sure he understood what being psychotic meant, we parted company. If I saw him again, what would be the point? I would have to act my socks off. The pressure of pretending and implementing all those tedious social checks and balances would be unbearable.

The philosopher, someone whom I had not contacted for three years since the psychosis, told me, "Quite frankly I am surprised that restaurant didn't ban you for life after the way you behaved."

"The way I behaved" – I reflected on his choice of words, as if I had voluntarily wanted to yell at people and acted in a way that was disturbing for all parties. I am glad this particular restaurateur, Mark Hix, didn't ban me. My artwork is still adorning his restaurants, but I haven't seen or spoken to him since, for that matter. We have had very little contact apart from congratulations on my first pregnancy via email. The stress and pressure I put myself under, when making the artwork in the restaurant, was one of the factors that contributed to the episode. I did write a letter to him and his business partner in 2013, trying – over earnestly – to explain what happened on that night. Neither of them replied. This was a hard lesson to swallow. Another slap. Perhaps they were busy, although inside I thought that being open and sharing doesn't automatically lead to compassion. All your previous impeccable, good behaviour counts for nothing. Why are drunken episodes more forgivable than mental relapses? The latter can be perceived as a temporary mental aberration, an ignominious period of your life to move on from never to be mentioned again.

After nearly five years, in 2014, I plucked up the courage to request a meeting with Mark, via his PA. Jo. This was the first occasion I had formally asked to see him and Jo wrote back saying he would be happy to meet. The use of the word *happy* was such a relief to read. Naturally, I was nervous before the meeting, it's been such a long time, and Mark's business has expanded exponentially while I continue to feel puny and battered. But it was important to allow me to explain what happened face to face, move on properly, and close the door of that memory for good. Privately I am, partially, resentful that I remain the one apologising, believing that being psychotic in a public place is an unforgiveable discomfiture.

Enough time has passed for him to know that I am not a psychotic monster. There remains the same person, fighting each day to stay healthy and well on the inside.

The day we were due to meet, I was sick with nerves. Meeting in his spacious, light office above his restaurant *Tramshed*, he smiled, we chatted and I said, "All artists are a bit bonkers aren't they?"

He nodded vigorously and said, "Yes."

Hesitantly, I brought up the fact that I had been psychotic on that ill-fated night. Growing silent in the room, I thought better not to talk about it. He gave me a signed copy of one of his cookbooks and told me to bring in the mobile next time. It was such a relief. Then I reflected on all the years wasted, being wedged between wall upon wall of false narratives, while life moved on and I vowed never to let this happen again.

Mark was one of a long list of people on the receiving end of emails that contained *damaging, ranting diatribe* and it is distressing to think of the scores of emails, written in a heated psychotic state, that destroyed relationships that had been years in the making.

Granted, I can understand why members of the public can't ingest mental illness in all its complexity or deal with it without a level of panic. Admittedly, when I was watching another documentary, *Diaries of a Broken Mind,* which followed youths afflicted with every mental health condition conceivable, rather than being engrossed, I switched off within the first few minutes. Each participant had been given a camera to keep a video diary. The way the film was edited made them seem like attention seeking freaks. Leaving a bad taste in my mouth, it consolidated pre-existing stereotypes of mental health conditions.

The best documentary I have seen remains Mr Fry's, *The Secret Life of the Manic Depressive* (2006), because there was a dignity and intelligence in his approach. The participants were treated as human beings with stories to share and you wanted to listen. There was none of this voyeurism, or *affected* drama, or choppy editing. I say affected, because the focus is often on the surface emotion, not the analysis behind the emotion. Just because you see someone in the throes of schizophrenia, or crying, or ranting, or being violent, doesn't mean you gain a greater insight. If anything, the sight of such behaviour makes you more detached and dispassionate. As I was cycling in London I saw one such man, talking to someone who wasn't there. He was pleading loudly and I stared at him, out of natural curiosity, before cycling on. There was no compassion on my part, no "Are you ok sir?" just the natural instinct to ogle and then flee the scene.

If being open with people is not necessarily a good idea, then surely confiding in the experts is more sensible? With my first pregnancy I experienced postpartum psychosis, with my second pregnancy I wanted to avoid it happening again. According to my research I was supposed to have a care plan in place. This ideally should be implemented from the outset of pregnancy, to help with the psychological preparation and to create an environment that reduces the chance of psychosis rearing its scary head. Because my original obstetrician saw how ill I had become after the birth of my first child, I assumed with my second pregnancy he would put all the relevant people in place to minimise the prospect of it recurring.

With two months of this second pregnancy to go and no definitive care plan, I find myself in a disconcertingly similar situation to my first. When I became mentally unwell, I emailed Dr H. He called leaving a *concerned* voice message, but he wanted to wait before discussing a care plan, which is why I thought he was too lackadaisical in his approach. Deciding to change hospitals, Dr H seemed offended. But at seven months pregnant, I wasn't confident in the psychological care and support they would provide after giving birth or that I would be left alone, for sufficiently long periods, to rest. I wrote a letter to Dr H rationally delineating my reasons for leaving. He didn't reply. He's a doctor; someone trained to care. The lack of response was disheartening.

As I rapidly lost faith in hospitals and doctors I began to panic, the flashbacks ensued and that's when I started reaching out and writing emails frantically. Most of my emails did not receive a reply. It's not that people don't care, often they genuinely don't know what to do or say – even, at times, the health care professionals. There are some exceptions. Dr Ian Jones specialises in postpartum psychosis, this is his area of research and expertise at Cardiff University.[31] Although I wrote to him and he tried to offer advice and reassurance, most of the hospitals I have encountered in Brussels don't have the resources to help mothers who have a history of psychosis.

After this I just shut down inside. It was almost easier to pretend everything was ok. Meeting a genial female friend for lunch, smiling and feigning interest in the prosaic subjects she wanted to converse about was simpler than talking openly about the difficulties I was facing. There was a cursory mention of my *condition*, but then it was swept aside, like an ugly dead fly from the table. That vacant look has become very familiar, the awkward silence when you speak about the visions and the prolonged pause when you mention the word *psychosis*. I am not in a mental asylum, although I have almost created one through self-imposed isolation. I live with the paralytic fear of the psychosis happening again. If I become severely sleep deficient that fear stalks me when I wake, when I sleep and when I go out and try to live my life. If I talk about the psychotic memories with family members, it is something they, often, can't deal with, so I am voluntarily silent. The keyboard and computer screen are always there to silence the constant whirr upstairs, but these modern devices have their limitations. Often, all I crave is to speak to another human being without being afraid.

That same friend called me up some months later, she said "I was worried because you didn't reply to my email and usually you write back straight away – how are you. Is everything OK?"

Utterly taken aback by the genuine care and concern in her voice I burst out with, "I'm not coping at all, I only had four hours sleep last night, I feel the psychosis is surging towards me and I am scared."

Her voice softened, she sounded concerned, "Do you want me to come?" she said.

I did, but I couldn't let her see me in this wretched, dishevelled state.

"I know a very good babysitter, she is quiet and good with children, I really do recommend her. She might relieve the pressure and allow you to sleep." I agreed to take the number and told her that if I was very tired I would call her and maybe she could come round to let me rest or we could have a cup of tea and a slice of cake. It was enough to just talk to her, to be honest and cry down the phone. People do care, if you venture to let them in. Maybe I should stop trying to be so brave and reach out more often.

After these kids exposed their minds and unadulterated pain on the BBC documentary – edited like a crazy pop video with an accompanying thumping sound track, as if to amplify their mental abnormality – what did they think about the final broadcast programme? Was it a positive experience for them? Was it cathartic? Or did it leave them more vulnerable and misunderstood than before? It's sad to see these fledgling people defined as *ill* and even sadder that some are on medication and/or institutionalised before their life has properly begun.

The pharmaceutical companies and some (not all) psychiatrists have a vested interest in diagnosing and prescribing – because it's their bread and butter. That is the easy part, to prescribe pills that will numb the symptoms and improve patients' functionality and, ultimately quality of life – although there is no guarantee of that either. Some of them might not even need medication, which means they are better off keeping quiet than getting addicted to superfluous pills with an array of unwanted side effects.

My former psychiatrist, Dr Bass, was very open in a recent email reply to questions I presented to him about psychosis. I wanted to know why I remained prone to episodes, despite observing my sleep, minimising stress and triggers, abstaining from drugs and alcohol, and living a healthy life style. He said that:

First, there is a lot we do not understand about psychosis (whether that means individual conditions such as schizophrenia, schizoaffective disorder, bipolar disorder or depressive psychosis or whether there is a common mechanism shared by all).

If, then, we can assume that the experts are struggling to find answers in the dark, then it's naïve to think they can offer a definitive solution by way of prescription or even talking therapy, which means we have to be careful before approaching professionals for help and spend considerable time trying to find the appropriate care if, at all, it exists. The brain remains the realm of the unknown and, as a sufferer, I know the mannerisms of my affliction better than anyone else ever could. A mental condition is specific to the individual; there is no *one size fits all*.

I hope that none of these kids get vitriolic emails or trolled after being open and putting themselves out there. I hope they get better and that the experience was helpful. I hope they never regret the decision and that they won't be stigmatised for *coming out* about their *different minds*.

After years of living with my *hot brain*, although hard to live with – day-to-day, tedious in fact, when this thing sucks the life out of you and compromises much that is taken for granted, such as family relationships, building a professional life, and interaction with strangers – I have concluded that the fewer people I talk to about it, the better. Writing about matters of the mind is easier and safer; it's out of my head and tucked up on the page; and maybe will be of some use later on. Talking to friends, colleagues, and people in the medical profession doesn't really help much either. Even talking to my husband can be frustrating, because he will never know what it is like to be submerged in a lacerated darkness that mentally rips you to shreds or to ride the crest of a colossal and mesmerising high, or combat with demons and visions that fire at you with indiscriminate zeal. What could reveal the hidden depths of the mind in any *real* sense? I think expression through words and the hand-created image come very close.

CHAPTER 7

Sleep, Cannabis, Psychosis and Hope

A colleague of mine recently wrote to me about his son who was experiencing psychosis and had been sectioned. When I read his email, memories returned of my own psychosis and the dread of being sucked into a parallel world that had no rules or limits, that was a complete mental fabrication and yet, so potent and inebriating, part of me never wanted to leave. To protect the identity of my colleague, I will call him Paul. I've only met Paul once; he came to an exhibition of mine in London in 2011. The first one I participated in after the psychosis. When I met Paul, the image that I had already carved in my head didn't tally with the one I saw. He seemed worn down, not by life, but by mental daily woes, something I identified with – it was all in the eyes, they had that hollowed out quality that comes from chronic battling with the demons that lurk in our heads. Yet, when we spoke on the phone, he sounded youthful, almost like a timid boy. The gulfs between sentences, the occasional stammer, the quietness of his voice, all resonated. It was as if he was speaking in code. The long pauses meant he was thinking about every word he uttered and the significance of what he said; the sporadic stammer the result of medication or previous psychosis; the quietness, a foil to appear gentle and safe to society when really he was angry and had something to roar about. I could be wrong, but this is what I sensed. Of course, I never relayed any of this to him. When I saw his artwork, the same decoding took place, each painstaking stroke, the hours that went into every drawing, the manic intensity of his shading – Paul and I were definitely carved from the same gnarled, ancient, and neglected tree. Both artists and writers, both sufferers of psychosis, both labelled with mental conditions that were stigmatising, both trying to engage in work that would attempt to answer the questions about the mind that the doctors were still trying to figure out and both parents to sons.

My biggest anxiety is that my son might, one day, be afflicted with the same brain syndrome as his mother. I'd already explained to him at the tender age of three that, "When Mummy's brain gets hot she shouts, but if Mummy's brain is cool, she's calm."

"Breathing helps too," I told him as he tried to emulate long inhalations and exhalations. He even knew the paramount importance of sleep and would often say, "Mummy needs to sleep" closing the door to allow me to rest. Such insights and understanding at his age seemed remarkable.

He would announce firmly, "Baba don't like shouting."

And I would reply, "Mummy doesn't like shouting either"

I loathe it, but when I become unwell I can start ranting, uncontrollably, like an automatic reflex response. It is something I have witnessed with my own mother and both my sisters. My rants never last long, they were like short, sharp, painful electric shocks, another sign of my inability to modulate the temperature of my brain, which heated up with such speed it was hard to nip it in the bud. I often long for a *no ranting* day, a day that is calm and solely full of laughter, affection and stimulating play with my son. There have been times when I am rested and life couldn't be better. It's when I am alone with my son for prolonged periods, coupled with paltry sleep that I can get into tricky situations – that's when I experience visions, am noise sensitive, impatient, and intolerant to the tiniest hint of mess. Add a new baby into the mix and it's a pressurised situation for anyone, with or without a mental health condition. My perfectly ordered universe ruled by the virus of control is now destabilised – allowing Fred to step in.

When Paul told me that his son had "got it", was it inevitable that my son would also "get it"?

We had both tried to do something productive with our very different sorts of brains: to create, to write, to believe that we were afflicted for a reason. Paul told me that his son wouldn't stop smoking weed. A previous dabbler myself, I never realised at the time that I was playing: *Russian roulette with my mental health.* The first time I tried cannabis was aged 18, it was a teenager's rite of passage smoking a joint, like losing your virginity. I had no idea that smoking weed could worsen my mental health problems.[32] The experimentation was brief, lasting approximately six months, and I didn't smoke another joint for ten years. Usually I wasn't entirely aware of what I was smoking, be it hash, weed or skunk – it didn't matter. I would describe myself as an occasional smoker. Refraining for long periods before bumping into a *friend* who would offer me what seemed to be an innocuous joint; I would swiftly resume the habit. I didn't stop smoking completely until I was thirty-six. The last joint I smoked may have contributed to the first psychotic episode I experienced. I don't know. It was most probably a combination of factors – stress, sleep deprivation, a series of traumas and disappointment – that all combined to cause a combustion in my brain. It was bewildering when I suffered a second episode, even though I had now stopped smoking cannabis. Was the second episode the result of the still smarting embers that swiftly became another inferno? It was when I experienced subsequent postpartum psychosis and identified patterns and clearly defined cumulative stages that I realised the neuroplasticity in my brain had *plausibly* changed. Just as someone who has had a knock to the head that leaves them permanently cognitively impaired, the psychosis had traumatised my brain, beaten it up, and altered it. Could I then repair the damage to my neural pathways? This is what I am straining to do. Dr Thys believes that because I use my brain intensely, with my art and writing, I corrected some of the damage caused by the psychosis and recovered more rapidly.

Given a certain set of circumstances, the descent towards psychosis can be swift. Such is my awareness of my condition that I am acutely conscious of the danger signs and now know what to do to stop the fall[33].

One psychiatrist told me that I would have developed psychosis without the cannabis; certainly smoking the herb didn't help. The extreme mania, hallucinations and voices only started after my cannabis use. Before then my mental affliction oscillated from mild mania to depression, to online searches of assisted suicide[34], to helplessness, to an inability to get up, brush my teeth, get dressed, wash, go out, and eat. These morbid, depressive phases continue to occur, and I can get manic and have problems sleeping, either sleeping too much or too little. I am walking on a delicate elastic string that could snap at any moment, avoiding triggers that can set me off into rages or mania, hastening a catalogue of very specific symptoms that all conspire together to lead to the same sinister, burning hole.

When Paul told me his son was a cannabis user I immediately blurted out, "He has to stop." An obvious thing to say, of course he had to, but if he didn't want to there was not much anyone could do. Paul also told me how his son was targeting him with his rage, something I had also done with members of family, friends and people who had been close. The main target was my husband. When you are deep in the throes of psychosis the people who are dearest paradoxically become the enemy and the only allies. I have said some unrepeatable things during these episodes, which fill me with abject shame. It is traumatic to be at the receiving end of such vituperative, rancid nonsense and yet you can't stop even if you want to. After I recovered, the residue of psychosis remained tattooed to my tongue, tainting thoughts and perceptions. After the psychosis you are not the same person and never will be or can be again.

Paul told me on the phone how his son had not been sleeping either and, although he'd been sectioned and put on medication, he wasn't recovering. The strain in his voice was evident. I listened, trying to offer words of encouragement, knowing that nothing I said would lessen Paul's pain. I sensed Paul's guilt too – that he'd passed on the *mad* gene to his son – and the apprehension for his child's future once he was deceased. In Paul's last email he apologised for not attending my exhibition, writing he had not been sleeping and that, "Trying to work out what best to do to keep myself sane seems impossible." I hastily wrote back that sleep deprivation for people with our brain composition was like gulping down a cocktail of potent drugs. In a recent email exchange with my former psychiatrist Dr Bass, he wrote:

A lot of people do subjectively attribute their illness to sleep problems... Objectively speaking I would concur that sleep problems often precede psychosis...but this often seems to be more an early warning and the way to deal with this is to ensure they have adequate antipsychotic treatment i.e. simply giving sleeping tablets would not prevent the relapse. But we also notice that unhealthy sleeping patterns (up all night and sleeping all day – "reverse sleep cycle") do often hinder recovery.

We don't really know what causes it (psychosis) to be honest (but genes are almost certainly at the root of the problem) so it is difficult to be sure how to prevent it overall.

Sleep was of pivotal importance, but it is only one factor to prevent psychosis. Personally, I will not stop trying to work it out and, at least, I had proven to myself that I could mentally prevent an acceleration towards psychosis when the symptoms began. This is something I have learnt to do by being smeared in psychosis and swimming in the very depths of it. If I am able to regulate the symptoms, then is this something that potentially others can learn too – including Paul's son? Or was he far too submerged in psychotic phlegm that was sticking to every corner of his brain preventing him from coming out the other side, mentally intact?

His son's illness also seemed to be infecting Paul. What if Paul became unwell too, then who would be there for his son? Each word I wrote seemed feebler than the last and then I realised, despite all the nuggets of perceived wisdom, I was powerless. Even the doctors were powerless. Paul had to sleep, his son had to rest and stop smoking cannabis. They needed peace, calm, nutritious food, access to nature and tranquillity – an exit strategy from the claustrophobic match boxes their minds had become. They needed to be as far away from the *toxicity* of the city and they needed time – copious amounts of it – to let their *hot brains* cool down. Yet, would they have access to such nature, food, quiet and tranquil calm? Or would the anxiety about his son and the crushing slow annihilation of the spirit that occurs when dealing with a loved one deep in the clutches of psychosis, impinge on Paul? Like lead hand cuffs, would the burden of worry stop him from doing what he had to do to bring his son back to reality? Right now, sleeping pills gave him little relief; Paul would wake in the night, plagued by nightmares and worry. He could only watch as the jaws of psychosis devoured his son, tore through his brain, reducing him to a ranting, raving, imposter. Even though I was not there, I could see what was happening.

For years now I was trying to keep my psychotic nemesis at bay, but Fred was there, watching me obstinately, jumping in if my brain got hot and turning up the heat for his amusement. Keeping Fred out of my life was my own daily crusade. My young son now knew about Fred. He wanted to infect his infant mind, just as Fred had got to Paul's son. To counter this perniciousness, I was creating a body of work to help my son understand the nature of psychosis and explain the fiend that was Fred: principally, what happened to his Mummy when Fred got inside her head; how Fred would maybe try to get into his head too; that if he wanted to stay well and be strong he must abstain from drugs or consuming alcohol excessively; and be vigilant about the people he surrounded himself with. How naïve was I? How could I stop him from teenage exploration? Would he care? Would he listen? Would he fall and not be strong enough to get up and fight, because each day was a battle for Paul, for me, for his son and maybe one-day my own son. As I write this, my second child is growing rapidly inside me, moving around in the snug safety of my belly.

"Stay in the womb, you are better off in that cosy cave than out here in the nasty glare of the world," I whispered.

Of course, this second baby would soon arrive and Fred would be waiting. All I could do was to maintain my crusade, to be the protector, the educator and never accept defeat, even when I was on my knees and weeping inside, begging for a different brain, and just a slender slither of peace.

As I near the end of this essay I think about Julia Donaldson's son, the children's author of the renowned *Gruffalo* books. Recovering from my first bout of postpartum psychosis, in bed, struggling to sleep, but unable to, I put on Radio 4 and heard her talking about her son on *Desert Island Discs*. She spoke bravely about his condition. Her son had also been diagnosed with schizoaffective disorder, but he didn't win the fight and died. She said, rather poignantly that in some ways it was a relief that she didn't see him deteriorate into some old "wino". She had the resources and love to assist her son, yet in the end Fred got him. It made me realise I could never be complacent; there would be no let up. Yes, it was exhausting having to wrestle with Fred as he tried to stop me doing basic human things (like going to the shops and buying food), and now he was determined to get at my boy and the baby sleeping in my tummy. Like Julia and Paul, words and art are all we have – that's our ammunition to fight this – not pills or dubious pharmaceutical concoctions.

Paul wasn't happy with the impact of the prescribed medication on his son. What would work then? Not giving up and continuing the war against

Image 36. *Portrait of Fred*, (acrylic on MDF block, size 10x10 inches, 2006). This painting sits in my studio and I use it explain what happens in Mummy's head when Fred climbs into it. I recall my son's expression when he first saw it – one of absolute unease. Mysteriously and unexpectedly, it has fallen numerous times. I am not superstitious, but there is something menacing about this painting. I think it is the closest I have come to painting the darkness that lives inside.

the illness, the disease, the condition, Fred – whatever you want to call it. I am reassured in the belief that everyone has a **Fred** – it's not just us. The problem is he's become a force so potent and destructive we have to rally together to keep him incarcerated or try to tame and befriend him. Fred will always be there, with me, with Paul and with his son.

"What to do Mummy?" my boy says quietly.

"What to do?" I reply. "Don't give up. Life is a big fight."

My boy stared at the portrait of Fred that sat in my studio; he stood up and said, "Go away Fred, go away. Leave my Mummy alone."

We hugged and played with Lego. I read him his bedtime stories and hoped that Fred would never climb into his head. Something told me that Fred wouldn't stop until he did and this left an acrid taste in my mouth and heart.

I end on this: Paul, remember that your son was not always ill. Remember your boy before the psychosis. Hold onto the belief that he will come back and speak to you in a gentle voice. The memory of the psychosis will always be a disquieting one. He will never want to go back there, however alluring Fred's world may seem, it is a rotten one where there is no hope. Hold onto that Paul.

CHAPTER 8

Living with a *Mad* Wife – the Impact of Psychosis on Relationships, Marriage, Motherhood and Life

My husband has often remarked, sadly, "You are not the same person since the psychosis." This is a strange thing to say, because I can't remember who I was before and even if I could, I am not sure it is possible to ever, fully, become that person again. Similarly after a limb is amputated, you will never be able bodied again, you might learn to walk but it's not going to be as it was. How could it?

Much of the emphasis in mental health, is on the person suffering from their specific disorder, rather than the partner or the immediate family. They get rubbed out as the spotlight shines brightly on the *mad* one. My husband has suffered and continues to suffer, at the hands of my condition. There are good days, peaceful days, quiet days and normal days. Days when he has to endure prolonged, rebarbative rants – insults of the most atrocious and unjustified nature. At its most lamentable he's accused me of being "emotionally evil". Then there's the selfishness, unkindness, joylessness…I could go on, but I won't. You might say, this sounds like a typically unhappy marriage. Doesn't the "putrefaction set in" after the purple honeymoon phase of a relationship subsides? The ephemeral newness of those tantalising petals withers like the fresh flower it was once.

We voluntarily choose to be together, despite the odds stacked against us both, recalling a time when life was harmonious, when ranting never occurred, and when we had a close relationship. After living together for ten, relatively content, years my husband has seen me metamorphose into another beast and witness an almost *Kafkaesque* transformation mentally, not from human to insect, but something altogether more perturbing. My mind, when I am ill, literally develops claws that verbally scratch out eyes and bite out chunks of my husband's flesh. It grows feet, with sharp spikes, that kick him in the shins until he bleeds with the stuff that comes out of my rancid mouth. And it becomes very rancid when I am having an episode; there is no filter either. It doesn't just pour; it surges leaving lasting stains that are hard for my husband to scrub from his memory. Not just attacking him, I attack each and every member of his family, treating them with verbal contempt that has no rational or logical basis whatsoever. He sits there stoically and endures the nastiness of it, knowing that it will stop, that I will emerge churlish and apologetic and promise to try harder and for it to not happen, ever, again. Except I can't promise that. I can try, faithfully, to go to bed early, take my vitamins, do my exercise, breathing, meditation and not stay up too late, writing, painting or watching a film, but there is no guarantee of a quiet life post psychosis.

There are times when my husband can't take it and fires back with equal venom or he says calmly, "Nothing that you say affects me." Sometimes he laughs and I laugh too, because laughter is all we can muster. More disturbingly I am overcome with a violent urge to attack him, my fists pummel his body and it is I who is left more bruised and hurt than he could ever be, with broken nails and searing pain in my hands and arms. You would have to be very thick skinned not to be affected or to opt out. He says he can make the distinction between when I am *sane* and *insane*. Some days the two states of being become conflated into a mush and then he describes me as simply "deeply unpleasant." Each morning I announce, "Today I will never raise my voice again," it's a short-lived motto, unrealistic and ends in failure. This irascibility only began after the psychosis. My brain has, it seems, irreversibly changed and I hanker after my old, quiet, reflective, morose brain. I could live in perpetual solitude, but then Fred (the voice in my head) would be my main companion creating quite a miserable existence since he's forever blaring at me to kill myself. My brain could combust, given a set of circumstances or exposure to specific triggers, but there is a litany. Each day you know that you could fall from the precipice to where the rocks await, eagerly, to smash your brain to pulp. Then there are those days when you become indolent, demotivated and don't want to do anything, those are the depressive days when attempting to live becomes futile.

This essay will explore how mental health problems conspire to destroy relationships with your loved ones and how the ultimate aim of Fred is to leave you isolated with only his interminable, chagrined commentary for company.[35] A good, solid, loyal partner/family, who is patient, loves you unconditionally and can see past the ailment, is key. But it is a big ask for a partner/family to live with the *beast* that roams the corridors of my head. Sometimes disconnecting is the easier path – easier for everyone concerned.

I will also explore:

1. Whether living with someone with mental health issues impacts on the non-sufferer's general and mental health?

2. Does staying with the mentally unwell partner become an obligation and a **duty**, knowing he/she will deteriorate without the stability and support that a solid relationship provides. My husband told me that this was one of the motivating factors of sticking it out. He couldn't live with the idea of me being sectioned and institutionalised. Naturally, I am slightly ambivalent when he says this. Should I be grateful then, that he saved me? Could I really not have managed my condition without his unwavering support? Alone, would it have been inevitable that I simply suffered multiple psychotic episodes and ended up an incoherent, dishevelled mess of a human being, homeless, filthy, impecunious, loveless, childless with cannabis as my crutch or become a sad, heavily medicated zombie? It doesn't bear speculating about. What is clear is that staying with me is a colossal commitment on his part that involves incalculable self-sacrifice.

3. Fundamentally, is there enough **support** for families and partners to help them deal with a *mad* loved one and cope day to day? Living with someone with severe mental health issues is not dissimilar from cohabiting with a person with a physical disability. It takes its toll, wears you down mentally, emotionally and physically tests you to your ultimate limits. I am under no illusion that I could get progressively worse or continue to be relatively stable, as I am now. I define stable as no longer having recurrent psychosis or engaging in threatening and perilous behaviour, rather I have episodes, which could be described as experiencing the beginning of the descent without fully falling. It's progress in my eyes, although painfully slow and incremental from my husband's perspective. He has sometimes urged me to pop a pill and pills do work for people. Tenacious in my belief that – because I understand the idiosyncrasies, shortcomings, and familiar entrenched patterns of my mind – I can dodge the psychosis, which can sometimes hurtle towards me like a rabid dog. Dodging is what I have, in effect, been doing and I'm working towards being a more pleasant wife. If I can do it publically then I can do it privately too. I do know one thing though – I will never be cured and life remains a complex struggle to stay calm.

4. The final question I will address is what is the **long term impact** of living with madness, mental illness, hot brain syndrome, whatever society wishes to call it[36], on the happiness of the partner, the stability of the family unit, and the children (if you have any)? And how can you live with the afflicted person, without steadily going mad yourself?

"An Untreated 'Ill' Mind Corrodes All that is Good, True and Sustaining"

I met my husband when I was nineteen and a reluctant student at the London School of Economics. It was a shock being in the filthy, heaving, intimidating throb of London and finding myself studying a degree that I didn't particularly want to study. My passion was art and messing around with the written word. Depression had already firmly set in growing steadily inside my brain like a thick mesh of bramble for years. And yet, teenage angst is nothing new, I never self harmed or had an eating disorder, I was moderately *blue*, just one of those *slightly lugubrious* types, but I still enjoyed laughter and remained the joker in the family, taking pleasure in cracking everyone up, despite the encroaching mental darkness. My husband to be stood out in his brightly coloured shirts, African jewellery, grey/blue eyes and tanned skin. I noticed him; we were staying at the same halls of residence at Passfield Hall. Perhaps I should have been thinking about changing my degree course or seeing a counsellor because my "mind felt out of sorts," but I didn't.

My mother once told me: "The problem with you is that you let the dog shit in your living room and then you hide the mess under the carpet. Clear the shit from the living room of your mind, otherwise the stink will never go away."

Often coming out with these vivid, precise metaphors, she knew something was not right, a mother's intuition perhaps, but her maternal concern had come too late and I didn't take heed.

When I moved to London a chasm began to grow, stealthily, between myself and the family and I barely spoke to my mother during these long London years. I've metabolised a huge proportion of my childhood baggage. My mother had her own demons to contend with and maybe I didn't want to burden her with my own. The problem with my mother is her heart remains with our late father and deceased parents in Pathuakali, Bangladesh. I have since called it her *Pathuakali Psychosis* because even though she has lived in the UK longer than she ever did in Bangladesh, her mind is held in that time – the place of her birth – and those childhood memories persist to haunt her. Whenever I speak to my mother she has a tendency to *go back*.

My mother believes, steadfastly, that we have a *worm* living in our head and once told me, "I was too critical and now you are too self-critical, we have to rid ourselves of this worm that is eating away at our minds otherwise life will be *dorbushor*"[37].

If only I could squash that worm, that continues to gnaw avariciously, with my big thumb.

Part of me thinks she loathed her life and being a mother. It was a duty to work and provide – she would much rather have shed all her responsibilities and watched TV, slept, cooked, shopped or gardened. She has since told me how much she loves us and never stops worrying or thinking about her children. She is trying to no longer torment herself with guilt about the past.

"It's ok, let it go, we have to find a way to move forward and bin those *dead* memories, there are no use to us now." I tell her.

It's something we both struggle with.

My mother was against me having a relationship and moving in with Oscar (not his real name – my husband is notoriously private and I would like to respect that). The relationship progressed quickly. It was escapism from the reality of studying at the London School of Economics and being surrounded by people who were hell bent on achieving their ambitions. Oscar was my second boyfriend; I was emotionally *green*. He was, by contrast, very sure of what he wanted and keen for me to visit Sweden, to meet his *perfect family* whose ordered home and perpetually vivacious personalities felt like a strange anathema. They were the complete opposite of my obstreperous, volatile, messy, dysfunctional family. Was I acting in front of Oscar's family from the very beginning and feigning to be someone I was blatantly not? They warmed to me instantly, but each subsequent trip to Sweden became harder for me to endure, the acting becoming more of a mental strain.

Back in London, I forced myself to go to my lectures and submitted one dreary essay after the other; part of me was dying a languorous death. By now I was living a dual life, a life of pretending to be the person I thought I was supposed to be and the inveterately depressed individual who fantasised about an end. Oscar glimpsed my darkness and tried to guide me out of it. He would dutifully pose as my life model so that I could keep up my drawing and whenever we were in Sweden, he would deposit me in the middle of the forest to draw the trees and gaze at the red squirrels, (I often wished to be one, searching for nuts and scampering about nibbling on blueberries and wild strawberries). Oscar didn't realise that he was providing emotional sustenance and yet things were becoming cloudier and blacker in my mind day-by-day.

Student days are supposed to be frivolous and carefree. Happy to be with only Oscar in his tiny room at Passfield Hall, he didn't think this was healthy and thought I should try to make additional friends. There were other ardent admirers lurking in the shadows such as an amorous stalker of German aristocratic descent who was six-foot-six with a mouth that resembled a wrinkled anus. Unable to revel in any of the male attention, I might have been passively curious, but the depression seemed to rob me of simple pleasures, such as enjoying youth and being desired. Not quite sure how Oscar put up with it, I have inferred that it was probably my teenage youthful looks that formed the initial glue to cement his commitment to the relationship, rather than my personality. The fresh bloom of beauty can provide an allure that makes people more tolerant, not that I thought I was anything much to look at, but when I started modelling at sixteen I could see how cleverly the camera lied and created a mirage. There was something quite compelling about knowing that with some make up you could literally transform yourself into this *other* being and con people into believing you actually were an ethereal goddess, rather than a lanky skinny girl with a sentient, albeit slightly dodgy, brain.

Maybe Oscar liked the idea of going out with a model. He certainly didn't hinder me when I joined a London agency and enjoyed success with a *Tia Maria* commercial, various magazine photo shoots or attending events like *London Fashion Week* when I sashayed down the catwalk wearing a huge hat and slick white suit. During my third year at university I won the first *Miss Bengali* beauty contest staged at the Theatre Royal, London in 1994, which Oscar proudly attended, and made forays into the Dhaka modelling scene under the guidance of Bibi Russell, a former model herself. But the experience was dispiriting, I had to sue the organisers for my prize money and although Bibi wanted to launch my career as a model in Mumbai I was ambivalent about being a model, ultimately disliking having my hair and make up done, finding the waiting around tedious and loathed the inherently vacuous nature of the profession. My dream was to be an artist. I recall finishing a photo shoot for *Cute* (shampoo and other

Image 37. *Paikpora (pen on paper, size A4, 2001)* An example of one of my roof top drawings created on site in Bangladesh completed as part of a wider project *From Briarwood to Barisal to Brick Lane.*

products) and rushing back to a Dhaka rooftop to continue drawing. When I felt the burn of the sun on my hand and the pen move with a spirit of its own my mind was free again.

During ten years of relative stability Oscar learnt to deal with my depressive bouts focusing on the good aspects of my personality instead. Calling him in tears saying, "It's starting", he would implore me to talk to a professional. My pride stopped me, believing I was beyond help. It was all a twisted mental conspiracy. This desire to hide my *sordid mental secret* was taking its toll. Letting the mask slip, I might say something that would give me away, feeling exposed I would then try to find a way to retract it. The story I spun to my parents was that life was good in London; I had two degrees from the LSE and at some point, was going to get a *proper* job. If I had pursued my art and gone to Art College, maybe the depression wouldn't have become endemic. Although living at home was tumultuous at the best of times, my art was a lifeline that I clung onto, losing all sense of time as I became submerged in the process of creation. It became my compass to steer through life and avoid the storms. There was a sensation that the desire to create would never end. It was the biggest and deepest love affair that nothing has ever come close to. In London my art began to take a back seat and this was distressing. Without my art I was incomplete and had nothing to live for.

After film school and a short career working in the media, finally, after much procrastination, I was accepted at Chelsea School of Art and Design and studying for the much longed for, art degree.

A few months into my degree, selected works (although not the pieces I wanted to show) were accepted for the *000* group show at the Whitechapel Art Gallery (1999). Excitedly, I shared the news with my tutor. Her acerbic reply was, "You are not there yet." I know that Art College is supposed to break you in order that you can reconstruct yourself into the artist you aspire to be, but I was too fragile for that brutal approach. Continuing at Art College would have killed any microscopic last shred of confidence and ironically, I dropped out in my second year. Instead I thought, *You can all go to hell* and decided to simply be an artist. Getting a studio in east London I embarked on an uncertain road, but I was determined to prove to myself that I could do it.

I believed my art was going to blast away the depression and generate a new *joie de vivre*. If anything, I was getting worse and this manifested itself in my behaviour towards Oscar and, subsequent, interactions with other people. He was tolerant, but he could see that a *disease* had set in now. When he moved to Brussels for his work and I stayed behind in London, shortly after we married, the shade of my mental complaint changed.

Image 38. *Bit of Brick Lane Onion Style* (pen on paper, size A4, 1999). I used to work from the top of the Truman Brewery, drawing for hours, this study evolved into a scroll of the panoramic view of east London, the first of nine. Much of what I drew does not exist anymore today, bulldozed down to make way for slick high-rise development. 1999 marked a year of frenetic output. Art was the only thing sustaining me.

Image 39. *The Lush Tea Gardens of Sylhet* (acrylic ink on paper, size A4, 2001). Painted from a sketch drawn on location in Sylhet, Bangladesh, I executed the actual painting in a hotel room in Calcutta on my bed when I was sick with diarrhoea. I can vividly recall being castigated by hotel staff for the ink splatters on my bed sheets. My art was taking me all over the world from New York, Kuala Lumpur and Jakarta and all the while my mind was inching towards an implosion.

He thought I would follow him, like a dutiful wife, yet I stubbornly stayed put. My mother commented lamentably, "You looked like the most miserable bride in the world."

The day I got married was not a deliriously joyous one – just pressurised. There was the oppressive burden to act in front of Oscar's parents, the heaviness of hiding my secrets that were accumulating, the compulsion to be this other woman – a woman I was not and could never be.

During our idyllic honeymoon in Thailand, when we ate like gluttonous kings, I spent most of the time reading Van Gogh's movingly, compelling letters to his brother Theo. If I was not reading, I was drawing painstakingly, almost photographically, rendered landscapes in a tiny sketchbook. I would say my mind was not present and I was simply becoming a shadow.

Oscar and I had our moments when the relationship was tenuous – when it could have gone terminally wrong. Like many relationships, it was not smooth, yet we stuck it out. The marriage certificate was supposed to staple us closer together, to stop me drifting in the sea and keep me firmly clamped to the rock that was Oscar. When he left for Brussels I jumped right back in and the sea became my new home, as if I enjoyed being thrashed by the waves and cavorting with carnivorous fish that wanted to consume me.

The eight years when we lived, effectively apart, in which I intermittently smoked cannabis; engaged in clandestine peccadilloes; and my mind, life, and relationship were tested to the brink – the depression deepened and morphed into something quite entirely different and unpredictable. I could go into all the sensational details, as a tabloid would, but it wouldn't give you any insights into the condition. Nor would raking up the past be cathartic, only a reminder of this alien that I had become. Most of the people I chose to surround myself with are also, notably, absent from my life now. Writing about these encounters could be the subject of a fictional novel, but serves little purpose here, apart from superficial, titillation.

Quite simply I was in self-destruct mode and testing Oscar with my behaviour, which was becoming more extreme. Even though I was an irregular cannabis smoker, the mild drug taking only aggravated my problems. The mental turning point was when I was in a club and a rather innocuous looking fellow, with a long beard, carrying a tray of cookies approached me.

"How much are they?" I asked hungrily.

"One pound" he said with a wry smile.

They looked delicious. I was with a work colleague and we both purchased one, gobbling it down in seconds. Like *Alice in Wonderland* who consumes the cake and grows gargantuan or shrinks to the size of a dot after drinking from the bottle, almost instantaneously, I felt a change in my brain. Laughing hysterically, my friend and I were dancing and generally being euphoric. It was delirious feeling unfettered, as if I was floating. The club, *Synergy*, did seem like a glorious, fantasy paradise and I wanted to skip my heart out, so I did. When the evening came to an end, I continued tripping for three days, calling people I hadn't spoken to in years, making them laugh with my ardent declarations, and generally being vivaciously enchanting. Even my parents seemed to prefer me elated and said, "Perhaps you should get stoned more often?" Then I crashed, spectacularly. Shaking uncontrollably I couldn't move my limbs, they felt like they were stuck to the ground and I was stooped and cried out, "What's happening to me?" What happened that night was my *Peter Green* moment. Things were not the same mentally after consuming that cookie. It seems almost ludicrous to imagine that a cookie could have caused such damage, but that trip was like someone stamping on my brain with spike-encrusted boots.

During these eight years in the mental wilderness my alter egos had also surfaced: Fred the Devil, Sophie the Cloud Catcher, and Mia the Diva. Becoming more pronounced at this time, it was Fred who I used to talk to when I was alone. Mia was the glamorous altar ego that I hid behind to entrance everyone I encountered, wearing ever more outrageous outfits with killer heels, travelling everywhere on a hand painted bike, which I named *The Spaceship*, always wearing a hat – the bigger and brighter the better. Attracting attention, much of it unwelcome, I was uninhibited, often, choosing to get into brawls with strangers and cab drivers, screaming at them to get out of the way, as I raced across London. Sophie would allow

Image 40. *A Bigger Brain Drawing* (pen and ink on water colour paper, size A0, 2004) Working flat on the floor I drew free style for hours and then became mortified when I thought I had messed up the drawing. This work is an amalgamation of ideas gleaned from my various sketchbooks.

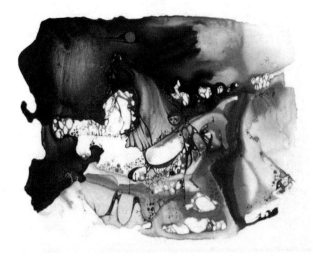

Image 41. *Volcanic Heaven* (acrylic in on MDF block, size 16x14 inches) Painted when I was very mentally unwell. I produced a litany of these paintings.

me to escape during those mindless, mundane moments that punctuate all our lives – when I was waiting at the airport, sitting on the bus, feeling rest-less at a dinner party or bored on the tube. I would start to draw clouds and trees and write down things that people said, or my thoughts in tiny scrawl. My sketchbook accompanied me everywhere and when I couldn't cope outside or deal with the people around me, I would retreat into Sophie's safe, magical universe of clouds and trees. Drawing in public places only drew more attention to myself making me more intriguing, weird and eccentric. I first met and properly spoke to the artist Tracey Emin at the restaurant, *Sketch* in 2005. When she saw my sketches she said, "Those are what I call *brain* drawings."[38]

Very soon after I began the *brain* series people would refer to me as mad. The more they pointed out my difference, the more dislocated I became within.

Each time Oscar and I met up he saw a very different creature embroiled in a very different life with many different people. It was hard for him to deal with, he began to build a new life, one that didn't include me and I don't blame him. I even gave him my blessing, but Oscar believed that without him I was doomed. Our old life of holidays, dinners, and cud-dling up together became a distant memory. He once wrote me a letter with the heading *Cloud* and described his life as a bad dream that he couldn't wake up from, that sometimes he would cry in the night when he thought of my behaviour, which could be insensitive and shocked him. He didn't know who I was anymore. He said it was tantamount to learning that your teenage, beautiful daughter was actually living a clandestine life as a drug addled prostitute. I didn't appreciate the analogy, but clearly I was changing into someone else. It was a frightening period when days merged into nights and I never thought twice about getting on my bike, in the early hours, and roamed London, fearless.

Our decade of relatively normality was now eclipsed by eight years of abject uncertainty. The mental problems that seemed manageable as a teenager were overwhelming and impacting on every aspect of my life. The first notable change was my abrupt estrangement from the family and a preference for certain types of people who encouraged me to stay in London, to be moulded into what they wanted me to be. Since I was adept at creating alluring masks, masquerading as other people was appealing. Arguably everyone wears a public and private mask, such a dichotomy is facile though, I was no longer a composite cohesive being but disjointed, fractured and confused, which begged the question – who was I? Even I didn't know anymore.

The relationship with my family is a bit healthier nowadays. At certain junctures, it completely broke down. They increasingly found my mental health condition difficult to cope with. Perhaps I was too demanding. My middle sister would spend hours on the phone talking, but she wasn't well either, we just fed each other's illness, which left us both wedged in a corner. My little sister, when I used to email her my disturbing poems, requested that I stopped sending her the material. My big sister visited me in London after a long period of non-communication and was incandescent with rage, accusing me of causing the family unnecessary worry and screamed, "If you want to fucking kill yourself go ahead."

My big sister and I have attempted to rebuild our relationship after intense bouts of correspondence, patience and a lowering of expectations on both sides. Families are designed to break down due to their inherent complexity, however disillusioned I became with my family, deep down I knew that the relationship was not beyond repair. Oscar was aware of my voluntary disconnection with them. Maybe he believed I was his only lifeline. But I was angry with him too, angry he had buggered off to Brussels in the first place. Also, I didn't want to relinquish my freedom and then, on other occasions, I wanted to escape London. By 2008 the situation was not tenable anymore. For the sake of my mental health I would have to leave London. I oscillated though, unable to stop my occasional weed habit and unable to end the dual existence I had been leading. The extrication from my old life was psychologically violent. This combined with stress, lack of sleep and some impetuous, ill-fated decisions created the perfect breeding ground for psychosis in 2009.

A Partner's First Encounter with Psychosis

Once we had decided that I move to Brussels, Oscar and I were fully committed to making it work. I knew it was my last chance, after previous failed attempts, like alcoholics attempting to wean themselves off the poison, but still sneaking a drink, when they thought that no one was looking. Possibly going cold turkey was too much for my brain to cope with. There was an inevitability about my psychosis, as if it had been brewing in my brain for years, cannabis was only part of the problem contributing to a complex mental state. I had been smoking the night before my first major psychotic episode, but not during the second or any of the subsequent ones. A psychiatrist told me that we have twenty to thirty thousand genes floating around, although not all are switched on. Something definitely was activated in my brain the night the psychosis ensued and I haven't found a way to deactivate it.

Oscar was there during both episodes. If he hadn't been present, I dread to think how I would have coped. Details of the psychosis have been partially recounted in previous essays, you might be asking why I don't just amalgamate all the details into one whole, but I want to demonstrate how difficult is has been to collate the memories. It would be disingenuous to attempt to write a tidy essay about what happened. Psychosis is messy, violent, illogical, incoherent, random and disturbing and I think the way I have written about it tries to mirror this.

During the second episode, which happened a month after the first, Oscar had flown into London realising I was gravely unwell. The day after the restaurant incident at *Hix*, we planned to leave London. I kept on packing bag after bag, insisting that I needed all these objects and things. Then I began talking to the Nazi (who was not there), apologising out loud and when I had finished I ordered Oscar to complete all my instructions. He carried the bags; there were at least ten. Then we stood at the roadside waiting for a cab. That's when I started singing at the top of my voice; a song that I composed called *I Don't Know*. Everyone who drove past was staring at me, their eyes agog, the cars slowed down, disappeared, then reappeared, and I thought that I was controlling it all with the blink of my eyes. The world took on an amber hue. Oscar implored me to stop singing but I refused. In the end he had to feign a heart attack to shut me up. We returned to my flat, because he didn't think we would be allowed to board the train. When I began to unpack, it was with a methodical precision and I was overly voluble speaking mainly about the family. I weaved a story that linked everything seamlessly to make sense of all the pain that we had endured.

All the while Oscar stayed calm while my neighbours were getting nervous. I haven't written about Oscar's loyalty before. He could see that I was delusional and this was the second time he was witnessing me in this state. The first time it happened, I was fixated on the numbers 3,6,9 and the colours, red, white and black. I, also, believed that my cab driver was trying to abduct me. He was an Asian cab driver, scrupulously overly friendly, giving me his personal number so that I could call him directly, if needs be. I should have been suspicious when he did that, but naively, I trusted him.

The Eurostar was out of service due to the heavy snowfall and I was forced to get a very early flight. That night, before the cab driver picked me up, he called on my mobile, reprimanding me sternly for booking him through the cab firm, which I thought was peculiar. He insisted that if I didn't cancel my official booking, he wouldn't come. I never thought of saying, "Fine, don't come then, I'll book another cab." Afraid of not making my flight I agreed, somewhat hysterically, because I knew I had to get out of London. When he arrived, two police officers were outside and asked if everything was ok. I nodded before getting in the car. I was far from ok though. I'd been ranting/singing, was sleep deprived, screamed at my mental health social worker and psychiatrist, because the latter had been an hour late, and was desperate to stop seeing all these patterns. They were ubiquitous – on my phone, in my head, and outside as we drove though the bitterly cold December's night. It was tantamount to being in fight or flight mode preparing for an imminent attack and not knowing where the attack would spring from.

It was December 23rd the episode lasted 3 days, it was 2009 and I had turned 36 earlier that year. I called my father and told him how the numbers 3,6,9 had cursed our family. They could be traced throughout our lives and that this was why we'd been struck, repeatedly, by tragedy. Speaking incredibly fast, spewing out numbers and facts that all seemed to link together, my stepfather was stupefied and almost believed me.

"How did you work this out?" he asked nervously. At that stage I felt as if I have been touched by a divine truth and wisdom. These numbers unlocked the answers to all our problems.

I kept talking to my stepfather throughout the journey to the airport. He sounded tired and old, I knew he didn't have his teeth in either, but he stayed on the line and tried to reassure me while the cab driver stole uneasy glances at me in his mirror. When he arrived at the airport, I saw terminal 3 and 6 and thought these numbers were a sign of imminent danger. The cab driver parked the car, but then it appeared as if he was pulling out to drive away from the airport.

I screamed, "Where are you taking me?"

Looking at me directly in the eye he spoke very slowly and said, "You should read the Koran". It was not so much what he said, but the way he said it that I became scared. It seemed sinister.

We were on the main road now and I insisted that I get out.

"Stop the car now," I yelled.

He did as he was told, but seemed agitated while I was completely hysterical. Handing over 60 pounds when the fare was 40, I remembered he told me he had 6 children. All I could see were these numbers. I fervently believed he was going to abduct and torture me. Running across the road, I grabbed the arm of a stranger. Appearing startled, he told me to calm down and then called the police. 6 officers approached me. One of them was Asian and this filled me with panic. My trepidation was linked to the fact that my show in London had been recently cancelled. When I saw this Asian policeman, in my mind he was affiliated with the group who said they would boycott my show if it went ahead. The Asian policeman was against me just like those who were, in my mind, trying to cast me out of London. I was sewing all these stories rapidly in my head and the absolute terror was becoming more acute. Two officers tried to call the cab firm and the cab driver. The firm said I had cancelled my booking and the cab driver didn't pick up his phone. Confused, scared and disorientated, the police insisted on escorting me to the plane and one of them called my husband. I am not sure what Oscar said but he reassured them, no doubt. Finally able to board the plane as I walked through Heathrow I saw numbers and signs everywhere. Believing people were cloned, I thought they were all in on it. My neighbourhood was a malevolent and surreal place. I walked slowly, breathed deeply and felt lost. When I was waiting to pick up my luggage in Brussels, there was a Jewish family standing in front of me, with a baby that looked drugged, the father was agitated and talking loudly. They were like cartoon characters. As I write this, my rational brain is telling me that all these thoughts were gobbledygook. Writing about it only serves to show how unhinged I was from reality.

Although relieved to see Oscar, when we were in the car I began to talk about the numbers, the cab driver that I thought had tried to abduct me, and the 6 policemen. I talked about how my family was truly plagued by the numbers 3, 6, 9 and that these numbers were linked to both our families. The famous quote from Shakespeare's *Hamlet* surfaced in my head in luminous green:

"There's a divinity that shapes our ends,
Rough-hew them how we will"
Hamlet Act V Scene 2

These correlations were not a coincidence. It was all preordained.

Then I began yelling, "Look, look at the registration numbers – see 3, 6, 9 – it's everywhere."

When we arrived at Oscar's flat I asked him if the flat was bugged convinced that he was the enemy. This went on for days, I kept on believing that I saw signs, a hair in the shower would curl itself into the number 6. When I was lying in bed I thought I had to lie in the shape of Jesus, as if I was on a crucifix; I tasted something bitter in my mouth; felt a sharp prickle like a vexed hedgehog rubbing against my skin; would have conversations with Oscar in my head and, suddenly, he would appear as if by magic.

The details return, going in and out of focus, receding and then blinking luminously at me.

Oscar, despite my alarming behaviour, didn't ask me to leave. He let me sleep for days and eventually the ranting and hallucinations ceased. There was a copious amount of accusation and unjustified abuse. This is when I changed and our relationship changed irrevocably. It was as if the psychosis had woven a narrative in my head that was so strong I couldn't dismiss it but clung to it stubbornly, refusing to accept that it was fallacious.

Writing gets this stuff out of your head. The purge provides a provisional cleanse, before the dirt returns to spoil your thoughts.

Oscar never received any advice from the doctors regarding how to live with a wife who was recovering from psychosis. He was just expected to deal with it. Post psychosis I became obdurate and belligerent, fixated on certain ideas. I didn't want Oscar's input because I would just ignore anything he had to say; I had to find a way out on my own. Oscar would sit as I unleashed the racing thoughts that scampered in my head. He could find it insufferable being on the receiving end of aggressive monologues, but he would endure them. I told him repeatedly that when the symptoms started we had to implement the code *3,6,9* with military precision to stop the fall. Oscar would go along with it.

I would scream out: "Do you get it,' and he would have to reply,

"Yes, I get it.'

Scribbling things down on pieces of paper I insisted that we were coping and grappling with it all, as long as we implemented this code.

At a recent exhibition I attended at the Hayward Gallery, I saw the artwork of artists working outside the mainstream known as *Outsider* art. Their work was never recognised during their lifetime, but is highly sought after and collectable now. I was struck by the prevalence of numbers, equations, some of them written very, very small. Then I recalled a documentary, which stated everything is predicated on maths, patterns and codes. During the psychosis, my mind then was scrambling for answers to unravel the mysteries of the universe. Of course I was not able to decode or unravel anything apart from my mind, but there was something noble about the pursuit of truth. For Oscar, it was draining; he just wanted me to shut up and stop talking about patterns and numbers. "You are talking complete bullshit," he would say to make me snap out of it.

I continue to find it hard to relinquish those numbers and their *preordained* significance. Depression was easier for Oscar to handle and less threatening. I was not violent or shouting, but he dealt with it all, the psychosis, the ranting, the abuse, the suicidal ideations – he always did in his own way, without consulting doctors or psychiatrists. Do other partners cope as well? I cannot say, although I imagine they struggle, too. Oscar has this inbuilt rational side that is unerring and he is inordinately patient. Perhaps it is pride that stops him from confiding with members of his family or mental health experts. Maybe part of him doesn't want to accept that I am *ill*. It is easy to keep it a secret and those that know only hear the words, "My wife is not well" – nothing more. He says he's trying to protect our family and me.

When the psychosis subsided and I fell pregnant, there was a period of relative stability, then postpartum psychosis struck and we had a new baby to contend with. This time I recognised the patterns and could see what was happening. Postpartum psychosis is the subject of another essay. Just because Oscar knew what was happening doesn't negate the enormous emotional toll on his health. He tries to get on with it, accept it, and to live with it.

Psychosis was in some ways easier to handle compared with the violent mood swings that he is now subjected to, because I am consciously aware of what I am saying and doing, rather than completely delusional. At the same time we both know that I can't ever descend into an all-encompassing psychotic state, because it takes days to recover and the trauma to my brain is profound. If I am suicidal and morbidly depressed, he doesn't have to be physically with me, we know these notions of suicide will eventually pass. His dogged belief that I will never do the deed has stopped him from being fearful and, maybe, that inadvertently makes me less fearful. That's not to say I might not do it one day, but after twenty-two years of him hearing me talk about suicide, perhaps he just can't give it credence like the boy who perpetually cries wolf. It's a fantasy that I indulge in and get totally consumed with (as a conceivable solution to end all this *tedious mental torment*), before I fend it off. Then it comes prowling and I get enmeshed all over again. Oscar lets me do the mental work, sometimes he just sits and listens knowing that nothing he says will assuage my state of mind. I usually have to find a way to break out of the darkness that I, habitually, bathe in. It's at night, when all is quiet outside that the din begins, the quiet simmer of thoughts during the day become a boiling mental pot of Fred's chagrin. My mind transforms into a super highway with cars that never stop, zooming and crashing and drawing blood. When I am like this, I go into the studio, lock the door, zip my mouth shut, pick up my pen and brush, or write.

Oscar has found his own ways to deal with me when I am psychotic, manic, depressed, angry, and foul. And he's done it all on his own. Time apart seems key, leaving me to do my art, to sleep, to garden, to go for a bike ride or he simply ignores his wife. Talking often creates heat, which is why he opts to listen more. Sometimes we shuffle past one another like strangers, I don't even say good night but Oscar chooses to forget about my rudeness, my moods, and my rages. After a sheepish apology on my part he will say quietly, "I am used to it."

There is a pain in his eyes, lines etched on his face that didn't used to be there, his body seems weaker and he has even told me, "I think I will die young."

This is a petrifying thought and gives me a *mental* kick. I must try harder. He doesn't deserve it. Oscar is sociable, popular, respected, successful, intelligent, handsome, gentle, a remarkable father, composed, fiercely private, and self-reliant. Perhaps I have put him on a pedestal, but then he has to live with this *thing* hanging over us constantly, like a noxious odour. I have told him that he could be effusive and praise me more. He has replied that he just can't do *praise* and I can't expect it of him. I have accused him of "emotional stinginess", he argues that, "If you are nice, then I will be nice back, but all you do is give me shit." We have been at a painful impasse; but we manage to find a way forward. He thinks I need to work on my mind more vigorously, although I am not sure how much more I can do apart from keep on believing that whatever we face we will always come through the other side, somehow.

For the last few weeks he's been abroad, far away from me, working very hard and eating fresh papaya every day in a sunnier, tropical climate. Now he is with his own family in Sweden. There have been times when he has implored, "I need to see my friends." My anti social demeanour (mainly towards anyone in his circle) affects him adversely. Being apart – having a break from me – has done both Oscar and my son some good, since the condition can be sapping and destructive. They are both being rejuvenated by some sun, laughter, good food and chat, all the things that are hard for me to enjoy without some level of affectation.

His family offer unerring support, even though he doesn't really talk about my brain issues with them, he can live the normal life he doesn't have with me. Should Oscar talk to someone, would talking make living with a *mad* wife more bearable?

Support for Family and Partners – Does It Exist?

There are support groups for family members living or caring for people with mental disorders. They are often the forgotten victims since the focus is usually on the sufferer rather than those that suffer at the hands of the condition. They just get on with it. The job is a thankless one.

My husband is one of those exhausted carers; he told me he has no life, "Every minute is either spent on childcare, work or doing things to make your life easier. It would be nice if you could do something for me."

Finding the image he paints unfair, I don't see myself as unpleasantly selfish. Outside the home and to strangers even, I take great care to be considerate, generous and thoughtful. Admittedly, the person that deserves this consideration and compassion the most rarely receives it. This is something that I am working on changing.

I am very grateful to Oscar, although he must feel taken for granted much of the time. Some carers and family members have complained, almost bitterly, that they never hear a "Thank you" and whatever they do "It is never enough." Their own lives are on hold. Caring for a person with a mental disorder can impact corrosively on your own mental health. Acutely aware of this, I have told my husband to, "Go to the gym," or "Do something nice." It is easy to say, much harder to put in practise.

The reality of the situation is that when our first son was born he let me sleep in and did the morning duties himself most days for months, unless he was abroad or unable to. He habitually dropped and picked up our son from crèche to ensure that I got adequate rest; this impacted, seriously, on his working life in Brussels. In many ways my husband is very similar to my stepfather. He does the shopping and takes my mother to most of her hospital appointments. He wakes up early and goes to bed exhausted. His whole life revolves around the family. In the morning he makes my mother porridge, he cuts the onions, sweeps the floor and keeps the kitchen tidy while my mother makes a colossal mess cooking. Since she took early retirement, my mother spends most of her life sleeping, gardening, baby-sitting my big sister's children, or watching Bangla soaps. And her health is slowly ailing. Without my father, she wouldn't be able to function as well as she does. On the occasions when he's been away from home, simple things such as getting the bus home become a feat; she might get off at the wrong stop, or even board the wrong bus. She needs my stepfather to be her guide, support and protector. It is a partnership, a union, and they can't live without one another. They can be found giggling and chatting in bed sometimes, speaking in Bangla, nothing can come between them; they have been through too much together. It's poignant to witness.

Sometimes I become overly dependent on my own husband; when he's around I regress. For example, he often does the cooking, although I am more than capable of cooking and very proficient in the kitchen. When I cook it has to be an elaborate dish that requires lots of pans, ingredients, and cleaning up, like my tofu noodle soup that has a list of ingredients too long to write here. It's extreme. Unable to tolerate any mess, everything must be cleaned, wiped, and put away before we can sit down to eat; something my husband finds very annoying when all he wants to do is enjoy his meal. If I have to take my son to crèche or pick him up, I must transform myself into an immaculate creature, to conceal my condition from the world. Everything becomes a project and it is tiresome for my husband to live with. If he puts things in the wrong place it can cause a row and quickly escalate into something else. My husband finds it impossible to live with me (most of the time) and unpleasant to talk to, and so I have to conclude why does he stay – out of duty or desire? I am not sure if I am exaggerating, maybe life with me is not as grim and there are puny moments of joy. Most marriages and relationships would plausibly collapse under the strain. Relationships and marriages are flimsy in this modern age, but with this to contend with, what chance does your relationship have of survival?

Is It a Duty or a Genuine Desire to Stay with a Mentally Unwell Partner?

My husband is the old fashioned sort, the adage: *In sickness and in health* resonates and counts for something. Why did my parents stick it out when family life seemed to consist of pointless rows about nothing? Shouting was part of the landscape of growing up and now I find myself raising my voice – something I abhor. A hot viscous anger erupts from the slightest, even trivial, incident. I long to tape my lips together, to be silent and yet I find I am, often, unable to contain that horrid voice.

I have told my husband, "Perhaps we should seek some counselling" but he is adamant we don't need it.

"Just be nice," he says.

A private man, Oscar doesn't think sharing or discussing helps. Choosing to say very little it frustrates his family, because they never know what's going on in his life. I have become invisible, shrouded in mystery, and none of his friends, family, nephews or nieces has seen me in years. They hear about me, but I never appear. I could, in effect, be dead. We are shielding ourselves from scrutiny, from the pressures and even the pretence of acting normal, which I find psychologically draining. It is easy for my polished veneer to crack and all that is left is green, glutinous gloop.

How long can I hide away? How long will my husband and children tolerate it? Or will I be accepted, but hidden from view, like the mad wife who is locked up in an asylum?

Unfortunately, many mentally ill men and women are cast off, isolated, left to twitch and decompose – even artistic geniuses. The artist Camille Claudel, Rodin's muse, lover and confidante, was admitted to a psychiatric hospital for 30 years of her life. Although her doctors said she was well enough to leave, Camille's mother and brother never authorised her release. Not only was she robbed of her freedom, locked up like a criminal, she was denied access to any art materials, not able to work, and died in the asylum a lonely old woman. Only 90 of her works remain. We all remember Rodin, but few know about Camille. Her story touched me and resonated, although I feel incarcerated in my own mind at least I have constant access to pens and brushes and colour that combine together to form the key that releases me from the jail my mind can often become.

"To live is the rarest thing in the world. Most people exist, that is all." Oscar Wilde

Essentially, art enables you to find a way to *live*.

My husband has accepted his lot. We don't talk about me visiting his family or even visiting my own, although inside I long to see my sisters and parents. I do not know when I will see my middle sister again for fear of her moods; although, recently she wrote a lovely heartfelt letter, which lifted my spirits. I can just about manage a Skype conversation with my eldest sister (although that has petered out now) and polite email contact with my little sister. My mother writes wonderful letters and cards with words scrawled in every corner, all topsy-turvy and brimming with love laced with superlatives that slide off my skin and fail to penetrate my consciousness. A breakthrough came when, my big sister, visited me during my second pregnancy. Full of trepidation, I hoped that there wouldn't be any clashes and that it would be a memorable, mutually beneficial, and emotionally enriching trip. Thankfully it went smoothly, she knew about my triggers urging me to go to bed when I opted to stay up too late. None of the rest of my family has seen me pregnant, this was the first time she had seen my bump – it was a momentous occasion for us, part of my recovery in re-building relationships that are crucial to life.

My stepfather is here now, assisting with the baby, who is almost five months. He comes once a month to visit, to speak Bangla with the children, to change nappies, and listen to my quiet tirades. I make home made carrot, sweet potato and ginger soup for him and charge the iPad so he can catch up on sport. I am glad that he is here. He deals with the various people that need to be dealt with so that I don't have to, letting me hide away and sleep. I am thankful to him for that. Yet any small incident, the whiff of rejection, perhaps a comparison with a sibling, the suggestion of criticism, and Fred makes me retreat into a sheath of mouldy silence, my family are rendered inert once more and I become intransigent and unreachable.

This condition has not only killed off relations with those once close to me, it has killed off feelings that used to come naturally – like desire and the passion to live. For now my husband remains a doting father, tolerates and endures, and chooses to cope and live with a mentally unwell wife without seeking advice or assistance. He made a recent promise, "If the second baby is a boy, we can try for a third, because I know how much you long for a daughter."[39] To consciously try for a third child in the, vain, hope of making me happy is quite something. However, when things have been strained he's renegaded on that promise. The dream of expanding our family hinges on my mental health, which can feel like a lost cause. Knowing, then, that perhaps I have to accept it would not be fair on my two children or husband to try for a third child – I am earnestly trying to be happy with what I have. This is hard since Fred is always sabotaging those fleeting moments of joy that seem to pass by, without letting me properly savour them.

Oscar is a unique, tolerant and emotionally robust man with staggering patience and abundant generosity. He shoots back bullets of light, when I fire bullets that aim to pulverise and draw blood. He doesn't worry or fret or regret, he loves his children and is a committed father, which compensates for my shortcomings. When he met me, I was a slightly sorrowful, confused, sentient, gauche creature – or a rough diamond, as he puts it. Now I am a woman, with an eclectically chic wardrobe, who knows how to mask the bags and gauntness that comes with ageing and hide behind clothes and oversized sunglasses. I have established myself as an artist, achieved a level of respect and, when I have to, can speak in articulate, coherent sentences. Behind closed doors I am antisocial and mumble. Shunning all my nice clothes, preferring black compression socks with holes, I write and paint for hours rather than talk. We constantly live under the shadow of psychosis, but when we are together mingling in social circles, I can hide all my mental afflictions, we can pretend to be a cohesive happy family, and no one would ever suspect a thing.

Oscar, does I think, stay with me out of duty and obligation, but there is a special, enduring, rare breed of love that few people experience and many crave, that has nothing to do with the physical or attraction or youth or personality. It goes beyond that and travels deep to the core of what it means to be human and frail and flawed. Perhaps he is the reason why I have not needed pills or been sectioned; perhaps he's the reason why I am striving to be well, despite the odds stacked, unfavourably, against us. He puts up with intolerable demands, antisocial tendencies, my impetuous, often destructive, actions and trudges on. It is baffling that it is easier to bite his head off than be nice when he really does deserve some niceness. My excuse always is, "Fred made me do it."

The Long Term Impact on the Security of the Family Unit – The Challenges, the Risks and the Reality

Living with a family member with a mental health condition can rip the unit to scraps. At least this is what has happened in my case, rebuilding is excruciatingly slow, but rebuild you can.

I do ruminate on the future. The children are small now, then I fast forward to when they are teenagers. Would they be embarrassed of their mother, would they find my mood swings insufferable, would they too develop the condition? Although genetically, children – born of parents with a mental disorder – are more susceptible to developing it, this isn't a tragic inevitability if they have a loving, secure and stable environment in which to thrive. How can I provide that if I can't modulate my moods or my ranting outbursts? My husband will be the calming presence in the family and provide the core stability. I *love* my children, but psychosis has robbed me of my ability to feel[40]. To experience emotions that people take for granted, I have to work hard at it. One thing that helps is to look into my children's eyes. When my baby stares at me, or sweetly cocks his head towards mine, he is willing me to love him. The pure lyrical gurgles that emanate from a baby's mouth counters the deafening din that Fred keeps banging on his toxic drum.

My eldest son, recently implored, "Please speak to my special, special Daddy nicely."

I sheepishly said, "I can't right now. It's not my fault, it's Fred."

"Oh yes, of course, of course. Go away Fred,' said my son resolutely.

I watched, not knowing whether to feel proud or despondent, as my son spoke to the wardrobe convinced that Fred was hiding in it. After he spoke, I was quiet for the rest of the afternoon and reflected on what had transpired.

"I have to keep calm for the children, I just have to do it," I whispered to myself.

The children have their grandparents too, their love and care has incomparable value. When I am struck down with the condition, I cannot give the children some of the essential things that they need and, rather than beat myself up, I try and entrust others to provide them with what I am, temporarily, unable to give.

Statistically, my husband should have left me then, and if he did leave me, he would realistically have custody of the children and I would live alone. This is the reality of the situation – isn't it? Why would you want to subject the person close to you to constant mood swings, highs and lows, suicidal visions, and sporadically bizarre, potentially psychotic behaviour?

A Good Example of this *Bizarre* Behaviour

I was in Paris over the summer just for a day, and I spent 1700 euros at Diane Von Furstenberg's boutique. These excessive spending sprees are specific to the condition, my friend who was with me had no idea that my behaviour was incongruous; she in fact thought it was marvellous that I was being so indulgent. Last year when I was in New York I spent an exorbitant amount of money on clothes and still haven't worn a fraction of what I purchased. When I got home I crashed, felt immense guilt, packed all the beautiful clothes and shoes away and opted to wear my black pants and socks, the ones I always wore, vowing never to buy anything ever again.

When I told my husband that I had indulged in some retail therapy, he gently castigated me, saying I should be careful. Outraged I tried to vehemently justify my behaviour, but when the call came to an abrupt end I recalled the behaviour of my mother. There were occasions when my mother bought clothes she couldn't afford when she had other pending financial pressures. Seemingly oblivious, she felt entitled to indulge in her retail therapy compulsion and, on rare occasions now, embarks on similar sprees. My stepfather tolerates them, the clothes pile up and become moth eaten junk. Aware of the symptoms, I can gag them most of the time, but sometimes they loom, knock me into submission, and I willingly collude. Then I blame it on Fred's insatiable appetite. How many times can I say sorry to my husband and declare that Fred's culpable? Although my eldest son knows about Fred, I don't think he realises that his mother is sick; there will come the day when I will have to tell my children. Although manic-depressive disorders are not bleakly degenerative and you can stabilise, even totally recover (according to some optimistic mental health care professionals) I find this hard to believe, because it is always there stalking you, in your head, your dreams, your thoughts ... this is the burden you have to carry for life.

Featuring a man with bipolar disorder, I recently saw a documentary. He was running a successful business and was outwardly happy. Without his friends and family supporting him, he said he didn't know where he would be. Living with his parents and partner, his father also had bipolar disorder, and yet outwardly they were coping well. The condition hadn't destroyed their family. The mother did recall the times when her son was manic and often didn't know where he was, the police would arrive at her door and it was terrifying. She could deal with the depressive lows; unless either of them spoke of suicide – then she would be forever vigilant. The condition does cast a burden on the families, even those that were coping. I never want my children to worry about me or to become my carers. My husband is my carer and has been doing this task thanklessly for years even when he is abroad, knowing I can turn to him, even during our non-communicative phases, stops me from completely sinking.

The Potential *Damage* to the Children and the On-Going Struggle for Normality and Stability

For now my son is largely oblivious to his mother's *hot brain*. He might not need to ask that many questions when he's older, I can just give him the essays; the poems, the journal I began after he was born and he can read them along with his sibling. I won't have to explain, but it won't be easy for them to come to terms with it, just as it has been hard to watch my sisters and mother become unwell at various stages with different manifestations of the same mood disorder. My family has stuck together; my stepfather has tolerated my mother's extreme ups and downs and always found ways to move past them. My husband and I have a family now and I have to keep it together and be a mother even when I am collapsing, triggered, or on the floor with fatigue. Perhaps I can't do things that other mothers take for granted; perhaps I can't be the wife that my husband would have liked; perhaps I will opt for isolation to protect my children and husband from the scrutiny and speculation of others. Ours will not be a typical family; my duty is to protect the children and keep them safe and happy. It's my husband's responsibility to shield them from me when Fred tries to strike out.

Already our infant son has seen me manic and raging and he becomes quiet and stares blankly at me. It's as if his inchoate brain can't process the *monster* that his mother has become and he blocks it out. We always try to mitigate any damage by removing myself, as rapidly as possible, from the scene, but he's still been present when I am deranged. These deranged periods never last long, like a series of short, abrupt electric shocks, I wince and then snap out of them quickly, give him a hug and say sorry. But has witnessing this damaged him? Or is his idyllic time in Sweden right now cancelling out all the bad memories that he's experienced during his short life. I am hoping that the love and stability from their father will supersede and obliterate anything *traumatic* that the children might have perceived now or in the future.[41]

I have tried to be the mother I hoped to be and will continue to try, even though the condition is a huge obstacle that sometimes I am unable to surmount. I must remain emboldened by my small daily victories like going to the post office, communicating in simple French and being understood. And I won't give up, ever. I can't fail my husband or children, I, unequivocally, refuse to.

As for my husband, will he be around for the long haul? Or will I decide that he should be allowed to have some proper happiness rather than live with a woman who is up and down, hallucinates, and can be deeply toxic to be with. Since the psychosis, I can't see many positive aspects of living with me. My husband has often told me how *joyless* life can be. He, more than anyone, deserves a little joy. Privately, though, I hope we manage to stay together forever, we haven't done badly thus far.

Right now my husband and son are experiencing a quintessential Swedish summer, eating crawfish by the lake, laughing and joking – tasting a happiness that appears tantalising and unattainable to me. I might try to grab bits of light, but they disappear before I can properly revel in them. Happiness can only be achieved though writing and creating and even then it's always about the next poem, the next brush stroke, it is never enough. Art is my third child, an unquenchable child who needs constant feeding.

Joy is not felt through family life and living life within a family unit. This condition makes you long for the unattainable, to live in a dreamland, to claw at your flesh metaphorically until you recoil in pain. People, friends, family, and children – they all bring me low in the end, because there is this feeling of failing them that follows me like a bad stench.

Why, then, have a second child? Perhaps I naively hoped that striving for normality and stability would normalise and stabilise my brain. To a certain extent his arrival has done this, excluding the occasions when I lapse. I have also learnt to recover from these lapses more quickly. Most of all his birth has given my husband fresh moments of pleasure and our families, too. That is something, then, to revel in.

Unquestionably this second baby has brought me rapture, because I have slowly learnt to open my mind up and receive all that a child can offer. This time I have vetoed Fred from obstructing that primordial mother and child bond.

My duty is to try and grasp this dark shadow that looms and use art and words to dissect it. This has become my life's work then, this is what will keep me going and I hope something good comes out of it, for those who were once close, for others who are suffering out there, and, most of all, my children and the children born of a parent with a mental health condition.

The birds are singing, it's 5.17am, time to sleep, time to rest my brain, time to stop and strive to be well.

The baby is sleeping, my son is happy, and my husband is building a better future for us in a faraway distant and exotic land. Despite everything after twenty odd years – we remain intact, pummelled, but not totally broken.

CHAPTER 9

Preventing a Recurrence of Postpartum Psychosis –
Are Hospitals and Doctors Helping Mothers or
are they the Trigger?

Written during my second pregnancy, at a time when I was becoming quite desperate, this essay examines my struggle to fend off a second episode of postpartum psychosis.

Thirty-one weeks into my second pregnancy, with a history of post-partum psychosis and a diagnosis of schizoaffective disorder I still don't have a hospital, an obstetrician or a care plan in place, only piecemeal bits and pieces. Fighting to get the right care for my own mental health and the well-being of my unborn baby is proving to be harder than I envisaged.

Since suffering from postpartum psychosis, I have tried to turn what has been a profoundly traumatic experience into a constructive one by writing about it and employing my art to heal a fractured mind. As the birth date looms, memories of the psychosis are returning vividly and I am scared it will happen again. Imagine visualising harming your child in the most odious ways possible. Imagine if this goes on for almost two years. Each day is a struggle – to be loving to your child, to be patient, to be benevolent, to stimulate and play with your baby, and all under the shadow of dreadful visions that don't relent. I won't relay the scores of monstrous scenarios that have played out automatically, in my mind. There are people out there who inflict terrible cruelty on children and I am, irrefutably, not one of those people. Personally, the idea of violence towards children is an abomination.

There is one, incontestable, truth that I have learnt about my condition – severe sleep deprivation makes me more of a risk to myself and thereby the children. I would like to qualify the word *risk* – although I, unequivocally, would never physically harm my children, the visions and symptoms of psychosis become more pronounced due to the sleep deficit and can be intolerable. Lack of sleep can affect the best of us, with or without a mental condition. It was due to my dire sleep problems that I felt compelled to send my son to stay with his grandparents, for his own sake. Being pregnant and with my husband abroad, I didn't have much choice, even though it was not an easy decision.

The media often implies that if a mother has psychosis, schizophrenia or bipolar disorder and is not on medication, it's almost inevitable that the mother will *seriously* harm her child – it is not. Women with mental health disorders are capable of making rational and informed choices about their own health and that of their children. What makes women ill is not having an outlet and someone to talk to openly who will, simply, listen. There are women who are exhausted, alone, who have slipped through the net, who in a moment of dark madness and in the throes of a psychotic depression, do something tragically regrettable. The fundamental difference between these women and myself is that I see the psychosis coming, hear its footsteps, and recognise the patterns. This evening, for example, after returning from the hospital I felt instantly unwell, my brain hurt, it was throbbing from stress and getting overheated. I hadn't eaten or had enough to drink, the dehydration was making me feel worse, the anger started to seethe inside and I began to write emails very fast – an elemental sign that my brain was heating up – followed by a vision to stab myself and jump off the roof. Starting to cry, I reached out to people driven by an overarching need to talk to someone. Then I misplaced something, couldn't find it and began to turn the flat upside down frantically searching for the irrelevant item thinking my whole world would collapse without it. A precise pattern was emerging. I was walking back and forth sensing, "It's starting, what do I do?"

I kept saying, "Eat something, drink something, listen to music, turn off your computer, stop writing, slow down and – just breathe." Gradually I ate some cherries, between the sobs, then I made something to eat, there was such resistance because it was about 3am by now, but I continued to fight it. Confronted with a potent urge to send off an angry email to my (now former) obstetrician, trying to restrain myself, unable to, I managed to eat some food, watched some mindless TV (which can often extinguish the fire in your head), played some music, and wriggled out of the mental strait jacket. If my rational self hadn't intervened, Fred would have trampled all over me, stopped me from sleeping, and conspired to exhaust me mentally until there was no rational ammunition left to fend off the incursion. You have to find your own strategy, not surrender to the blackness, not let it smother you, not let it pierce your heart, mind and soul. Unable to reach anyone, I had to do it on my own. Not an advocate of medication, especially during pregnancy, even I know that I am in a vulnerable position and, if I really feel that the mania is going to curb the desire to sleep, I will take something to knock me out like a kick in the head. By 4am, I thought falling asleep naturally was not going to happen and if Fred had his way, I would be up all night writing or painting. Deciding to take half a sleeping pill (at a very low dosage) soon my eyes closed, and the over-heated hard drive of my brain shut down for the night.

Before I went to sleep I spoke to the baby and explained what was going on. I said, "That doctor was really horrible to me, that's why I am upset, he just wouldn't listen, but don't worry, just let Debussy's *Reverie* soothe you, we will be ok, I promise."

Talking to my protruding belly seemed absurd, but it worked, reminding me that I have a responsibility to the baby and myself to stay well. Lamentably, the hospitals and doctors have been exacerbating my stress levels? And that's, fundamentally, not right.

When Dr Ian Jones asked me how I dealt with the visions without the aid of mediation, I replied, "I just fire bullets of logic at them as they come zooming towards me and give them no credence; then I flick them away as if they are annoying, buzzing mosquitos."

He commented on my use of metaphor, saying only an artist could come up with such a vivid description of what was occurring in my brain.

Finding the Right Support Structure to Ensure a Healthy Mind

Since suffering from psychosis I have been in touch with various doctors who specialise in this field. On the whole they have responded positively to my letters, essays and questions and I value this contact. It has given me insights to help manage my mind a little better. When I found out I was pregnant a second time, I was determined not to suffer from postpartum psychosis again and to do everything in my power to ensure this. Equipped with knowledge and insights, I was also seeing my new psychiatrist, Dr Erik Thys.

Dr Thys always had a serious expression on his face, which vanished when he opened his mouth. He spoke so softly and slowly that sometimes I would have to ask him to repeat what he said. He would also answer the phone if it rang during a consultation and accepted my request to put any incoming calls on hold, since it disrupted my flow and made me uneasy. He would often doodle as we talked, as I would, too. Crucially, I felt I could be relatively open with Dr Thys. I say relatively because I think it's preferable to hold some things back and not to divulge your whole self to a health care professional. Why? Because if the relationship breaks down such openness can render you more vulnerable, which is never a good position to be in.

The main problem with Dr Thys was I saw him more as a colleague than my doctor, since he supported my first art project in Brussels with patients suffering from mental health problems and my first solo show at

KAOS, the sister organisation of TrActor. I found it hard to talk about the pregnancy and all the issues surrounding it. Inside I became conflicted between our creative working relationship – that I valued – and that of a patient, exposing herself and her most personal issues. I couldn't reconcile the two.

I was hopeful that the medical team at my hospital, St Luc, would be well-equipped to deal with me second time around, after witnessing the psychosis during my first pregnancy. I read that patients who had experienced postpartum psychosis were susceptible to it developing again after the second birth, but if a care-plan was implemented it mitigated chances of this occurring. As the weeks went by, conscious that the appropriate psychological support was not forthcoming, I expressed my concerns to Dr H, my obstetrician. He said that we could delineate a care plan later; but I needed one now. Each time I returned to St Luc I got flash backs; the hospital had become a trigger. Anxious before entering and anxious after leaving, I began to dread the next appointment. Believing that Dr H was not taking my concerns or condition seriously, I wrote to him, candidly, saying that I was going to leave and find another hospital. He didn't accept this news well and, at our final meeting, he was aloof and almost hostile. As I tried to explain my reasons, he cut me off mid-sentence and said, "You don't have to explain." But I did. He had a duty to implement this care plan early on in my pregnancy, so that I could get sufficient psychological support and feel assured about the baby, the pregnancy and not be afraid of the post-birth outcome. After this meeting, I wrote to him explaining my reasons for leaving:

Regarding the care of pregnant women with bipolar or schizoaffective disorder, this is what they require, according to my research:
1. *The patient needs a structure of support that comprises a GP, obstetrician, psychiatrist, and hospital psychiatric/psychology team that has specialist knowledge of pre/post-partum disorders.*
2. *The patient requires a clear health and pregnancy plan that is outlined from the very outset of pregnancy, especially if they have a history of psychosis and postpartum psychosis.*
3. *The mental health of the patient needs to be monitored closely throughout the pregnancy and in the weeks after the birth.*
   ...I am writing this email so that, if you come across another pregnant mother who is suffering from this condition, you will know what to do and how to provide the best care plan, to minimise the risk of them getting ill.
   After seeing how ill I was post my first delivery it seems quite odd that you didn't feel a need to implement a plan earlier. I was hoping

you would have devised a structure of support. Instead this pregnancy has been marred by the fear of postpartum psychosis recurring.

Postpartum psychosis and depression during pregnancy are dangerous for both mother and baby; the onus cannot be on the patient to do all the begging for help. Although I appreciate your phone call, what I needed was an immediate appointment with a hospital perinatal psychiatrist when I felt my psychological state was deteriorating and to be more closely monitored in the months prior to the birth.

You asked about my sleep, it has been getting worse and I hinted at that. I don't think you realise how detrimental lack of sleep is for me, it can trigger the nascent symptoms that lead to psychosis...

I know mental health is not your area, but I just needed one person who has specialist knowledge to assist me through this difficult time. Although Dr Thys is my psychiatrist, he is not specialised in post and pre-partum psychosis.

I was disappointed by our last appointment...It gave me a bad feeling...

I find hospitals and doctors very difficult to handle at the best of times, which is why I wear a mask of politeness or am appropriately laconic. It's hard for me to establish a good relationship of trust when I feel disenchanted most of the time.

When Dr H didn't reply, I put my experience at St Luc behind me. Both Dr Thys and my GP, Dr Dechamps, recommended another hospital, St Elisabeth and a new hospital psychiatrist. I sought a perinatal psychiatrist, but have yet to meet one in Brussels. My GP was very supportive and attentive during my pregnancy. Her GP practice was on my street and I always enjoyed seeing her and sitting in her spacious, wooden floored office. Giving me her mobile number, in case I needed to speak to her in an emergency, she was unlike any GP I had ever met before – tall, blond with a very warm-hearted face– she always had time to listen.

When I visited St Elisabeth I took to the hospital immediately. It was modern and spacious, unlike St Luc, which was hectic, with people smoking outside when you first entered it. Upon meeting the midwife I told her briefly about my history.

When I began the sentence, "I suffered from postpartum..." she cut me off and interjected with, "depression", nodding as if she already knew me. And I said, "No, postpartum psychosis." Her expression changed and she said, "Oooohhh".

It's always testing meeting new people and divulging such information. I said that I needed to see a psychologist, was in the seventh month of the pregnancy, and felt psychologically unprepared. I had been very low and, for reasons that I found hard to explain, was not optimistic about the pregnancy.

She recommended the psychologist, Mrs Achermanns. I also requested that after giving birth I preferred just one or two midwives to be assigned to my care. Later I received an email assuring me that this would be the case.

When I saw my new obstetrician, Dr D, there was a student doctor in the room holding an ominous looking notebook. The student soon left because I insisted upon it. Speaking briefly about my history of postpartum psychosis I told him, "The need to sleep after giving birth was of paramount importance." Dr D decided, on the spot, that I should be induced, to control the time when I gave birth and ensure that I rested afterwards. He never explained what induction entailed. I just said, "Ok". Not questioning his judgement, I was just glad not to be at St Luc anymore and hopeful I would get the right care.

Later, I wrote to him stating that I needed as few midwives as possible disturbing me, since the crucial time would be the period after I had given birth. He wrote back saying, "I don't know any midwives who have experience of psychosis." That wasn't what I was asking.

"The psychosis is going to happen again," I said out loud. "Why aren't they listening to me?"

It was when I went to Paris to meet my old midwife, Anne, that she related all the negative sides of induction. Anne and I had become friends; she'd been there after the birth of my son and witnessed bouts of postpartum psychosis. Ironically, it was Dr H who had passed on her business card. Often she'd been afraid and anxious for me, but always believed I would pull through and gave me sincere words of encouragement. An energetic and youthful woman for her age, it was always a pleasure to see her. To Anne, an induction was absurd. Since my first birth had been easy – a swift and painless one – it was likely that the second delivery would be quick too. If anything, she said, "Maybe you have to go to hospital a little earlier this time." Once she informed me about the *downsides* of induction I decided against it. This was after my own online research, consulting with other mothers and seeking the advice of Albertine, one of the mental health social workers at TrActor, with decades of experience in this field.

Questioning the Professionals

When you challenge the authority of a doctor they don't like it much, with the odd exception. Postpartum psychosis is rare and the Belgian health system does not appear equipped to deal with it, which is surprising, considering how much they invest in health care. Postnatal depression is widely known and is not to be confused with postpartum psychosis, although I think confusion does occur, making it harder to create a proper treatment plan for the afflicted. The *support team* for women at risk of postpartum psychosis, delineated by Dr Ian Jones and the Royal College of Psychiatry, also does not exist in a systematic way over here. The onus is on the mother to find a psychiatrist, a good GP, a good hospital, a good obstetrician and a hospital psychiatrist or psychologist with knowledge of the condition. Although my GP, Dr Dechamps and Dr Thys tried earnestly to find such a team of people, even they struggled. It was very much a hit and miss approach. If I had said I was vulnerable to postnatal depression, perhaps my case would have been handled differently. When you mention the word "psychosis" it can create a mild form of panic or over-reaction, which is unhelpful.

When I told Dr D that I didn't want to be induced, he said that he respected my decision, but that this was the practice at St Elisabeth and all his colleagues agreed with him. If I didn't concur I had to leave St Elisabeth and find a new doctor. I tried to reason with him, asserting that mine was an unusual case; that I was not on medication; and that I had learnt to deal with the threat of psychosis using my own cognitive strategies. A support structure was in place, which included home help, and my husband was taking time off in the first weeks to assist. All we needed from them was the assurance that, after I gave birth, I would be allowed to sleep, since sleep deficiency was the biggest trigger for psychosis. Psychosis is a cumulative illness, I told him. It would only happen several days after giving birth, not immediately, if at all. After the initial post-birth euphoria, rest was essential because I could succumb to mania, sleeplessness and expend too much energy, leaving me mentally exhausted and, thereby, allowing psychosis to set in. Unmoved, Dr D remained unyielding; in fact when I relayed the views of my midwife and her reservations about induction, he said they made him "mad". Beginning to question his approach, which seemed aggressive and unsympathetic, I felt he wasn't listening to me at all.

My husband said that some of my emails were perhaps too assertive and maybe the doctor felt professionally challenged. Nevertheless, stress can also contribute to episodes and dealing with Dr D was more stressful than going to St Luc. Swiftly and silently I began to despair inside.

I was referred to a new psychiatrist (number 39). His name was Dr L. He was white haired, round faced, portly and sixty plus. He looked more like a banker than a psychiatrist; I suppose psychiatrists come in all shapes and sizes. Instinctively I thought, *Will I connect with this man?* Dr Thys had recommended him in good faith, therefore I was hopeful. Unfortunately, he didn't fare much better than the rest.

Upon arrival there was another psychiatrist seated, smiling and poised, with a notebook in her hands.

I asked, "Who is this?"

"Oh she is just here to observe," replied Dr L.

"Can you ask her to leave please?" I said without hesitation.

It was not a good start. Feeling exposed already, the conversation was immediately awkward. *Here we go again*, I thought. All the rudimentary information he had was incorrect about me, forcing me to go into skeletal detail about my past, which is never easy. He might be a psychiatrist, but these people remain strangers.

I began correcting him. Small details began to spill. Briefly, I told him that I had been sexually assaulted multiple times, as part of my narrative history. He misheard and asked, "So, you were sexually abused?"

I said "No," but he insisted on repeating the question.

He then asked, "What do you mean by psychosis?"

This was almost too much. Why did I have to explain myself in gruesome detail? Scrawling something down, I wanted to read what he'd written. Then our session came to an abrupt end and I asked, "What now? Should I see you again, what is the procedure for women susceptible to postpartum psychosis?"

He was evasive in his answers, as if eager to get me out of his office.

"Yes, you need to sleep after giving birth and you need care and monitoring. If you want to see me again it's up to you."

Up to me to do what? Feeling drained, I thought *this man really can't help me*, despite his obvious years of experience.

He ushered me out of the room and I was none the wiser. Should I have plucked up the courage to see Dr Thys instead? Right then I was weary and confused. Albertine was waiting and I just quietly cried while struggling to eat my cake in the hospital café. Desperation was beginning to set in. I needed my mother, stepfather, sisters, a friend, my husband, my son – I knew he would give me a kiss and a hug – but there was no one. Fred was cackling at me, saying, "It's going to happen again and this time..." Refusing to let him finish his sentence, instead I wrote a letter to my unborn baby explaining that:

Mummy is going through a hard time, but don't worry, we can listen to Beethoven, Bach and Debussy. We don't need the doctors, as long as Mummy sleeps and eats and goes for a bike ride when things get too much, we will be ok. Actually, Mummy is a warrior, a fighter, too, and physically Mummy is an ox. It's just Mummy's mind can go a bit gooey. Mummy won't listen to Fred, even though he keeps on kicking her head in. It didn't help today that the doctors were jumping up and down on Mummy's head, too, leaving it squashed and crumpled.

The baby kicked enthusiastically and I thought, *I will get the care I need; I will keep on searching for it until I get it and my children are not going to be afflicted with this bloody gene. They are going to have a good family life and so will I.*

When I saw the psychologist, Mrs Achermans, she was a benign faced, softly spoken lady, but she didn't speak English. Another mental health social worker, Jean Pierre, was on hand to translate and from thereon, with the aid of Google Translate, I tried to communicate with her. Jean Pierre was a jolly man, enthusiastic about his job; we often had interesting discussions about the mind and mental health approaches. I could see he was struggling, though, to translate my English to Mrs Achermanns.

Mrs Severin, her colleague, was on holiday and not back until August. Mrs Achermanns asked if I needed help before then; I said I would wait. It was emotionally draining seeing all these new people. She was, unquestionably, a very personable, serene lady, which is exactly what I sought. I began to think what a difference it made to be accompanied to the hospital. TrActor, the mental health organisation, was invaluable in that sense. When I said that I found using cabs in Brussels stressful they said, "Don't worry we will take you to the hospital" and, naturally, when you are in the car you can have a chat which often helps you get out of your head. My usual mental health social worker, J, was off sick, but Albertine and Jean Pierre had stepped in and were there to assist. Before they dropped me home, if needs be, they would let me do my shopping. Such practical provision made life less heavy. It's not only meds that patients need, or sitting in a stuffy office talking about issues, it's about the day-to-day practical living, keeping appointments, and having enough food in the house. Fortunate to have such people in my life, at that moment I thought about their unerring patience; how they were doing an arduous job; and that they should be lauded for when they have got the level of care just right.

On 9th August 2013 I went back to St Elisabeth for a final meeting with Dr D and the psychologist, Mrs Severin. My due date was officially 8th October; if Dr D had his way, I would have been induced on 25th September 2013. As I sat waiting I started to visualise the induction, arriving in the evening, waiting around, feeling claustrophobic and restless in the hospital, then the artificial process beginning, the poor baby not knowing what was going on, happy to be in the womb for a little longer. The cervix was not dilating, they fiddled some more, pumped me with drugs, the baby was getting distressed and agitated, the hours went by, I was in pain and then suddenly, "We have to do an emergency C- section." I was distraught; the baby was out; I began to sob, was angry, couldn't sleep and became inconsolable. An induction was supposed to diminish my chances of having postpartum psychosis, if anything it would have increased the probability of an episode. *No way*, I said to myself. There was no justification for this procedure, maybe they were just covering their backs or advocated an interventionist approach. The more I thought about it, the less logic there was to their decision. My body was tense and all hunched up; mentally I was bracing myself for a confrontation with the doctor.

My appointment was at 3.30 pm; by 4 pm I still had not been seen. I asked the surly receptionist if it was going to be much longer, recalling the way she had once spoken to me on the phone. Calling up the hospital, a few days previously, I declared, "I want to cancel the induction."

She said, "It's not up to you, it's up to the doctor to decide."

Hearing her say this was infuriating and seeing her in the flesh I had to contain myself. There was no point saying, "You need to work on the way you speak to patients, because your telephone manner is appalling."

Dr D appeared. He was an unassuming slight man, but his modulated tones could quite rapidly become agitated and his eyes would squint and flash in a menacing way.

When he came out of his office, he was friendly and said, "Come back at five and knock on my door."

He walked me to Mrs Severin's office and, as we spoke, he reiterated his stance regarding induction and would not budge. Mrs Severin caught the tail end of the conversation, seeing I was upset and on the verge of tears. I couldn't understand why he was being this stubborn. Didn't he realise the birth was not a problem? It was afterwards that was potentially risky – all he had to do was ensure I slept.

He doggedly asserted the argument, "What if you arrive in the middle of the night and people are not here to assist you?"

For me that sounded like a good thing, the fewer people the better. I only needed a midwife, my husband and one doctor – that was it.

"What if you become psychotic?" he said.

"You don't become psychotic just like that, it's a progression, a downward spiral that has to be magnified by something – usually prolonged sleep deprivation that has lasted a couple of days." I said.

It was irredeemable. He left. Then I lost my composure, momentarily, in front of Mrs Severin; it's excruciating breaking down before a stranger. Very empathetic she listened and tried to speak from Dr D's point of view. Mrs Severin was small with a face that was docile and knowledgeable. Then we talked about all the issues that were bothering me. Stuff I had been anxious to offload. It's never easy talking about the visions and when she asked, "Have you ever harmed your child?" I felt like screaming, "Of course I bloody well have not."

Then I paused and said, "Sometimes, when he's very naughty and I am extremely tired, I have had the urge to smack my son and this has shocked me, I never thought I would ever feel that way."

I didn't feel proud about admitting this information. Actually, it was deplorable. You are under the spotlight, being scrutinised, but I was doing the right thing, being honest. It was a relief to talk to her. I even sensed a slight connection forming, showed her the book of drawings of my son, and explained all my strategies – she was impressed. It was encouraging. She wanted to know more about TrActor and said she could find a midwife to visit after I went home with the baby. Then she accompanied me, along with Albertine, to see Dr D. Having two women by my side I felt stronger. Earlier, in the car on the way to the hospital, Albertine had been vociferous in her opposition to induction, "It will cause more stress for you and the baby and it will be painful."

I thought, *Ok, the doctor won't listen to me, but he will surely listen to Mrs Sevrin and Albertine.* When we got to Dr D's office, another student doctor was present I asked him to leave, which he did, refusing to have another stranger hearing my business. Albertine tried to assure Dr D that, if he believed there would not be enough people available at the birth, they could send their people, who were trained to assist.

Mrs Severin said, "She's not on medication, she's been living with this for years, she knows what she needs."

Albertine intervened, "She just has to rest and sleep after giving birth."

Dr D nodded, but clearly he wasn't listening. His position remained unchanged. It was as if he was putting a gun to my head saying, "If you don't agree to the induction then get lost."

I then asked, "Have you had experience of women who have suffered from postpartum psychosis?" The question left him incensed.

"Yes," he said, his eyes ablaze, "I know one woman who threw her baby out of the window" and then he divulged that his mother had experienced it with her fourth child.

With all his knowledge, why was he being so intransigent, refusing to listen?

Albertine and Mrs Severin left and the atmosphere became more frayed. He was agitated, just like Dr H was when I had challenged him. I told Dr D that all this pressure was stress inducing. Now nine weeks from giving birth, on top of that, I had to find another hospital.

All I wanted was a natural birth, to which he replied, "If you prefer all things natural, why are you wearing lipstick?"

I thought, *This guy is absurd* and it was lip balm actually, and what did that have to do with anything?

When I left, there was no handshake, just a closing of the door and I was back to square one. Despondency and exhaustion set in. I was hungry and thirsty with no desire to eat or drink anything. The good news was that the baby was in the right position and despite the fact that I had only put on six kilos the baby was going to be three and a half kilos. *At least the baba is all right*, I thought. Struggling to be positive, mentally I was on the brink of a meltdown.

After I got home, becoming instantly agitated, I began writing emails, firing them off with a bang and then was overcome with regret immediately after pressing the send button. I sent two angry ones to Dr D, knowing he wouldn't reply. I also wrote to Dr Ian Jones, to Dr Thys, and members of my family – saying to the latter that it felt as if I didn't exist. I started crying. The symptoms were starting. Although delirious with fatigue, I just wanted to write. It was 1.39am and I hadn't eaten or drunk much. What had caused this spiral? Dr D and the way he spoke to me – which was wrong. I was angry. Could it have also been pregnancy hormones making me even more emotive?

Writing all this down has helped to vent my frustration with doctors and hospitals. Maybe it is better to conceal truths behind meticulously painted facades than be honest due to the pervasive lack of understanding? If I had not said anything about the postpartum psychosis, they would have left me alone to let nature take its course and then, once I was released from hospital, my husband and I could have implemented the care plan I needed.

All I wanted was to give birth naturally – the assurance that I would be able to sleep, together with a few people to keep an eye on my mental state and make certain nothing went too awry – ensuring that this second birth was a memorable experience and something to look forward to rather than dread. Was that too much to expect?

Waking up the following morning, bleary eyed, as if I was hung over, my eyes were stinging and then I groaned when I looked at all the emails I had fired off.

"Christ, not again."

I didn't want to re-read the emails; most of them were tirades. Pacing up and down, I tried to stop myself from pressing the send button and called a few people, but no one picked up their phone. Now I was alone again, Bach was blaring. I had to start the day, which was like a heave and a chore: a slow and sluggish trudge through the tangled mental undergrowth, before I could get to the base of the trunk and climb the tree of life. By the early hours of the morning, I would be dangling from the branches with a paint brush in my hand, finding some small pleasure in the brush strokes and the parallel magic universe I was creating, that was a far safer place than the one out there. For now, my second child was sleeping contentedly in the womb and the least I could do was to play soothing music, be calm, and wait until the baby was ready to enter the world. Whatever problems we encountered, we would face them together.

12th August 2013 – The Aftermath of a Mental Assault

It had been three days since I saw Dr D. During that time, my sleep had been lax, my eating patchy, and I had been plagued with anxiety about the next hospital and doctor that I would be forced to see. Part of me had no willpower. Although Dr Dechamps told me not to worry, when I should have been resting I was on the phone to the new hospital – Edith Cavell – speaking to various people, in English and pigeon French, getting more and more weary. Not only that, St Elisabeth called me saying that Dr D was on holiday and they needed to re-schedule my appointment. I told the receptionist that I was no longer seeing Dr D and to cancel everything. She asked if I wanted to speak to another doctor, I replied, "Only if it is a good doctor."

She said, "All the doctors here are good."

I said, "No they are not."

Uneasy with the way I was talking, she told me another doctor would call, which he did shortly afterwards.

"I'm an assistant to the doctor," he said. I wasn't sure what that meant.

I said, "I would like a second opinion and want to know if the decision that I should be induced is final and considered the best course of action by the whole department, including the head of obstetrics."

He said he would make the enquiry and call back in the afternoon.

He did call, saying, "Hey, I am just the messenger, but everyone, including the psychiatrists, the obstetricians, and the psychologists all believe that induction is mandatory in this case."

I knew that this was blatantly inaccurate, because Mrs Severin hadn't agreed with this decision. I didn't much like the doctor's tone either.

He did say, "If you want to make a complaint regarding Dr D you are free to do so."

I replied, "Do you have a name of the person I should lodge this complaint to?"

He said, "No, but you can look on the website, ciao, ciao."

Who trained these people I wondered? I managed to speak to another obstetrician at Edith Cavell. She said I needed to make an appointment with the psychology department and the radiographer – that was three new hospital appointments. Mentally shattered, my eyes were stinging; I was ravenous and yet had no will to eat. How was I going to go to London the next day and conduct my meetings professionally? I began blasting off emails, tidying and cleaning, pacing up and down, desperate to talk to someone – and get out of my head. Managing to speak to Dr Dechamps, she calmed me down – as she always did – and said she had spoken with another doctor. Her name was Dr Deleuse. Interestingly, Dr Deleuse didn't believe that being induced would prevent postpartum psychosis. Dr Dechamps said it was also unnecessary to see the radiographer, which was one less appointment to deal with. Dr Dechamps said she had a good feeling about this doctor, I trusted her. I just wanted to find a benevolent, empathetic doctor. Since the one I had spoken to emailed me later and said, "I don't feel equipped to deal with your case," Dr Deleuse was my last option.

After speaking with my GP, the fleeting sensation of calm was soon eclipsed with debilitating rage. Having barely eaten, my blood sugar level had plummeted, which was why Fred's voice was amplified and my thoughts were becoming more confused and disjointed. Telling me to mop, to wipe, to clean, he was draining me. Fred demanded that I write another angry letter to Dr D; I resisted the urge. Trying to reach my husband, we spoke briefly and I retained composure momentarily. As soon as I put the phone down, the fury returned and Fred was in the driver's seat. Unable to walk properly, with a stooped head, I was becoming deranged. Getting quite frantic, I knew the longer I didn't eat, the more manic I would become and the symptoms would intensify. I started to break down, afraid of the damage all this stress was inflicting on the baby. Texting Albertine, J and Jean Pierre I asked if there was a mental health social worker I could speak to at TrActor. J got back to me and texted a number. Guilt ridden for reaching out, I knew that if I didn't, Fred would completely dominate my actions.

I had to find a way to eat and sleep as soon as possible. For the last few nights I had been going to sleep progressively later and later, the previous night I hadn't fallen asleep until 5.30am. Usually, if I sleep eight hours it is not a problem; if I don't, then I slip into mental quicksand and am unable to function properly. That morning I had woken up after four hours of sleep – not enough for most people. Dr D's face and inimical voice kept on replaying in my head. I am glad that I maintained a modicum of decorum and did not lose it. Part of me believed he revelled in my distress (improbable, although it appeared that way at the time). Knowing that Dr Thys was on holiday, I didn't want to disturb him. Patients were constantly demanding his attention. Also, I didn't want him to see me *unwell*, since it might undermine confidence in my professionalism. Yet, I had to contact him. Even though he was in Italy, he said I could call him and the familiar sound of his voice was instantly reassuring. Relaying a truncated version of what had been happening he repeated that:

"There is no evidence that induction prevents postpartum psychosis."

He then warned me about the sleep medication prescribed by Dr D. At my last consultation, I asked him how often I should take the pills and Dr D said, precisely, "One per day."*

This didn't sound right. Because my relations with Dr D were fractured, I didn't quiz him on this. I did seek a second opinion, though. My very conscientious pharmacist warned me not to take them frequently, in fact, only to use them in emergencies and for no longer than two weeks.

Dr Thys also said, "You must not take one a day, because the baby could get addicted."

The thought of making my baby addicted to sleeping pills made me incandescent. As the conversation came to an end, although much better after talking to him, my wrath returned.

Pacing up and down, ranting, getting flashbacks, crying, cleaning, tidying, and disorientated, I wanted to scream at Dr D and say, "This is your fault."

Calling my husband, he tried to calm me down again; I didn't want to worry him. He was far away in Asia, what could he do? It was too late. Fred was in the room and I was getting scared, not so much for me, but for the baby, thinking about the rise in cortisol in my blood stream. What was that doing to the poor little thing? I tried to talk calmly to the baby:

"That doctor was really bad: I knew I shouldn't take a pill a day, these doctors are making me ill. I am sorry, it's not my fault, I will put on Debussy's *Clair de Lune* and it will be ok, Mummy is going to try to eat and then sleep."

Feelings of sorrow hit me in wave upon wave – sorrow that the baby's mother was *mentally ill*.

"These poor children, I should never have become a mother, it's not fair on them..." I said out loud.

My mood was becoming darker and bleaker. "Snap out of it," I tried to tell myself. Calling the number that J had given me, I spoke to a woman who said I should call in the morning.

I said, "I need to talk to someone now!"

Sensing the desperation in my voice, she told me to call again in fifteen minutes. I did and heard the voice of a tired man on the other line. At first I was vigilant, gradually I opened up to him.

He said, "Don't listen to Fred, stop cleaning, try to be calm and eat something, getting angry is not going to help the baby."

"I know, but I am so livid, I go to hospitals and see doctors but they just make me worse."

He asked me about medication, I said, "I am not on medication, I am very strong, but right now I can't quite take what's been happening. It's too much for me to cope with mentally."

He said, "Do you have friends or family, anyone you can turn to?"

I said, "No, my husband is abroad, my friends are far away, my family too. The friends I have here don't really know how to handle my condition. There is no one, I am alone and I am frightened. I can't get out of this hole. Fred wants to exhaust me, you see, he doesn't want me to eat or sleep. I have to eat. Then I can take a pill and sleep."

He listened attentively, I asked his name and he said his name was Ken, then he asked, "Do you have food at home?"

I said, "Yes" and started to open the fridge and put some soup on the hob and cut vegetables. As I prepared the food a shred of hope returned.

"Listen," said Ken "try to eat and if you want to call back, don't hesitate, I am here the whole night."

I put the phone down and, for a second, I thought perhaps I could fight this and be ok.

Then the symptoms began to change. Sliding further, the sounds outside became acutely amplified. I kept on hearing sirens and planes, consolidating a sense of paranoia – a clear signal that I had go to sleep immediately. It was as if I was in hell and my brain was melting. In my mind it was Dr D who had poured the petrol and lit the match. The scary thing is, he had no idea of the damage he was inflicting. Doctors are supposed to be the allies and hospitals a place of sanctuary; in the end I had to restore my mental equilibrium.

It took another hour to sit down and eat some food. Fighting the urge not to sleep I cleared up the dishes, cleaned my face, brushed my teeth and stared at the pill, resentful that I had to take it. I had been doing so well, painting and writing. I shouldn't have beaten myself up for this mental lapse; it was no fault of my own. Dr Thys had promised to call Dr D, which made me feel less powerless.

It takes enormous mental fortitude to keep Fred locked up in the cell in my head. Imagine a boulder teetering on the tip of a mountain. Imagine it falling and using your bare hands to stop it crushing you – that is the level of mental stress I am under. Tomorrow was another day, for now Fred did not get his way; the baby was tranquil and at peace. It was time to take half a sleeping pill and rest my tired, weary head.

What if I had not been able to fight the symptoms? What if I had developed advanced psychosis? What if I had jumped off my terrace balcony and listened to Fred? Do you think that Dr D would have felt any culpability? The assistant doctor I spoke to demonstrated the same professional indifference, while the head of obstetrics at St Elisabeth didn't even bother to talk to me.[42] As far as they were concerned, they had washed their hands of my case. These people have a duty of care, whatever their code of practice. Dr D's methods of communication made me severely unwell, putting my unborn baby and me both at risk, the very thing that Dr D asserted he wanted to prevent. Left picking up the pieces, it was as if I had been beaten – actually, bludgeoned mentally – like a seal with a sledgehammer. I don't think they would have listened to Dr Thys either and I feel sorry for other women with my condition who are subjected to this lazy *one size fits all* treatment. It is such a facile and negligent approach. Later Dr Thys told me that his colleague, Dr L, was actually worried that Dr D had been assigned to me. If this was the case, I find it odd that no one talked to Dr D and told him that his approach was heavy handed and counter-productive. A self-evident, complacent conspiracy of tolerance existed that was impossible to penetrate. I consider myself lucky because I understand the specific traits of my condition, better than any doctor could ever profess to.

As promised, Dr Thys wrote to Dr D, telling him that his handling of my condition was wrong. Dr Thys received a reply from Dr D. Apparently, Dr D was perturbed by my emails, which left him apprehensive. He had thought about my case long and hard but, in the end, believed his stance was justified. Asking for a copy of the email (which was in Flemish) I never received it. Maybe Dr Thys thought it might fire off my brain. I would like to read it one day. Also, I don't understand why he wouldn't listen to Dr Thys, or Albertine. Dr Dechamps also spoke to Dr D; again he wouldn't budge from his stance.

If another pregnant woman with schizoaffective disorder had received the same treatment, would she have been strong enough to stand up to the doctors and demand to be heard? Whatever your mental health condition, it is a woman's fundamental right to have a natural birth, if she is able to do so. I was trying to avoid a repeat episode of postpartum psychosis. In effect, the hospitals almost precipitated a psychotic episode during my pregnancy. Hospitals and doctors cannot be solely relied upon to assist pregnant women with a history of psychosis. These afflicted women have to examine their minds, to identify the main triggers and symptoms. Armed with these insights, they can be mentally equipped to tackle psychosis if it strikes postpartum. Doctors and hospitals also need to listen to mothers, working in tandem to create a proper care plan that meets their needs.

Loramet

*Since reading about Loramet, the medication prescribed by my former obstetrician, I have thrown the pills in the bin after reading online:

This medicine may be harmful to a developing baby and it should be avoided in pregnancy ...this is particularly important during the first and third trimesters of pregnancy...regular use is not advised, as the baby could...suffer withdrawal symptoms after the birth. If this medicine is used in late pregnancy...it may cause floppiness, low body temperature and breathing or feeding difficulties in the baby...

Dr Thys told me that it is a balancing act. Despite these side effects, he wrote:

Regarding the medication, things are not black and white. Most medication should be avoided in the first trimester of pregnancy because they could influence the development of the baby. In the last trimester, the baby is fully formed, so medication doesn't influence the general development of the baby, but can have side effects just as in adults. The main concern about sleep medication is that the baby could also feel the effects of the medication and, secondly, that frequent use could cause an addiction in the baby. With moderate and irregular use, this should not be a problem. These possible negative effects should be weighed against the possible negative effects of sleep deprivation, stress, anxiety, and so on...sleep is crucial for you...you should avoid a vicious circle of sleeplessness that provokes even more sleeplessness.

Who is right? The best-case scenario is to fall asleep naturally and only take such pills in emergencies, when all else fails, yet I also respect Dr Thys's views.

Although I have retrieved the medication from the bin, I remain ambivalent about taking the pills, viewing them with extreme caution.

It's past 5am and I should be asleep. Does Dr Thys, then, have a point? I will go to sleep now, without the aid of any pills and I will endeavour to deal with my condition, keeping Fred well away by using my own cognitive strategies for now.

My son and husband return in a few days that is something to look forward to and it's not long before the baby is due; I will just hang on a little longer until then.

CHAPTER 10

Why Do Some Mothers Experience Visions or Voices Telling Them to *Kill* Their Baby and Can You Make Them Stop?

Kill is a very provocative word and I don't use it lightly. This essay has come to me in many forms and now, at 2.13am, almost three months since the birth of my second child, I sit down to write this. There has been an urgent need to convey my thoughts on this polemical subject while, simultaneously, a torturous desire to avoid it.

Addressing a taboo that, I believe, many mothers endure in silence – because the support often just isn't out there – I have seen enough psychiatrists, psychologists and mental health practitioners to make this assertion with confidence.

Shortly after the birth of my first child in, October 2010, I experienced the first horrendously intense visions and (Fred's) voice telling me to harm my baby. I did not understand what was happening: as a new mother, everything was alien. Naturally, it was alarming and incomprehensible. My head ached afterwards, leaving me bereft and confused. Engaging in an analysis of what was happening, it was plausible to assume that having such ideations was directly correlated with the psychosis.[43] Long after escaping the sticky psychotic web, the visions and voice did not abate, even when I was calm and stable. Through a process of dissection and mental pattern identification, I've worked out why I suffer from auditory and visual hallucinations. My discoveries could help other mothers in need of more substantive answers.

When I asked my psychiatrist why such thoughts were occurring she said, "It's normal for mothers to have an urge to harm their babies" – as if it was commonplace, just something that we have to go through, along with the fatigue and initial shock of motherhood.

Speaking manically and anxiously to another psychiatrist, who specialised in postpartum psychosis, I relayed how I was witnessing up to thirty visions a day that involved vivid enactments of violence.[44] As I told him how I dealt with the visions and bullying voices, I was none the wiser about why it was happening. Of course someone could interject with, "You have schizoaffective disorder – that's the reason why you see all this horrendous stuff," but I wanted something more substantial than a nebulous mental health label that I no longer wanted to be defined by.

I started a process of deduction; during the depressive phase of my condition, I visualised my death by hanging or jumping in front of a tube. A normal feature of my life, it was an automatic reflex response of my brain. Once I became a mother, the voice was now telling me to harm the baby and/or myself. Unquestionably, the children were safe. It is a mother's instinct to cherish her children, yet it was, at times, very hard to reconcile my desire to love, nurture and protect my babies with the obscenity of the voice and visions. Such thoughts are barbaric, making me shudder every time I experience them. I would never do anything to harm my children. I only ever wanted to shield them from Fred (the main voice in my head) and all that is nasty, to raise them into strong, confident and resilient human beings who are sensitive and curious. This is why most days seem like I am locked in a war. Although some days are less turbulent and more peaceful than others, each day presents new and often colossal mental challenges.

Fred's sinister focus on the children remains acutely disturbing. On the occasions when I was tired, as I cleaned the toilet with bleach, Fred would tell me to feed the baby with bleach. If I was cutting carrots, Fred would tell me to stab the baby with the knife I was holding. My conclusion is that some form of *inverted transference* was taking place, which caused more internal torment than telling me to kill myself. Deducing that what I am experiencing are a series of mental anomalies, I can ignore them. A mother's instinct is also to be vigilant towards danger. My brain sees the danger then it mutates into something else. When I am on the terrace, the voice tells me to throw the baby over the terrace rather than saying, "be careful and don't get too close". Or, due to the persistent fatigue – as the brain goes into fight or flight mode – telling me to throw the baby over the terrace could be my brain's extreme way of saying "You need to rest now." Rationalisation does not diminish the hideousness of what I see and hear. Emphatically, I can say without a shred of doubt, I would never act on these thoughts.

Initially, I found the visions and voices so disturbing I could not mentally deal with them. Having such ideations is abhorrent. It was impossible to share these experiences because people simply would not be able to digest them. At times I thought it was unfair that someone with amnesia or Alzheimer's would get more empathy. Something had gone awry in my brain and yet assistance to deal with it was elusive. Desperate for the thoughts and visions to go away, how could I banish them? Or would I be living with them, in some form, indefinitely? If this were the case, I would have to find a way to manage and process what was happening in a detached, logical manner that did not involve pills or anti-psychotics. Living medication free, I wanted it to remain that way. Breastfeeding was the primary method of both bonding and nourishing my baby. That closeness would psychologically counter the visions and voices. Staring into my baby's eyes, listening to the coos, stroking that soft scalp, enjoying those intermittent smiles, and that unflinching, penetrating baby's gaze became part of my ammunition. My baby was helping me, inadvertently, to ignore Fred's voice and push the accompanying visions aside, as they inched ever closer. It was a case of psychological push and shove. Fred was never far and keeping my baby close became a form of protection for both of us. I was not a potential baby killer; I had a psychiatric condition and had to find a way to overcome it. I might have discovered the equivalent of a mental limp rather than a sprint, but at least I wouldn't be mentally paralysed and refused to cave in.

Gradually, I established that the visions and Fred's voice became more acute when:

a) I was sleep deprived
b) Alone
c) Breastfeeding
d) When the baby was crying
e) Or when I was stressed

I tried to go to bed early, to nap if I was tired. When I was alone, I would put on the radio and if *trapped in my head* I would try and climb out by going on the terrace and tending to my flowers. Having a pen or brush in my hand was an effective form of mental escapism. If the baby was screaming, the noise felt like a baton beating my brain. The swiftest solution, to avoid getting triggered by the shrill sound, was to cuddle and nurse the baby or reassure and explain. I used my rational voice to silence the other one. When my rational voice became almost inaudible, smothered by Fred's rants, I have had to find ways to amplify it and fight back. When experiencing visions during breastfeeding, I employed an array of strategies to dodge the mental bullets and avoid a complete assault. Fred wanted to break down a padlocked door in my head, with kicks and pounding fists and I was pushing against the door, attempting to stop him, knowing that, if the door did break open, I would end up flailing in the waves of a psychotic sea that was on the verge of flooding my brain. How can you push away the sea with your bare hands and stop your mind from being flooded?

Build up your mental defences, be aware of all your triggers, and handle them carefully.

The nature of the visions and voice differed greatly. When I breastfed, there was often, not always, a correlation between the intensity of the visions and when my baby latched on. Reducing the feeds made them wane. With the birth of the second baby they started again with a vengeance as I nursed, becoming more severe when I was nursing lying down in darkness, rather than nursing during the daytime, sitting up. Maybe the darkness created a perfect incubator for the imagination to play devilish tricks on me? When my baby latched on and I closed my eyes, like an edited movie with jagged jump cuts, the visions played out in rapid succession, darting out at me. Convulsing and recoiling as each one leapt out, I squinted, clenched my fists and tensed my body as if preparing myself for the mental barrage. As soon as my baby finished feeding the visions ended abruptly. Recently I discovered a name for this phenomenon – Dysphoric Milk Ejection Reflex (D-mer)[45]. When the baby latches onto the breast, the surge in oxytocin and dopamine can induce feelings of dysphoria in some women. The website devoted to D-mer provides a *scientific* explanation and an accompanying long list of testimonials. It also suggests that D-mer is treatable if the dysphoria is the result of inappropriate dopamine activity at the time of milk ejection. My new midwife, Jo, sent the link to the website. Discovering a specific physiological explanation for what was occurring, rather than the glib "it's just a chemical imbalance" line was a revelation. Grateful for the link, I avidly read all the testimonials. Women spoke of a wave of melancholy, depression and gloom when their baby latched on, which would subside at the end of the feed. Their feelings fitted in with the definition of dysphoria.

No one wrote about the violent visions I experienced. Was I simply an extreme case? Mothers were probably too afraid to disclose such gruesome thoughts, for fear of the consequences, shame and stigma.

Certain questions came into my head. Did this make me a monster; severely mentally ill; at risk of harming my baby; or just an unfortunate minority?

After the birth of my second baby, I spoke about what I was experiencing to the hospital psychiatrist, Dr V at Edith Cavell, telling her that I was looking for strategies to deal with the visions I experienced when I breast-fed. Several days after the birth, her response was to share personal emails I had written prior to giving birth with a hospital social worker I had never met. Apparently this was standard procedure. If I had known this, I would never have been so open. I was in an emotionally distressed state when I had written the emails. I turned to the doctors terrified that postpartum psychosis would strike again. Unfortunately, I did not receive much meaningful input to alleviate the mental confusion that ranged from suicidal thoughts to profound feelings of negativity and hopelessness. The hospital social worker never met me personally, yet she proposed sending me home and keeping the baby in the hospital; implying that I posed a potential risk to my child. Dr V, after seeming initially satisfied with my maternal competence and mental state post giving birth, now concluded that I could not be alone with the baby at home. This was after I relayed the experience of mania, OCD, garrulousness, heightened energy, increased creative activity, amplified sounds, paranoia etc. – which she concurred, were the first signs that I was descending into a psychotic state. The symptoms began three days after I gave birth, exactly what happened after the birth of my first-born. Although aware of the patterns and parallels, after giving birth it's normal to feel tired, brimming with emotions, oscillating from euphoria to something darker to sheer numbness. I stopped an escalation of symptoms through the implementation of my key strategies, the most effective one being *sleep*, by leaving my baby in the care of the midwives at the hospital when I was mentally sliding. Pumping milk every three to four hours, by listening to the radio or watching a movie to provide mental distraction, I ensured I was never alone in the darkness with my thoughts. Avoiding any superfluous social interaction, I also kept my OCD in check, which was kicking in. The visions were, oddly, non-existent when I pumped milk. Was it the nature of the baby's sucking action and proximity that created the mental disorientation, in conjunction with the surge in oxytocin?

Dr V was the 40th doctor I had seen since my mental health journey first began. Feeling distrustful, I concluded she was covering her professional back and that of the hospital, rather than providing me with the care I needed. Misunderstood, exposed and vulnerable, I projected a protective shield of normality to facilitate a swift discharge. In hospital for eleven days, it was a marked improvement on the one-month stay imposed upon me in 2010. To this day I loathe hospitals, avoiding them if I can. Remaining sceptical and nervous around doctors, I am suspicious of their questions and unimpressed with their often tactless and heavy handed probing into my maternal competence and complex mental health issues.

Dr V had never heard of D-mer. If there was a scientific explanation for these visions, oddly, why didn't any of the psychiatrists I had seen know about it? Now, when my baby latches on, it is better to breastfeed sitting up in a light room, ensuring that the visions and voices are less acute. Night feeds remain unavoidable. Although I have concocted my own explanations for the varying intensity of the visions, a scientific one would be welcome. When the visions start, if what I am seeing, becomes unbearable, I repeat the following sentence,

"These disgusting visions are not my fault, it's the surge in oxytocin and dopamine."

Repeating this sentence helps to dissipate them. I also employ another strategy. To detract the mind from discordant thought patterns, the focus needs to shift onto the sound of the breath; when my baby is feeding I listen to the unalloyed sound of the gulps of milk, the rasps of air, the sighs, the snuffled breathing, the snorts, the sensation of the milk let-down, focusing on everything that is real and not the mental mischief that serves no end. There is an incredible drive to shield my children from Fred, to stay well and never give up trying to be a better mother. There are times when I am on the floor, mentally and physically, from exhaustion, and I tell myself, "Just get up and do it." There is also something gratifying about nourishing a new life, knowing that your body is helping a burgeoning being to thrive – an incontrovertible truth that I cling onto.

Isolation can compound the visions and voices, which also occur when I am not breastfeeding. These are quite different in tone and complexion. When I am alone – painting, writing, gardening, cooking or cleaning – it's Fred's distinct masculine voice that creates intrusive disturbing thoughts. They are also harder to cope with when I am sleep deprived because I have to deal with the initial symptoms of psychosis, which ensue rapidly. The solution is, always, to sleep, even if the sleep is not in one chunk. Now, for example, it is getting late, I have been alone with the baby the whole day, without a second to sit down with my thoughts. If I don't go to sleep soon, I will suffer tomorrow: I must stop writing. Hard to implement when the ideas are flowing and naturally falling into place, there are discordant forces within, yet I must exercise discipline, stop, and resume work when I can; since sleep – and getting enough of it – is vital to keeping mentally robust and healthy.

I tried to explain to one mother who knows about my condition – although I don't think she understands it at all – how sleep deprivation intensifies the visions and psychotic symptoms; she dismissively retorted, "Everyone acts funny when they are sleep deprived."

Staying quiet, I carried on being cordial rather than trying to educate and illuminate. That's the fundamental problem, the necessity to *act* rather than express what you are going through truthfully, without fear of the repercussions or how people will react. There is, regrettably, a level of social vilification of mothers with mental health problems. Am I being over-simplistic, or generalising? Perhaps, but there remain very few platforms, other than social media, available to have an open discussion about this topic, without your views being grossly misconstrued.

My assessment of what is happening in my brain is supposition and it does not make what I see or hear easier to metabolise. Imagine if someone flashed images of child pornography in front of your face – grotesquely different images in quick succession – and you were forced to look at them, even when you would rather eat your own vomit? That is tantamount to what I go through. I often think, *What kind of mother am I to see such stuff?* There is this innate belief that you are evil, sick, or severely ill to see such things. Bizarrely, the oxytocin and dopamine that surges through and brain while breastfeeding makes you feel incredibly relaxed, while spitting out these visions in your head. It is somewhat saddening that the neuropeptide of "tend and befriend", the brain's natural hormonal response to induce safety and trust, the "molecule" of maternal love, produces something so grossly askew in my brain.

My GP, who has had some basic psychiatric training, advised that I pray, when I explained what was happening. I looked at her and said, "Prayer is not going to help me."

I found her advice mildly offensive. Experiencing such thoughts, sensations, visions – call them what you will – is alienating. On the few occasions I have dared to be open, people listen and you instantly see pity in their eyes. Instead, I opt to write a poem, paint, or draw, transforming the toxic, unpleasant and difficult into something with resonance that is visually or conceptually potent. Even when I confide in my family, there is often a prolonged silence, which I interpret as, "Please don't tell us these things."

My husband doesn't know what to say either; no one does. That's why it is emotionally devastating. To cuddle, kiss and care for my baby while having visions and hearing a voice telling me to do unspeakable things is intolerable. Who could deal with that?

The principle way I cope, in my everyday life, is by having external order to counter what is happening in my head – which is often a vicious babble. This need can be all consuming. When I walk into a room my eyes scan it, looking for any misplaced detail and I notice things that others don't in the quest for an elusive, aesthetic equilibrium. The tea towels must be folded the correct way, stacked up into uniform, tall towers, all items placed in a *pleasing* position; the skirting boards dusted, especially those places that people don't see – they seem to matter the most: the corners, the edges, the dark parts of the flat that never get tackled by a feather duster. As for the smudges, they must be wiped without trace immediately. It is fastidiousness to the point of being maniacal. My OCD is intolerable, all-consuming and an exhausting waste of time.

Living with and working for me can be oppressive. I demand that my husband clears up straight after he has prepared some food, keeps his desk tidy and his shoes in line. Often he doesn't do it, asserting his will and right to do things his way, but then my mind becomes totally disorientated and I can't cope. His absence abroad means I can arrange my external environment without interference or disturbance and am much calmer for it. When my husband and son return home, I will have to deal with the chaos in my head and the external chaos inflicted by a toddler and a tired husband.

Initially, I couldn't tolerate having paid help in my home. It always felt like an intrusion. There were times when I thought I was trapped in the Harold Pinter play *The Servant*. Silently these strangers mocked me and surreptitiously I was being usurped in my own home. The worse moment was when my husband employed a perfectly amenable Spanish woman, shortly after I came home with my new-born baby. He allowed her to drive his car to do the school run. And as my husband, eldest son and this woman ate supper at the other side of the flat I was alone in my studio breastfeeding, able to hear their chatter and laughter. Then she would lie in bed with my son, as instructed by my husband, and read bedtime stories until he fell asleep. It was intolerable and I told my husband this wasn't the sort of help I needed. Instead the situation brought me low and made me more unwell. Needless to say the Spanish woman didn't last long.

Eventually I dismissed the various people my husband employed to do the school run because they, *all*, triggered me. I usually got into an emotionally exhausted state before I had even received them. Just opening the door, saying hello and making small chat with them required considerable effort, putting a strain on my already overheated brain. Maybe they detected a modicum of mental unsoundness through my body language and the way I avoided eye contact. Possibly, I over compensated to hide it, terrified that they suspected and might report me, which was nonsense. Yet, the terror was real and paralysing. My husband wanted to inform them about my condition, but I refused, because my instinct told me that they would not understand. Those you confide in, I strongly believe, must have the training to fully grasp what is going on.

Since my husband is abroad a great deal, leaving me alone with the children, it would be irresponsible not to have a support structure in place. Wendy was our last hope. She was employed through Family Help[46]. When Wendy first started working for me, if she didn't do things the way I required them to be done, my fragile mental coping mechanism would collapse. Sometimes I would push her away, preferring isolation, which created the perfect breeding ground for Fred to take over. Having said this, it felt natural to tell Wendy about the visions and Fred's voice because she had some training and experience of assisting women with postnatal depression. Wendy's presence gave me a few hours a week to draw, paint, work, run errands and rest. She proved to be a real lifeline.

With time and additional training Wendy began to understand my needs and the importance of sleep and became attuned to my symptoms.

Rarely complaining, she has inordinate patience and never asks "Why?", completing the tasks that I tell her to do, which are usually related to regulating my OCD. Often finding fault in what Wendy does, even though she is doing her utmost to follow my exacting instructions, I apologise to her profusely saying, "It's not my fault, I didn't get much sleep and am easily triggered today."

Wendy says, "I know, don't worry, just rest."

She accepts my condition and works incredibly hard. When I think I am tiring her out, I tell her to drink some tea and take a rest. Only twenty-two and mother of an infant son, Wendy has overcome great adversity and a challenging upbringing; perhaps that's why we connected. Supporting and praising each other, we created a strong mutual respect. Crucially my baby adores Wendy, offering something I don't instinctively possess inside and I will sorely miss her when she leaves.

Family Help, the company she works for, is not insured in case I have a psychotic episode. They are, principally, equipped to help women with postnatal depression and offered a short-term, interim solution. They made an exception in my case by offering six months of support. Wendy used to come two full days and one half day. Her time has officially come to an end.

Wendy's departure sent me into a panic. I even asked Dr Thys to argue a case, on mental health grounds, to extend the help. Since I am on my own, with no family here, and Dr Thys's organisation is unable to offer me the specialised care I require with two small children, Wendy seemed like the only option. It is very hard to employ people privately that meet my specific health requirements; this remains a constant source of frustration. Unfortunately, despite my arguments, my request for an extension was refused.[47]

A recent storm killed my roses when the buds were on the cusp of blooming. Spending three futile days trying to salvage the plant, I watched as it withered stem by stem. It was torturous. Lamenting its passing made me realise my children were tiny inchoate buds, my role was to ensure they bloomed, but Fred was trampling on my nascent maternal feelings before they had taken time to root. I couldn't let them be trampled upon.

Bonding with my babies was always going to be hard. What can you do to consolidate that connection with your baby, while battling with something this corrosive? You have to find your strategies and mine are complex, exhausting and unrelenting, but they work. I know I am not a threat to my baby, nor capable of harming my children, yet the sheer barrage of images is mentally debilitating. Fred's voice can be so loud that I sometimes talk back in a non-aggressive fashion to assert my own power and control over the situation: even stripping Fred of his name, for a short time at least, to reduce his potency. Occasionally this works but, more often than not, it doesn't, especially when I am tired and then I lapse into a form of servitude to his edicts. This is why an empathetic support framework is crucial to offload the mental heaviness and break the cycle.[48]

I can't kill off Fred – he's someone I have to live with for the rest of my life because he's essentially an intrinsic part of who I am. Increasingly, I have come to realise, then, that I might have to make peace with him, tame him, try to understand Fred's anger and see that we are actually, on the same side. This will be my biggest challenge yet.

CHAPTER 11

Should a Mentally Ill Mother be Left Alone with Her Children?

The short answer to this question is, "no". A mentally ill mother should not be left alone with her children exclusively. For short periods it is endurable, but other adults – preferably the father[49] – need to be present, as long as he doesn't have mental health problems, too. When I say mentally ill, I am referring to mothers who have experienced psychosis or visions that involve harming their children. It is too much of a mental strain and risky, not only for the mother, but also for the children.

Ideally, someone has to be available for the mother to speak candidly about what she is experiencing without the anxiety of the children being removed from her care. Finding the right support structure is not straightforward when you have complex mental health needs, as illustrated in my last essay. Paid strangers in your home, purporting to help, is stressful; and yet without them the mother can struggle.

Imagine this scenario: a mother, with a history of psychosis and a diagnosis of schizoaffective disorder, is left alone for three weeks with an inquisitive, boisterous three-year-old and a three-month-old baby that has a voracious appetite and is being exclusively breastfed. On the morning that the father leaves, the mother is already anxious. Doing all the night feeds and experiencing disturbing visions each time she breastfeeds, she knows these are evanescent symptoms and if she sleeps she can deal with them, just about. Alone with two children, she is tested beyond her limits almost immediately.

Her eyes are stinging she should be sleeping. It is nearly midnight and her husband has been away for barely one night. Her stepfather will be coming in a few weeks. She just has to hold on and put the children first. When her mind is rested she knows she's a good mother; when she is ill, she must sleep and let others take care of the children. It feels like a maternal defeat to make such an admission. Her paranoia has set in: she thinks she sees people in the shadows, thinks the neighbours are watching, thinks an intruder is about to enter to rape her and murder the children; she sees it all and is petrified that people suspect she is mad – she doesn't know whom to trust.

Her former mental health social worker is the only person she used to be able to speak to. She always said, "You are doing well," but this is not sufficient anymore and she's gone now. The mother starts to think of all the dreams this mental disorder has robbed her of and gets incensed. Yet, she wants to believe she can cope. Flinching, she sees someone moving…Psychosis is straining to bust open the door in her head and the knocks are getting louder…

The above is just a snap shot of the rapid mental deterioration that occurs due to sleep deprivation, the pressures of two small children, and social isolation. It is too hard to make an open admission that the mother is *myself*, because often I don't recognise that mother. She is an alien – a complete anathema.

My overarching conclusion is that I cannot be alone with the children unless I have had adequate sleep. There was a time when I thought, with night feeds and a toddler who wakes up at 6am most days, this would be impossible, and yet I find a way. Some days I do not want to get on my bike, but I have no choice; I have to do the shopping and I have to get my son to school. Cycling is the most viable option and the lack of sleep might make me manic on the road, so I focus on my breathing. If I have to deal with an aggressive driver I swear quietly under my breath. When I return home I sleep with the baby, even though sleep is the last thing I am interested in. The reality of the situation is that there are many mothers like me, who have mental health issues and are, for whatever reason, alone with their children. The negative implications for the mental health of these children are a cause for concern. The hugs, cuddles, kisses and breastfeeding on demand might mitigate the adverse effects of when I am unwell; ideally, though, my children should be protected from my condition. Being psychotic is a form of mental violence that no child should witness. Even if I am able to exercise restraint, control the visions and the ranting – these are simply not acceptable forms of behaviour. This is why I *choose* to send both my children away to a safe, nourishing and nurturing environment that I sometimes am not able to provide, leaving me to replenish my drained energy stores.

Since I couldn't persuade Family Help to extend Wendy's duty of care, my son will go to Sweden as soon as the school term finishes and the baby will go to the UK with my big sister, a painfully difficult decision. My dream is to take both the children to see my family, despite my anxiety that psychosis could strike due to the pervasive triggers. If it doesn't work out I can always scurry back into my hole. We are determined (my parents, sister and I) to achieve this goal. However hard, I have to try, at least once. We need to create new shiny, upbeat memories for the children to hold onto; these will give them strength in the knowledge that my family loves them and that they have much to offer that is good.[50]

Coping with a Challenging Day

Today I was faced with one challenge after the other while Fred fired his taunts saying: "If you died would anyone notice? Do yourself a favour and go kill yourself – now."

Refusing to listen to the voice I explained to my son, when he arrived home from school, "Listen, Mummy is on her own here, Daddy is far away and no one is coming to help Mummy. The tap is broken and the heating, too, so you have to listen to Mummy and be good OK, otherwise Fred will come."

"OK, Mummy, I understand. I don't like Fred,"

"No, we don't like Fred, but I think Fred just needs to cool down. Let's put him in the cupboard." I watched my son knock on the cupboard door timidly,

"Go away Fred," he said angrily.

"Don't worry he's scared and won't come out." Scooping him up in my arms, I give him a kiss and a hug, doubting if being open about *Fred* was such a good idea.

After supper I cleared up, made the pack lunch and prepared his uniform, now I am lying in bed with the baby breastfeeding, and the visions appear periodically. I can barely keep my eyes open. After reading the bedtime stories, my children fall asleep naturally and quickly. When I wake up, for the next feed, it is 1am, I wish it was 6am. Gravitating towards my computer I write to Dr Thys in a plea for help. My writing is frantic and this is what pours out in five minutes:

Dear Dr Thys,

I understand that resources and manpower are very tight, but I am in a difficult situation ...

I have no heating, and the tap in the kitchen sink is broken making it difficult for me to cook and wash...I am wrapping up the children to ward off the cold...but at night it's freezing.

Wendy is off sick tomorrow. Family Help sent a replacement yesterday...When she sat down, her trousers slipped, revealing half her backside. It was disconcerting that she didn't pull up her trousers... she didn't know about my mental health problems, barely spoke any English, and I ended up doing everything. Becoming very disturbed, I told her to leave early. By the evening I was shattered and holding on until bedtime.

My sister cannot come, because her daughter is sick, my stepfather, now, is also unwell...My husband does not return until the end of the month and I do not know when Wendy is back...

I am trying to hold on, to stay calm, yet I feel...very unsupported.

I called TrActor several times, breaking down on the phone and was told there was no one to help me yesterday; I was hoping for a proposed solution in the coming days, I emailed you, called and texted...

Your lack of response is compounding my sense of isolation, Fred is telling me to take pills, end my life and harm the children, because I am "a waste of space". I am used to these ideations, they recur daily, and I can deal with them but, mentally, it is – extremely – heavy and the pressure is taking its toll. There's only so much a person can take before they break and I am rather battered.

I have been without a mental health social worker for some time even though I have, repeatedly, requested a new one. It is no one's fault that J is a trigger now, however this is sadly the case. Mine is an irrational condition; it is what it is.

I do need someone to help me sort out these practical problems, to receive the electrician and plumber...so please can someone get back to me. I cannot afford to get triggered by strangers who do not understand my complex mental health needs.

Yesterday, I called the CHS mental health line and no one picked up in the morning, I am going to call them now to see if they can calm me down...

...Sometimes I see no way out of this perpetual cycle of sleeplessness. My eyes are like two burning holes and my mind is smarting. I need someone to put a big fat anti-psychotic pill on my tongue to knock me out for 48 hours, then I will be alright but what about my baby? I am so worried, I keeping falling and falling and I reach out for a branch, hold on for dear life, not daring to look down, then I manage to climb up again only for Fred to push me down. I am delirious with fatigue. Tell me what to do?"

Fred is telling me to do so many things, but I can't listen to him. If I just sleep, eat and lie down and feel the earth pulling me down and breathe I will get through this.

I know I am strong...but I am starving and dehydrated with no desire to eat or drink my weight is going down even though I force myself to eat. I am completely and utterly spent. It's going to be trying these next days. I don't have much left in the tank...although somehow I stay afloat...*There are always others worse off; I know that...*

Although I am in hell, I concede that it is a comfortable hell, an endurable one, yet I think I need some support to take the edge of what's going on in my head.

Please, can you write back and, together, we can find a workable solution?

Tomorrow, I will be on my own with the children, not knowing if Dr Thys can assist. I haven't done any painting, but that's ok: my life is not going to collapse if I don't pick up a paintbrush. Right now, I have to go back to sleep. For an instant I have the urge to call the CHS helpline and decide not to.

"There is no one here" I say out loud, "these problems are only big if I say they are, if I make them small in my head, they will shrink and go away."

She gets up,
Lies down,
Closes her eyes and sleeps.
She wakes up again,
Can hear the loud rumble of the boiler
And it sounds like Fred's wrath,
She starts writing,
Has a shower,
Eats something...
Time is ticking away,
She can't sleep...
Sends some emails she shouldn't have...
Too late now...
She is worried...
Wants the noise to stop...
Feeds the baby...
At least the children are sleeping,
She thinks...no point sleeping now.
Her brain is too hot...
In the end she picks up her pen,
Starts to draw
And gets transported to another place where no one can touch her,
She will find a way out,
She always does.

What happened yesterday and in the early hours of today sums up everything I have tried to convey in this book. It's not about blame – my mental health needs are intricate – people are well intentioned, and Dr Thys's organisation did try to call back several times; I was so lost in my mental woes I didn't notice until the next day. Despite knowing that I shouldn't be left alone with the children for prolonged periods, when overly tired and stressed, if the specific help is not available, I have no choice but to help myself mentally, which is what I did. Ultimately it was the pen and paintbrush that has guided me out of the mental maze.

It's Friday 21st March 2014; the crisis on Tuesday is almost a surreal memory. I don't recognise that scared, panicky mother.

As I paint at my desk, I call the CHS Helpline just to ask, "Am I doing OK?"

The Pat on the line, who yawned occasionally, said, "Yes, I think you are doing really well and it is clear that you love your children." Then she paused before adding, "Do you think you have a loving voice?"

"A loving voice, what's that? I don't think I know what that is."

"You do have that loving voice, I can hear it."

"Is that loving voice when I put my eldest on the breast, to console him when he wakes up screaming, or when we work on the scroll, or when I draw a dinosaur to make him smile?"

"Yes," she said.

"Oh, I see, I think I understand," I said.

For the last few weeks, I have found myself thrown, mercilessly, back in that stench of a hole. Yesterday evening I became utterly desperate and laid out all the sleep medication I have accumulated over the last five years. Counting 166 pills, in total, I wondered if that was enough to kill me. I laid my head on my desk and sobbed, then I emailed my neighbour and told her how I was feeling, she said she would come up and see me for a cup of tea and a chat tomorrow[51]. I told her "I am Bangladeshi, I am tough, I have been here before." She advised sensibly that I should flush the pills down the toilet, but I don't think I will. It was strangely soothing to look at them.

Instead, I ended the call and executed another two paintings in the early hours, watching, transfixed and lost in the fluid Tango dance of the colours. Creating a tangible thing of beauty temporarily dispelled the sour garbage brewing in my head. The following day I could not wake up, despite hearing the cries of my baby, I trudged through the day as if the seconds were piles of mud, telling my neighbour that it would be entirely selfish to inflict my black morbidity upon her. I cancelled teaching a scheduled Pilates class with a private student making up a mendacious story about my baby being feverish. When he took his nap I reached for the Helpline, like an alcoholic craving that mid morning drink to dull the pain that never seemed to wane. The man I spoke to said,

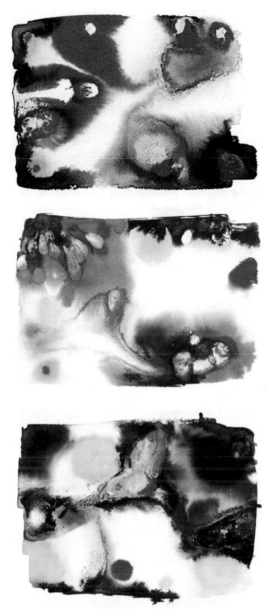

Image 42 (triptych). *When I Beat My Drum I Thought of These Colours*: *brain painting* 3,6,9 (acrylic ink on canvas paper, size A3, 2014). Sebastian Rochford, drummer of the group *Polar Bear* contacted me, a few years ago, saying he saw one of my abstract paintings in a hotel in Bristol and couldn't forget it. Recently when he was composing his album he thought of that same painting. He subsequently commissioned me to create several paintings for his forthcoming album cover. That night, after the brief email exchange, I made twenty paintings, after a few more nights I made twenty more and they kept on coming like turtles hatching and scrambling frantically to the ocean's shoreline.

"Listen, in my eyes you are a real hero, you do your art, you raise your kids, you do everything alone. You have to stand outside yourself and admire what you do and what you have achieved."

I told him, "I'm sorry I keep on calling, but there's no one else I can turn to. The problem is in my life I let people break me and I don't know if I can fix the damage. Sometimes my eyes are closed and my heart shuts down and I can't see what my baby is trying to teach me about life and what it means to be alive. I have to focus on him, his spirit is free and I know he is trying to guide me by the way he looks straight into my eyes and rests his head on my lap."

I thanked him and said his words had helped me a lot. *No one has ever called me a hero before, am I really that?* I thought, *maybe I am.* If I learn to believe in myself my children will believe in me and grow up to be poised and secure. It's a steep learning curve, but I am a willing student. The reconstruction of my paltry self-esteem will be a life long mission, although well worth it if I succeed.

CHAPTER 12

Schizophrenics Can be Good Mothers Too

It's January 2013 and the gaps between when I am able and not able to function *normally* are growing wider. This Christmas I stayed at home, while my husband and son celebrated with friends and family in Sweden. Barely seeing or speaking to anyone during these eight days, I woke up late and painted until 4am most nights. Exhilarating to be alone with my paint-brush, I listened to the radio to silence Fred's haranguing in my head. As I worked, the walls of my brain caved in and Fred's voice grew ever louder and all consuming. Unable to re-establish a healthy sleeping pattern since the return of my husband and son, my body clock remains welded to the nocturnal way of life I indulged in. After a week of barely sleeping, I am nervous about tomorrow. My husband will be in London for the day and I'll be alone with my son. Without my husband there is no buffer; no one to take the little one when I need a break, to lie down and stop the throb. I should rest my brain, although this essay has been gestating for a while; exercising the mind can scrape a way out, temporarily.

There are countless books on parenting and how to be a *good* mother, but relatively few books for mothers who have mental health problems. The internet is littered with accounts of the perils of becoming a mother if you have a mental health history. There are dispassionate scientific essays describing the negative impact of mental illness on the ability to parent and stories of mentally unwell mothers who have abused their children or, trag-ically, even killed them when gripped in a psychotic state. Rarely do we hear success stories about those mothers who manage to contain their men-tal disorder and remain good mothers.

What is a good mother?

We all just get through the days, even the super-organised, pro-active ones amongst us. During my interaction with mothers, I am affecting my behaviour; hiding my other self. Several mothers know about my problem-atic mind. When I divulged my secret malaise, during a fleeting spontane-ous desire to confess all, as soon as my mouth opened I regretted saying anything. With the first mother I confided in, her eyes widened with interest, then narrowed with a blatant awkwardness. Not knowing how to respond or what to say, maybe she would have preferred not to know.

"I never suspected," she said, "and if you'd told me at the beginning, I probably wouldn't have been friends with you."

I have since told her, disingenuously, "My temporary dip was just linked to being in London, everything's fine now."

After the revelation I see her less. When we meet up, we talk about the children over a pleasant lunch or tea, rather than anything mentally related. It has become the white elephant in the room. Once I announced that I was completely cured, that the visions had stopped, and that I had never been better. Brimming with endorphins from a gym session, feeling mildly euphoric with a gush of optimism, it was a transient sensation, fading once I reached home.

It is preferable to hide rather than disclose, for fear of the wrong type of people knowing. This particular friend was inclined to agree, "Better to stay quiet." All this hiding and pretence doesn't make your mind heal – instead you become entombed in perpetual darkness.

Addressing the conflict of reconciling my mind with the toughest, loneliest, most rewarding, yet least valued job in the world that is motherhood, this essay explores why I have a such a corrosive voice in my head; the impact of these mental health issues on my pregnancies; the onset of postpartum psychosis and its consequences on the ability to parent; and how these protracted mental frays have shaped every aspect of parenting life.

The compulsion to write this essay also stems from the need to convince myself that *schizophrenics can be good mothers, too*. It will be uncomfortable to write.

To paint a picture of a mother with schizoaffective disorder, I will assume that the reader knows nothing. There are sensational accounts of mentally ill mothers who have done something regrettable during a state of mental blackness. They have to live with the devastating consequences, in lifelong shock, pain and numbness. Newspapers report such cases as headline news, in a cursory sentence: "Mother stops medication and smothers child" or "Deranged mother stabs baby multiple times."[52] These are unhelpful descriptions. The headline might be accompanied with a photograph of a woman who is blatantly unwell and a shadow of her former self. Or, she is concealed under a jacket to hide her identity and avoid a backlash. If read online, in one of the less salubrious daily papers, the story will be accompanied with readers' comments: "Lock her up and throw away the key"... "She's not fit to be a be a mother, women like this should be sterilised"... "Murderer, I hope she rots in hell." Sometimes, a member of the public might demonstrate more leniency and say: "Clearly she needed the correct care and medication – what a tragic and sad case." That's exactly what these are.[53]

There can also be confusion between postnatal depression and post-partum psychosis.[54] The latter involves visual and auditory hallucinations, paranoia and strong false narratives. The former induces strong suicidal ideations, but both conditions generate thoughts of harming your baby. I recently read one tragic case about a mother who had not slept for days, as her baby was sick and crying continuously. Believing the TV was bugged and her husband was a government agent, she became acutely paranoid. Eventually, she snapped, drowned her baby and threw the tiny corpse over her terrace, convinced her baby had wanted to die. Although reported as postnatal depression, I would infer, from the case description, that she was in a psychotic state when she unintentionally killed her baby. If she had known that her symptoms were directly correlated with sleep deprivation and feasibly breastfeeding too, then infanticide could have been prevented. She needed to sleep while someone else took take care of her baby;[55] and for someone to explain the chemical changes that occur in the brain when the milk lets-down as the baby latches on to feed, which can lead to subsequent visions of harming your baby. Unfortunately, Fred climbed into her head and she listened to his corrosive voice.

The vast majority of mothers would never willingly hurt their offspring. Infanticide is one of the most appalling crimes known to man, with only a small percentage of mothers who actually end up killing their child. However, mothers with mental health problems, who do not seek or receive appropriate support, can damage their children, physically and emotionally. I will be the first to say this, after unwittingly suffering at the hands of my own, long-suffering mother despite all her concerted efforts to give us the best start in life.

My mother sought help. This was in the 1970s, and the cocktail of pills she was taking did her more injury than good. They certainly didn't improve her moods at home, although they allowed her to function at a professional level. Being widowed in her 20s and losing the love of her life was one of the pivotal factors that precipitated a change in her moods and subsequent relationship with her children. Recently my mother told me that once she felt such joy, she declared out loud, "I am so happy, I have never been this happy in my whole life" and, a couple of days after saying this, our father died. Since that moment she has been unable to say she is happy for fear of what might happen. This is heartbreaking and also plausibly explains why I, too, find it hard to experience joy in its most basic forms. It's as if any potential joy is tainted before it can ever be realised or fully experienced.

I can also understand why she was angry during our childhood.

"I used to terrorise you and you were all scared of me," she has since told me. She even, albeit fleetingly, considered putting us in care. Her GP dissuaded her, asserting she was doing her best – and she was, in light of the circumstances.

Most of the *terrorising* has been blocked out. As a child I was robust. I could take the intermittent beatings and frequent shouting, grew a thick skin, watching it all rebound off, seldom crying or displaying a shred of weakness. It's only as the years take their toll and strip away at your mind that the problems arise. The formative robustness is replaced with a pre-carious frailty, creating the cracks that allowed Fred in. But perhaps this frailty is essential to human existence, you certainly need it to be creative.

Memories can get skewed. When I think of my own childhood the darkness, however real, can eclipse all that was good. I marvel at the way my mother held down a career; always sartorially elegant in public; forever smiling and affable; hosting the most sumptuous of dinner parties despite being quite asocial – it's remarkable how she did all of this. Focusing on the good half of my mother and not lingering over the darker side that inhabits her is more beneficial psychologically. I recall a beautifully illus-trated Hans Christian Anderson anthology that my mother bought (I am not sure when she found the time to peruse bookshops), which she just placed on my bed to discover, which was always a delight. There were also piles of *Beano* comics, an abundance of Lego, the necessary art materials I needed, the classical Indian dancing, the Bengali singing lessons, the Ban-gla school my mother set up, the piano she bought for us, and the harmo-nium she provided which I learnt to play by myself. And there was always music: the soundtrack for the classic Bollywood film *Pakeezah*, the Beetles and Elvis were some of my earliest musical memories followed by Fleet-wood Mac, The Police, New Order, Elvis Costello, Peter Gabriel and there was always contemporary music playing in my stepfather's car, which my middle sister and I would energetically sing along to. There were the poi-gnant stories my mother would tell us about our late father singing in his VW Beetle, but most of all I remember my mother's out of tune humming – it was as comforting to the ear as her home made rice pudding was to eat. Clearly there was much that was good in my childhood and it's important to acknowledge this.

Guilt ridden for years, my parents recognise their mistakes. There are occasions when we attempt to discuss tricky subjects. Interestingly, much of what happened at my parents' hands, they can't recall, making it harder to attain closure. I have to believe in my own memories and move on. In retrospect, my mother didn't seem in control of her mind – which, meta-phorically, was a sumptuous garden with glimpses of colour that became overrun with the violent mood swings that overshadowed all that was wonderful in her life. Older and more docile, as my parents approach their twilight years they look back at that era with a sense of bewilderment. As grandparents they are different people and much more patient. My mother, almost seventy now, confessed, "I have very low self-confidence and I have directly passed that onto you." She's still trying to address this issue, as I am, too.

Perhaps it takes a lifetime to learn how to be a good parent; I don't want this to be the case for me. We can unwittingly replicate parental and childhood patterns; awareness of these patterns empowers you, facilitating intervention and prevention. It's easier to lose your temper by giving in to the rage than to take a deep breath, pause and reflect. We all face these daily struggles. But, with a mental health condition, the propensity to lose it is swift and can be devastating, especially on the little ones.

Before my son was born, I was naively confident that everything would be fine. Out of London, no longer smoking cannabis, I thought the worst was over, psychosis would not recur and the diagnosis was not set in stone. Residing in a less hectic environment would eliminate the stimuli that fed the condition, curtailing certain behaviour. A miraculous recovery would dawn as motherhood approached.

Leaving all that was familiar and relocating to Brussels unfortunately created another breeding ground for negativity. With the infrequent presence of my husband, the lack of close friends and inconsistent family presence, the language/cultural barrier, and piecemeal mental health support (apart from the CHS Helpline) anyone who is left alone, for prolonged periods, with small children would probably crack up at some point. Believing I had to endure the blows rather than stop them, my mind continued to be thrashed on a daily basis

Nostalgically, I look back to the time when I was sixteen and the year my little sister was born. Wary of my parents indirectly damaging my little sister, I took it upon myself to shower her with love and stimulation, even reciting Chekhov to her a few days after she was born. Balancing the stresses of my studies with the new childcare responsibilities for my younger sibling was effortless. I don't recall raising my voice, only having inordinate patience and spending hours building fantasy towns with wooden bricks, while eating digestives and oranges, or going for walks in the woods at the front of our house, looking at the bluebells.[56] Disengaged in the early years of my little sister's life, my mother openly told me, "I am not the maternal type" and if my little sister cried in the night, I would race up the stairs and rock her back to sleep in my arms, creating soothing chants to assuage her. For the initial three years of her life, arguably the most vital ones, I was present. By nineteen my mental landscape changed dramatically. Nonetheless, this early parenting experience gave me the confidence that I would be able to handle a new born with ease. A sibling, however, is very different from tending to the needs of your own child.

The pregnancy hormones protected me throughout the nine months of my first pregnancy and I was fairly stable. Coming from a household of all girls, when I discovered I was having a boy I wondered how would I raise my son into a *good* man after encountering so many insalubrious ones during my life? Throughout the pregnancy, I worked on my animation film *White Wall* for the UK Film Council. Although aware of my mental disability, no concessions were made. Any stress was due to deadlines, not the pregnancy. I spent long hours drawing all the backgrounds, turnarounds, flowers, trees, bats, cats, individual layers of waves and clouds. The workload was unrelenting. The exchange between London and Tehran (where the animation team was based) was fraught. I delivered the film two weeks before giving birth.

From the very outset of my first pregnancy I told my British obstetrician, Dr H, about my condition. He'd perfected a gentle way of talking that was designed to allay your unease. Timid and subdued during our consultations, I let his words glide over me, preferring my husband to do most of the talking. The psychosis gouged big holes into my brain and I was still recovering from my 2009/2010 psychotic episodes. There was the initial trauma to the brain, the time it takes to stop the mania, the delusions, the hours of sleep to catch up on, and then the flash backs. During my first

Image 43. Sketch 2 for animation film *White Wall* (pen and ink, size A5, 2010) commissioned by the UK Film Council, a few months after my second psychotic episode. The little girl in the film has special powers, when she screams she can make bombs fall from the sky and explode cities with a blink of an eye.

pregnancy I was affecting a level of recovery. At least making this animation film kept my mind occupied and my mental delicacy contained. After revealing I had schizoaffective disorder, Dr H responded awkwardly. He said he didn't know much about mental health issues. *Why don't you educate yourself then?* I thought. Appearing flustered, he decided to speak to the hospital psychiatrist, who subsequently told Dr H a meeting was unnecessary and that I should continue seeing my, then, psychiatrist, Dr R.

My ambivalence about having a boy was becoming more acute as the pregnancy progressed. These incongruous feelings stemmed from my late father's obsession with having a son and initial disappointment with the consecutive births of his three daughters. He would have preferred it if all of us have been aborted and instead start a family when he was more economically established, according to my mother. My mother has since assured me that our late father loved us and was inordinately patient when we were small, never raising his voice.[57] My mother wishes he had lived a little longer for us to experience his paternal care. "If he had been alive, you would have all been alright," she says.

Experiencing multiple sexual assaults at the hands of men, much of my interaction with the opposite sex was fraught with complications. Nor did I want to have a cloyingly close relationship with an only son, something I had grave misgivings about since writing *Hidden (2006)* – a book about women suffering from domestic violence – and learning that most of the male perpetrators had perversely close relationships with their mothers. My perceptions of men were skewed and how would these distorted views impact on my relationship with my baby? Wrestling with myself to resolve these complex issues with Dr R, I saw her throughout my pregnancy.

Regarding the nature of the sessions, we also dealt with a lot of London stuff and I enjoyed watching the leaves rustle in the wind out of her office window. My husband would question what we actually did during these sessions, unconvinced that talking was constructive. Working through these emotions, many of which were irrational and absurd, I was consumed with dispelling blocks of mental rubbish. I say rubbish, because, over three years into motherhood, most of it seems unimportant now. Somehow, I had forgotten the most elemental fact of pregnancy: that there was a budding life inside me, another being who would be entirely dependent on his parents for everything.

After the initial excitement of being pregnant had abated, the final six months were a more subdued affair. I might sense a kick, observe a slight indentation in my skin with each foetal movement and try to think positively, yet this was impossible to sustain. Relishing the quiet of home and neatness of the flat, knowing that soon this would all change, sometimes I thought, *Perhaps the baby won't come*. It was a perplexing and difficult time. Occasionally, I might ask my mother a question or email my sisters for motherhood tips. Few were forthcoming. My pregnancy was an isolated and lonely affair.

The night when I felt my first contractions, I'd been painting a portrait of my unborn son, based on the hospital 3-D scan. He looked like a little blue alien, now he was telling me to put down my brush and preparing to make his grand entrance into the world.

After my waters broke in the early hours, I puked and excreted feeling his head pressing down. Somehow I applied some make up and put on a pretty floral dress, before we made our way to the hospital. A flat tyre made the journey torturous. Quietly wailing with the pain, which wasn't that acute, but strong enough to make me wince and unable to walk, my husband procured a wheel chair. People in the lift stared as I whimpered. Finally we entered the delivery room, teeming with people wearing green coats. In a pitiful voice I said, "Help me, please."

Dr H was on vacation. A calm and quietly spoken male obstetrician took charge and told me that my cervix was fully dilated and the baby was ready to come out. I remember the indignity of another doctor and my husband removing my clothes. Powerless and entirely in their hands, I closed my eyes throughout, breathing and pushing, doing as I was told, until the baby was out. Considering myself very fortunate, the birth was swift, painless and relatively easy. The doctor commended me on my composure saying, "I think you come from a different bygone era", perhaps because I didn't make a peep during the delivery. When I saw my baby, it was a peculiar feeling, not one of breathless joy. Noticing his thick crop of hair and how small he was, everyone around me appeared indifferent. I was just eager to get out of the delivery room.

Placed in a private room to recuperate; my baby was dressed in dreadful hospital clothes (ours remained neatly packed in my case). He looked pitiful in his cast offs. Midwives streamed in insisting on opening the curtains. The bright morning sunlight made me squint. I needed to sleep, but their only concern was the baby, who needed light. Was it usual for the midwives not to ask, "Are you ok?... Are you tired?... Do you need to rest?" Then a doctor came in and poked me until I woke up. Worse, a student doctor strolled in, asking with a smile to examine my private regions. All these strange faces, all these people who spoke varying degrees of English – and all of them were focused on the baby, not the mother (apart from inspecting my vagina to see if the incision, from the episiotomy, was healing).

The steady disruption continued for three days. During this period I was writing, painting, drawing, barely resting and becoming increasingly manic. The enduring sleep deprivation culminated in psychosis with all the symptoms; a pattern that unravelled like clockwork.

It was early evening. I vividly recall the kettle sitting beside me: they'd put one in my room because I repeatedly asked for hot water; soon this innocent kettle became a sinister, metallic monster with teeth. Watching as the kettle rose into the air, it travelled over to the baby's crib and slowly began to pour. Fred was telling me to do it. There were no screams, just the sight of pouring, scalding, boiling water filling my son's crib. It was sickening to see – the first of multiple visions. Realising what was happening, I called my husband immediately. Fred was not in control, the baby was safe and yet it remained a harrowing experience.

Impossible to sleep by now, I had completed four drawings of the baby, thinking this would be an effective way to combat the visions, but I just became more exhausted. Fred demanded that I draw the intricate view from my hospital window and I obeyed, completing two more paintings. Placing all my belongings in an exacting fashion to counter the alarming chaos in my head, if anyone came to see me I spoke without pausing to breathe. These were all classic signs that I was mentally deteriorating as the mania gathered momentum.

The inveterate, despicable visions went on for months until my son was two. Simple household tasks become traumatic. For example, when I put a pan on the hob to boil some water, make rice, or heat up some soup, Fred would tell me to pour the scalding liquid over my son and I would watch, helplessly, as I saw an image of him screaming with his skin peeling off. A horrifyingly visceral image, it unfolded in real time. As I tried to sleep and breastfed less, these images became more sporadic, but with the birth of my second baby they started up again with renewed alacrity. Learning to flick

Image 44. *View From St Luc Hospital Window*, (pen and ink on paper, size A4, October 2010), painted after the birth of my first child during the first days of postpartum psychosis.

Image 45. *The First Year of Life* (oil on canvas, size 10x10 inches, 2011). Part of a series of portraits that I am completing perennially until my children turn 18-years-old. Positioned together consecutively to create one composite portrait, the eighteen portraits will depict their psychological evolution. By scrutinising each contour of their delicate faces, I can get under their skin and almost touch their souls.

them away, I used my cognitive rational side to dismiss them as a mental distortion; experiencing them makes you feel subhuman, suicidal and unworthy to be a mother. Had it been a mistake to tell the midwife about this first vision, because as soon as I did they refused to release me from hospital. My rational self did not pose a risk to my baby, but could I say the same about my psychotic self? When you are in the throes of psychosis, you are capable of doing things that you never imagined. The first two psychotic episodes trained my mind into knowing how ill I could become and never to let it become that bad again. Looking for early signs and patterns, I dissected the condition. It didn't take long to identify eight consecutive stages that culminated in the same outcome. These were:

- Obsessive-compulsive disorder (OCD), needing objects to be uniform and for the inhabited space to be as perfectly ordered and pristine as possible. If an object is mislaid, hours can be spent locating it; failure to find it causes acute anxiety.

- Fred's voice becomes incessantly vituperative.
- Mania manifests itself by increased volubility, lack of impulse control and the subsequent partaking in rash, hazardous behaviour, working late, flight of ideas and insomnia.
- An intensification of sounds, usually police sirens and planes flying overhead, leading to paranoia of being pursued and/or under surveillance.
- A fervent desire to reach out to family members or significant people from the past.
- An unwavering belief that the baby and/or myself are in danger.
- Self-proclamation of being *the chosen one,* on a clandestine, government mission to eradicate global evil, accompanied by a persecutory complex.
- Ranting and repeating phrases with physiologically impeded movements.
- The resurfacing of the obsession with the numbers 3, 6, 9 – numbers that signify a code that if cracked will lead to the formation of a utopian world.

When psychotic I would see evidence of these numbers punctuating the history of my life and that of the world. They held all the answers to my problems and the global ills. A preoccupation with these numbers signified the onset of full-blown psychosis. Bouts of postpartum psychosis were shorter and more intense. Occurring very fast, the predominant feature of the symptoms was the recurrence and promptness of morbid visions. Aware of what was happening and equipped with the knowledge that these were irrational, impermanent flashes of a brain that was temporarily malfunctioning, I have found ways to pull back mentally and function normally. Nowadays, once the symptoms begin I implement measures to stop the rapid mental decline. These have ostensibly worked effectively, without the aid of medication.[58]

Throughout my two weeks at St Luc, the midwives taught me how to breastfeed and use the breast pump machine correctly. My output soared as a result and I was buoyed by the copious amounts of milk that my body successfully produced. Removing my son during the night to be fed by a nurse allowed me to sleep. I continued to breastfeed my baby, eventually surmounting the agonisingly painful phase of the cracked, bleeding nipples. Gradually they healed. I was never left alone with my son during these first crucial two weeks, while all manner of *professional* strangers handled him.

Being forced to stay in hospital was traumatic. The initial weeks of life are supposed to be special. I revelled in the tininess of my son's hands and feet, his extraordinarily long nails and his delicate torso. When I bathed him for the first time he squirmed and peed all over me in protest. I looked at him, this tiny being making strange expressions, gangly, delicate and utterly enchanting and found myself laughing at this little bundle of life that was totally dependent on me. These first moments of joy were tempered by the fact that I was not able to go home.

Becoming attached to a Scottish midwife at St Luc, I hoped to stay in contact with her after I left; this never happened. At one point I invited all the midwives for tea; looking back I feel quite embarrassed. My over-zealous conviviality might have scared them away.

Finally I was admitted to a mother and baby psychiatric ward at St Jean. The ward at St Jean was noisy and the nurses intimidating. They would weigh the baby and check that I had bathed him properly, but barely conversed with me. Pulling the curtain around my bed for privacy as I breastfed, the cleaning lady pulled it back aggressively. She was obstreperous and hostile. Becoming upset and agitated, I complained. This only made the nurses defensive. One of them smelt acutely of stale sweat. When I took issue with the smelly nurse and her aloof manner, she was offended. All the while you could hear the wails of babies and the obtrusive footsteps of mothers pacing the corridors – it was tantamount to being in an asylum.

I was getting worse, not better. Ultimately, as the mother and primary carer of my child, surely my health should have been prioritised? Perhaps the knowledge of psychosis remains rudimentary and health practitioners don't know what women afflicted with it need. I know what I craved: someone to listen, to tell me that I was not a bad mother for seeing such sick images, to be reassured that I would get better, and that someone would visit regularly to check I was bonding with my child and say:

"You are doing ok, the drawings you have done of your son are beautiful, keep up your art and occupy your mind with helpful pursuits. Don't worry, you will get through this, other women have, we are here to help not judge."

Seeing various psychiatrists and psychologists, many only French speaking, I explained the estrangement from my family and why I thought the psychosis was happening. They listened, assiduously took notes, and didn't say much apart from that they were impressed with my insights. Some even appeared uninterested. Like a caged, scared animal, forced to endure the unremitting pokes and prods, I needed an escape route.

The condition of release was that my mother-in-law came for several weeks. Pining for my own mother, she couldn't come because of health issues. During my psychosis, prior to the pregnancy, I'd requested to see my father-in-law, believing he was the only person who would understand. I'd always been the polite daughter-in-law, concealing any mental health problems. Witnessing my psychotic state, he was unable to handle it. I have seen him only a handful of times since. With sparkly eyes and a permanent smile, my mother-in-law is an ebullient personality. She bakes cakes, is up early and full of beans – the complete antithesis of my own mother. My mother goes to bed late, wakes up late, makes a mess in the kitchen and she can shout and be unkind (although such outbursts are infrequent these days). Each time I saw my mother-in-law, she reminded me of everything my own mother was not. This created a huge internal tension making it difficult to be in the same room with her without being triggered.

Eager to dote on her new grandson, my mother-in-law was at home waiting for me with a smile. Believing she judged me because of my mental health issues, I was constantly paranoid about what she was thinking. During the time she stayed, I shut down when she was near, barely able to say two words. Instead, I skulked around her, avoiding all eye contact. Although she made a valuable contribution, I was relieved when she left. Nowadays, if my husband speaks to his mother he has to take the call discreetly because when I hear her exuberant voice it creates a violent incomprehensible reaction.[59]

When I have been ill I have engaged in rants about my husband's family. Most of my beliefs are unfounded. During the histrionics I feel aggrieved and misunderstood calling them all manner of awful things; afterwards I apologise.[60] My mental health issues have, in effect, alienated me from my husband's family. When my son goes to Sweden with his father it is always without me. His parents and siblings are aware of my diagnosis, but that does not mean they understand what it is like to have my brain. Since my disability is invisible, outwardly I may appear very capable, but imagine running a marathon without legs or trying to lift trees without arms? Imagine that – it is not possible – and yet I feel, often, that the impossible is expected of me.

Voluntarily, I stay away to protect my son. If I am not able to control my moods at home then imagine what it would be like if I had an outburst in front of my in-laws? The humiliation would be unendurable. But family is integral to life, isn't it? There are plenty of families who are estranged and/or dysfunctional. My husband's mother is a perfectly good woman. His whole family are decent people, yet my mind concocts such strong false narratives that when I see them they automatically mutate into the enemy. Like a machine that has been re-wired incorrectly and keeps on malfunctioning, smashing the objects it is supposed to covet, my brain is not too dissimilar. When I finally saw my parents-in-law in 2011, it was briefly, for a few minutes, on the condition that they didn't hug me. Managing a subdued, "Hello", only after becoming almost hysterical beforehand, in the end I sat there silently and they left within minutes. It was awkward, regrettable, and soul destroying. My inability to see my husband's family is an adverse consequence of my disorder and will, inevitably, impact on my children. With time, maybe relations can be salvaged.

I've reached a point where if I can't have honest communication, I'd rather not have any at all.

I am, however, in touch with my husband's aunt and daughter, for some reason I identify with them (perhaps because they have overcome various life and health struggles) and am able to write to them truthfully about my mental health issues without fear. I value this contact, hugely, and they often say how fond they are of me, which is touching and bolstering.

The effect of the condition on my blood family has been equally corrosive. As my postpartum psychosis worsened in 2010, my stepfather came to visit, but soon became a trigger. He couldn't keep up with my need for faultless order and the more we talked about family, the more heat it created in my brain. Although genuinely happy to see him, he had to walk on eggshells around me. My mother visited, too. They both tried, earnestly, to help by looking after my son to provide a much needed interlude, yet I ended up cooking, cleaning, talking too much and exhausting myself. All the hard work I put into rebuilding the fractured relations with my family collapsed after a long-awaited trip home to Manchester. They couldn't provide the fastidiously ordered environment I needed and, despite their concerted efforts, I was more isolated at home than when I was alone in Brussels. A series of events and disappointments contributed to a major psychotic episode where I behaved in a way that was disturbing for my family. My husband returned, earlier than expected, to take us home. Recalling my behaviour shocks me; at the time the rage was so intense it bled through me. I was, temporarily, locked in one of Fred's complex faux narratives, designed to destroy those relationships that were dearest.

It was a sad day when I left home that summer of 2011, in deadening silence, refusing to say goodbye to either parent. Having inconsistent contact via email, letters and texts was hardly satisfactory. My family were worried about my welfare and profoundly saddened by this period of self-imposed isolation. Crucially, they understood why I was doing it – I was putting my health above everything else I might yearn for inside.

The birth of my second child thawed the psychotic ice block that had thickened around my heart and mind and I allowed my stepfather to visit in October 2013. This was a turning point. Realising how much I had missed my family and the huge void created by their absence, my big sister also visited. We laughed liked our old teenage years – when we were close and seldom exchanged a cross word – and I cooked for her. Last Christmas I spoke to my stepfather on the phone, my middle sister called, my big sister

Skyped and I even turned the webcam on, something I never do. Regularly writing to my little sister, I helped facilitate an exhibition of her photos in London this year. Slowly we are repairing the damage reaped by my condition.

It was not lack of sleep that brought on this psychotic episode in 2011; it was the conversations, fake beliefs, and firmly entrenched narratives that I couldn't shift. Before I was ill, despite the usual fluctuations of family life, I never would have believed that I would no longer see them at all. Yet, the idea of going home remains risky and would be tantamount to stepping into a living room of invisible bombs that could detonate in an instant. The words of my eldest sister still resonate:

"At least I never wanted to kill my baby," she screamed.

I fired back, "It's not me who wants to kill my baby, it's Fred."

Although I am happy at the resumption of family contact, I have to err on the side of caution. Something might cause a spark in my brain, forcing the mental gates to come crashing down, making me retreat and break off communication. We will have to work hard as a family to stop Fred's spiteful mischief from destroying what we have re-built in recent months.[61]

During the three years of family estrangement, my husband and I had to find a way out of the dark, entangled mess in my head and raise our son.

Still experiencing visions, I'd had no follow-up support since my release from St Luc. Because of a loss in confidence in Dr R, I stopped seeing her. Although I liked and respected Dr R, she neglected to forewarn me that I could be vulnerable to postpartum psychosis and she prescribed medication that exacerbated the psychotic symptoms I was experiencing months after I gave birth.

At times I was afraid of what I might do. My tiny, innocent son blinked, looking slightly bewildered, knowing something was wrong with his Mummy. Often I had to call my husband or midwife, when unable to handle what I was hearing and seeing.

In my case, before my son was born, Fred was consistently telling me to commit suicide; after the birth of my child, a process occurred where Fred's attention focused on the baby although it would vary, day-to-day. I had to rationalise it in my head and say:

"Imagine pressing a button which releases a dagger that tries, virulently, to stab you – that's my brain. Innocuous words become claws in my consciousness and are stuck there for days, impossible to dislodge. If only I could place my hands into my brain and fix the faulty wiring, but I can't because that part of my brain is broken. Can I fix it? I'm not sure – I can avoid pressing the button, though."

Creating visual scenarios like this, to explain what was happening in the brain, was my own method of creative mental logic that stopped me asking, "Why is this nightmare happening?" I could accept this was part of me, deal with it and move on.

The impact of my condition on my marriage, daily family life and ability to parent, has been devastating. The prognosis, on the surface, does not look good. Despite the negatives, I hold onto the good moments – when I create thirty-foot scrolls and scores of paintings with my son, play *bouncy-bouncy* on the bed, pull funny faces that make him giggle, draw a dinosaur to make him happy, potter around on the terrace garden watering the plants with his snail watering can, and tell him stories about the moon to get through the difficult times – not my bouts of irritability and short temperedness that stem from sheer exhaustion. I've created a book of drawings only of him, with words of wisdom, to show how hard I try to combat Fred.

My Bosnian friend told me, "You are not ill, most mothers experience the same pressures and stresses due to the daily, solitary and unrelenting grind of parenting."

Although a platitude, modern parenting is demanding. Our ancestors brought up families in a tribal environment with an abundance of hands to assist. In Western societies, mothers often live far away from family and become disconnected. Interestingly, my sisters have manifested similar threads of behaviour as the ones I am experiencing since becoming parents. It's as if we are trying to live with the same worm inhabiting our heads.

How Do you Bond With your Child and Deal With your Mental Health Issues, Especially the Visions?

There is a causal link between the hallucinations and sleep deprivation. Stress makes them appear, too. Or depression. My eldest son, at three-and-half-years old, refuses to wean. Who am I to deny him the breast, when he clearly needs it for reassurance and closeness? Letting him suckle if he wants to has ensured a strongly cemented bond and a sense of security that he feels deep inside, despite the voices and hallucinations I have endured. Others may disapprove of the duration of my breastfeeding, but my son is a confident and happy little boy today.

One psychologist, in London, asserted that, because I didn't get enough of my mother's milk I never established that, crucial, core bond with her. My stepfather said he was never breastfed and it didn't do him any harm, but he received unconditional love from his father. A child needs consistent love from at least one parent. I have no recollection of my mother cuddling or kissing me, there are no photos of her holding my sisters and I in her arms. My mother often says, in fact, that we never properly formed an attachment like she did with her own mother, [62] although she has since asserted that she read to us and established closeness in her own way. Her eldest sister said that affection spoils children and my mother, unfortunately, listened, opting to eschew affectionate embraces. I can only speculate about whether being breastfed would have protected me from developing the *mad* gene. Breastfeeding certainly established a connection with my son that I was finding hard to forge naturally. As my second baby suckles, looking up at me, with his long-lashed blue eyes, I draw his hands, feet and the folds of his clothes, watching as he falls asleep in my arms.

Images 46 and 47. *Sketchbook for Baba No.1* (ink and pen on paper, size A5, October 2010-2013). I decided to create this book to help relate to my baby, which I found challenging during the postpartum psychosis. Creating the drawings during these lonely, confusing, dark times provided a much-needed form of escapism and something tangible and poignant to present to my son when he's older.

Seeing my face in the mirror of his eye, I draw this image repeatedly, making me believe that we are inextricably linked. Whatever Fred hurls at me, he can never break this mother and child attachment.

During my son's early years, my husband let me sleep in the mornings, eventually putting our son in crèche three days a week when deemed old enough. Crèche exposed him to social interaction with other children, allowing me to work and providing a crucial break. My husband also enlisted a cleaning lady. I was scared of the previous one, Marta and used

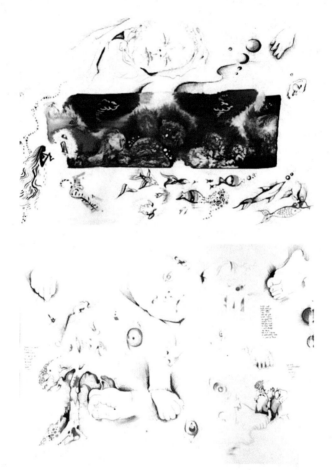

Images 48 and 49. *Sketchbook for Baba No. 2,* started immediately after the birth of my second baby (pen and ink on paper, size A5, 2013). As soon as I began to draw my baby, Fred's voice diminished in power. When I am having a testing time, drawing my baby calms down an overheated mind and reminds me of what is important, keeping me anchored to the *now.* All the answers seem to lie in my baby's eyes. The longer I look into them, the more I try to unravel the mysteries locked within them and the stronger I become.

to hide from her. The new one triggered me, I tried another, and she didn't work out either.[63] It's hard to find paid help with whom I feel at ease.

Working from a studio at home certainly reduces the anxiety, because my hours are flexible. Project work and commissions boost my flagging self-esteem, making me believe that my art and writing count in the world and yet the pressure I put on myself to create is acute.[64] Teaching Pilates keeps my body strong, focuses on my breathing and helps other women. Because of my OCD, sleep disorder and child care duties I can be late for class. Some look irked when I relay my *pseudo* excuses. Knowing it would not go in my favour to tell the truth about my disability, I don't bother, focusing on the advantages of teaching for my mind, instead.

I believe art is the only thing that soothes my mental woes. Art is pure. It doesn't involve anyone else and I can assert complete control, unlike people who are slippery, unreliable and unpredictable. Meditation empties the head, although I can only manage fifteen-minute bouts at the end of the Pilates classes I teach. My mind continues to remain a noisy place. Mindfulness is something to develop and consolidate over time, extending the periods when I am still, slowing down my breathing, focusing on the subtle nuances of the breath as if it is a gentle breeze. When negative thoughts intrude, using the strong and steady undulation of the breath, I blow out all the useless mental clutter from the room of my mind and try to stay in the present. During the class I teach, meditation comes naturally, at home I find it hard to put into practise.[65]

There continue to be times when I have *lost it* and not been able to control the mental volatility – putting colossal strain on my husband. Since the psychosis and birth of the children we have more storms than bright blue sunny days, yet I think we are managing, in spite of the circumstances and odds stacked against us. Today I spoke to my husband via Skype and stayed calm throughout. Although Fred tried to sabotage the conversation, I didn't let him intrude. I am undergoing an experimental phase, currently in the infant stages, of trying to tame his acerbic tongue. But, I will admit, it's a struggle since Fred's voice remains loud, intrusive and destructive.

I have written a journal from my son's perspective called: *My Mother is Mad,* to help him understand what it has been like growing up under Fred's shadow. He knows when "Mummy's brain is hot" blowing on it to cool it down and says, "Baba don't like shouting" and I keep on trying not to. Our current art project: *1,000 Postcards* entails my son creating squiggles on individual postcards. Instructing me what to draw, I create something out of these random, almost anarchic, squiggles. We have made 150, to date, with a plan to exhibit them at my next shows, in London and Brussels in 2015; we have also completed a new scroll, our third thus far. Producing art together allows us to stay healthily connected and keeps Fred in check.

Having a second child was a risk, but I wanted to give my first born a sibling – to not be alone in the world. Although a challenge to cope with two children and my mental health problems, I can't give up. I have a vested interest in continuing to dodge the bricks that Fred hurls and trudge on through the mud in my head, while searching for the stars above.

The first three years of my son's life have been up and down. Without my husband and the initial childcare he provided, it would have been difficult for me to parent. Requiring more sleep than the average person to function, mornings are hard, since I can be a zombie. Battling with persistent insomnia, I often end up writing and painting in the twilight hours, when I should be in bed. If my son glimpses me when "Mummy's not well" it is soul destroying. Since my second child turned three months and with my husband abroad for three weeks of each month, I've faced difficulties managing two small children, for the most part on my own.

Doing the school run by placing both my son and the baby in a buggy attached to my bike is far from easy. If the weather is good, I get a kick of endorphins and a dose of sunshine to start the day. Yet cycling on roads that are not amenable to cyclists is hazardous. Any benefits are destroyed by the onset of hypomania, which mutates into an extreme hyper-manic state, due to the surge in adrenaline.[66]

Doing the shopping, taking the baby with me, often going to five different shops to buy everything, I can be loaded with so many bags it becomes farcical. When I pick up my eldest from school, he can be

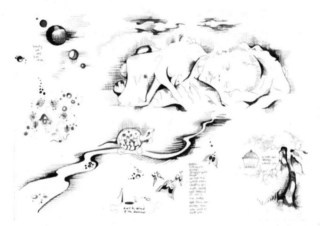

Image 50. *Get Well Quickly Baba (pen and ink on postcard, 2013)* This was drawn when my baby was in hospital recuperating from bronchitis. Creating the postcards is a mind diversion technique and an alternative to medication. One of my mantras is: "A drawing a day keeps the doctor away."

curmudgeonly and might have a tantrum; it is not always pleasant. When we get home there can be more tantrums (not always) before I prepare supper for the children. Ensuring they are both well fed, all the food I cook is made from fresh ingredients (sometimes the lengths I go to are excessive and taxing). After reading them stories and putting both the children to bed, I try and work. My eldest can test me, finding any excuse to get up; it is tiring and frustrating. If things get really bad, I call my parents or the CHS Helpline to vent. My husband gently advised, "Perhaps you should stop working," but I can't do that, making art and writing sustains me. The propensity to work when I should be asleep is a habit hard to break. Fred also instructs me to do things, mainly cleaning, before giving me permission to retire. It can all get very exhausting.

For a few weeks I found a solution requiring supreme discipline. Going to bed at 7pm with the children and waking up at 3am offered a panacea and an escape from the sticky, thorny holes I get caught in. Nine hours later I was transformed – patient, tolerant and competent. Showered and hard at work in my studio until the children woke up, I then dressed and fed both the children and even had time to play a little before depositing them in the bike buggy and ferrying my eldest to school. Rather than feeling frustrated in the morning, I was ready to be a mother and fulfil all my duties (even the interminable domestic ones) – happily.

Unable to maintain the new routine, I soon reverted to my nocturnal ways. Asking my son politely to play with his Lego or watch *Mr Men* on the iPad so that I can grab a few minutes more shut eye, he's happy to oblige, but this is not the optimal solution.

Often the desire to sleep deserts me. I just can't go to bed until I have emptied and soothed my head with a creative fix. Yet I would like to return to the early to bed routine, since lapsing into a bad cycle of sleeplessness has negative consequences. Tiredness reduces my appetite, induces mania, transforming my husband into a trigger. Subsequently, I lose control and Fred takes over, easily wreaking havoc. My sleep deficit is becoming huge.

I have not yet found a way to silence Fred. He is forever waiting to pounce at any opportune moment, but I am armed and ready for mental combat. If I can manage my sleep, I can manage my mind, manage what spews out of Fred's mouth, and manage my life.

During the summer of 2013, my husband was working abroad and I was quite heavily pregnant and alone with my son. The sleep deprivation developed rapidly and as the symptoms started to unfold I instinctively knew that my son would be better off in a safe environment with his doting grandparents. As much as it felt like an admission of failure on my part, it had to be done. In Sweden he is happy and thriving, enjoying an idyllic natural environment, picking berries and fishing for crawfish. It saddens me that I can't go berry picking with my son in the beautiful, ancient Swedish forests and, instead, I hide myself away from those that care.

I briefly saw a new psychologist, Mrs Severin, during my second pregnancy. We spoke about my relationship with my son and how the postpartum psychosis had impacted on our bond. It is hard saying, "I have to fake it sometimes," and that often, "I force myself to be affectionate and cuddle him because it doesn't come naturally."

She asked if I missed him during the weeks he'd been in Sweden over the summer of 2013, and I didn't know how to answer the question. Why should I feel inadequate for admitting, "I am not well and sometimes I don't know what or how to feel anything much"?

My former mental health social worker, J, often told me that she had seen mothers who were more detached than I was, who couldn't engage or interact with their children in any meaningful way. She reassured me that I was not one of these mothers and that I was doing an "amazing" job. That's what our old GP in Manchester, Dr Bodie, told my mother, although she was just coping much of the time.

When my eldest son was small, the breast seemed to eradicate all my shortcomings as a mother. Sending him to crèche and the time he's had with his father meant less time with me, meaning there was less chance of him being psychologically harmed. With my husband away, we spend more time together and, with a small baby to handle too, I am under pressure, especially when the children have been sick. Somehow, I get through these long days and nights.

I try and hold onto all the good things that I have done with him: the art, the maths, the elementary science, the reading, the music, the chasing, the jumping on the trampoline, the blowing raspberries on his tummy, the creation of a roof top *jungle* and the expansion of the increasingly complex Lego town, replete with spaceships, robots and dinosaurs. Sometimes, when we paint I get irritated, when we read I get bored, when he refuses to eat the nutritious food I prepare for him frustration sets in. Yes, it gets repetitive and lonely; this is an intrinsic part of motherhood and, with Fred constantly tearing me down, being a good mother seems an elusive prospect. I can't relinquish that dream nor give into Fred's malicious tongue and sick ideas.

In the days leading up to the decision to send my son to Sweden, I prepared for his departure. If he stayed another day, I was afraid of what might happen. The previous night I was dying to sleep, while my son was unsettled and Fred was telling me to get a meat cleaver and chop him into small pieces. It was horrific. I knew I would never do such a thing, but visualising it was a severe mental strain that I could no longer support. The lack of restorative sleep contributed to the erratic moods and I was worried about the impact of these moods on the unborn foetus. I also wanted my son to be in a safe *happy* environment and that meant being away from his mother. These were the difficult decisions I was forced to make. When his grandfather came, it was partially humiliating. I'd written a long list of instructions, as if this was proof of my ability as a mother, but I couldn't show my face and say hello. My son was none the wiser, oblivious to my torment. I hugged him and then listened as he ran into his grandfather's arms, all facilitated by one of the mothers I had befriended, who didn't ask any questions.

Sending my son to Sweden has become an incumbent precaution to keep me mentally on an even keel. I have accepted that bonding with my children takes a long time and a great deal of effort; I wish it was instantaneous, but it's not. I am prepared to put the time in, determined to love them as much as my mind allows me to; who would have thought, something that is instinctive, would be so elusive?

There are many poems I have written explaining my emotional state and what I went through during the time when my son and I were apart. It also allowed the second pregnancy to progress without additional strain. Children are not possessions, they deserve the best care possible and, if a mother cannot provide it, then she has to accept that the child is better off in an environment where they will receive it unconditionally. Perhaps my parents were too proud to admit they were failing us, maybe they thought they could behave in whatever way they liked, irrespective of the consequences. Or maybe it was the best they could do at the time.

Solitude, rest, art and words are all I need and I will be a better and healthier mother for it.

My husband believes I exaggerate my shortcomings, asserting, on occasion, that I am an affectionate and loving mother. These memories fade in the distance, as I focus on the bile my mind generates, defiling all that is worth coveting. Maybe, then, he's right and my mind is tricking me into thinking I am a worse mother than I actually am? Repeating the positive things I have done makes them stick a little longer, and they become less likely to be trampled upon by Fred's stomping feet.

This book I have written for my children, so they can fathom what has transpired in my brain. It is my attempt to show a mother's love, when Fred has tried to turn me against my children. I am doing my very best to protect them from him and to make them understand him, too. Fred has issues: maybe he's an angry child that's why he's overtly aggressive, maybe we have to befriend him so he stops biting us?

My mother said that everyone has a Fred inside their head and that I have just identified the discordant babble that we are all living with. Is this true? I don't know, but it was comforting when she said it.

Image 51. Detail from *Squiggle on a Scroll* completed with my three-year-old son (pen and ink on 30-foot-scroll of paper, 2014). My son creates the initial squiggle, telling me what to draw. His squiggles guide me, taking me to a special place in my son's head. He seems to derive great pleasure looking at the postcards and scrolls we create together, all this artwork we make is one way of beating Fred with the baton of beauty and imagination.

When I prepared to see my son again, after the two and half months apart in 2013, I imagined squeezing him very tight and narrating made up stories; set in Pathuakali in Bangladesh. Stories based on my mother's childhood tales and the pink house she used to reside in, behind a green lake with a snake.

However hard Fred tries to destroy my bond with my son, I don't give up hope. You have to continue to do normal things to counter the depraved stuff you see and hear in your head, like letting him run and roam unfettered, patting the gnarled, wise tree trunks, eating ice cream on a hot summer's day, playing football and devouring home-grown strawberries. If the weather is good, we go for a bike ride or the dinosaur museum, which is his favourite. All the while, Fred is near, all the while he whispers in my ear, and I try to ignore his taunts.

The dark poems I write purge me of all this negativity and the inadequacies that come from living with a mental health condition. By emptying it from my mind, I try to be free of these *twisted* feelings, refusing to let them come between my children and me.

Blank Ink describes some of the visions I have endured.

Black Ink

She was lying next to him
The sound of his breath
His sudden movements,
They were reassuring
"He's still alive," she would say silently
Do all mothers have visions?

Crossing the road
One car doesn't stop
She's holding him proudly in her arms
Only seconds before they exchanged a kiss
The car rams into her and his body goes flying
She's semi conscious,
Cars start moving again
Not caring
Where is he?
His pathetic body parts ripped to nothing
A smear on the pavement like unsightly dog shit.

He's crawling towards the door
And it slams
Slams hard
His skull gets crushed
Was it the wind that slammed it?
Or was it her foot that kicked it like a small football?

"No," she gasps in the middle of the night,
"Stop it," she says knowing there are more visions to come
Sewn together in colours that appear
Graphically twisted.

The other night
She lay awake
Unable to sleep
Like the past seven months.

He was sitting in the middle of the living room
And she was throwing black ink
On the cream sofa
And the white walls
Then finally she stripped her son naked
He thought it was a game
Laughing as the ink splattered on his
Very tiny body
He wanted to join in and reached for the large black puddle on the, once,
Ash wooden floor.
He lifted his hand to his mouth to taste the delicious looking ink
Then she dipped a large brush in the puddle
Began to paint her baby

In black
He starts to scream
His trembling black body
Grows into a monstrous hard lumpy mass
With a mouth and white teeth
She instantly crawls inside
As he closes his jaw and swallows his mother whole.

The flat is as it was
Once more
With a cute baby playing on his mat with his many toys
She stares at him
Trying to comprehend what's she's just seen
Her son can stand now
Likes to lean against his bed railings
Her husband has warned her
"If he climbs onto the duvet or pillow
That will be it
He will go right over the edge."

She's seen it happen
He falls
There is a terrible crack
And he's dead
Then she's as good as dead
Promptly stabbing herself
Very badly, with a sharp knife
That leaves a mess that her poor husband
Has to clean up

Is this motherhood then?
The joy
The pain
The black ink of love
That spreads
Within and without
That leaves a stain that is visible from the moon.

He's breathing
Sounds like music
Something wise
Simple

Peaceful and
Beautiful
Listen to that sound
Listen and believe
Believe that you are mother not a
Killer with a black ink stain for a heart.

The sweet and innocent stories that I make up – about my son on the moon, for example – counter the dark, often unrelenting, visions and make me believe that there are other universes in my mind that I can retreat to that are safe, cosy and friendly hearths to inhabit. Writing these stories is just as soothing to me as it is to narrate them to my children.

Is There a Risk that I Could Harm My Children or Myself?

The risk of killing myself is greater than that of killing my children. *Killing my children,* is the worst thing a mother could ever write down, but this is what I have seen in my head, multiple times. It doesn't follow that I consciously want to harm them, however the horror of seeing such stuff takes its toll. No matter how hard I rationalise the visions, nothing can diminish their horror.

Should I ever tell my children that I have envisioned such things? Or will this remain my dirty secret? It does feel dirty. As if I have already committed an unforgiveable crime. I am not alone and other mothers live in silence, distress, and shame for the things they involuntarily see and feel. My brain wants to tell me to protect my children. These images are warning me of the danger they could be subjected to, but somehow they have become skewed and distorted, like a painting that has been vandalised, senselessly and brutally. I won't tell them, unless they ask me. They might feel alienated, though, and, in the end, retreat further away from me, just as I have retreated from my own family at times. I am prepared for this.

When they are older, they can read my poems dispassionately and understand that my occasionally bizarre behaviour towards them was not my fault. I hope they accept that it was the result of a faulty brain and recognise how hard their father and I have tried to give them a happy, loving childhood.

A few days before my son returned from Sweden, he told me that he was missing me and wanted to come home. He blew a big kiss, making me think – he must love me and, perhaps, *schizophrenics can be good mothers, too.*

CHAPTER 13

A Sane Response to an Insane Situation

Mental health resources are being cut and tested globally. I listened to the psychiatrist Dr Lynne Jones on the BBC World Service. She sought to help a single mother from the Philippines in the aftermath of the 2013 hurricane known locally as *Yolanda*. This woman was sleeping rough, a victim of sexual abuse and vulnerable to sexual predators, the main one being her stepfather. Mentally, she was in a precarious state. In collaboration with the authorities and local psychiatrists, Dr Jones found her protection and shelter. When she asked the woman what she thought of her new temporary lodgings she replied, "It's special."

It was just a bed on a wet concrete floor.

There are many more, isolated, mentally unwell mothers out there, tackling Fred in his multiple manifestations and getting on with it. More than 350 million, according to the World Health Organisation, suffer from a mental illness and it will be the main global health crisis of 2020, with all age groups affected. People will have to develop strategies to overcome their condition, since treatment will not be readily available to all.

I would like to imagine my brain as a majestic cathedral with stained glass windows. Multi-coloured rays of light stream through, painting a blue haven in which to create alchemy with my fingers, stirring up boundless energy from within, revitalising my tired bones, letting me soar with my children, taking them to another place that is magical and safe.

I am at war with myself to remain a good, calm and loving mother to my children. To keep this *threat* away from them without the aid of medication, I will do whatever I can. Even though I am trying to tame Fred, if I am tired or stressed, I know Fred will, eventually, come out and attack me – with bombs that explode into scores of images and rockets that splinter into a thousand screams – urging me to do awful things. This is why I have to win this never-ending battle: and I will and in order to win, Fred has to become an ally, not my foe.

Today, after three months of doggedly drawing and painting my baby, writing poems and essays to fend off the visions and Fred's insidious voice, I realised something very simple. I looked at my baby, stared right into those blue eyes, saw my reflection in those glistening tiny irises, listened to the gurgles, kissed those cherubic cheeks, held my baby close, stroked those perfect fingers and toes and said:

"I won't ever harm you, you know that don't you, because Mummy really loves you," and then I held my baby very close, so close we almost became one.

Finally, I am enjoying the little one and revelling in that magical baby's smile, his laughter and his generous cuddles. We are a team and having my baby near makes me strong. When I remember this Fred is far, far away, even if only for a short while.

This poem conveys an on-going mental struggle and the continued fight to stay well. I will carry on fighting for the sake of my family and sanity. Fred is not going to win; I won't let him.

Am I Slowly Going Mad?

Am I slowly going mad?
Is this *thing* eating away at my precious brain?
That worm that feeds
With its very sharp teeth
Each night I clean out
Fred's excrement
He's defecating in the living room of my mind
Polluting the air I breathe
The place where I would like to sit
and listen to the sound of the sea
Plant flowers in the garden
Fred pulls them out
Wretched weeds grow with claws for leaves
They scratch out my eyes
and scratch at my heart
Now he wants to get to them
Those two
Who sleep.
They don't know that Mummy is fighting
The little one sucks
The big one sucks
They are sucking me dry

I am shrinking
Fred is getting stronger
I am weak, small,
Very small now
Am I slowly going mad?
Am I?
Fred grabs me by the hand
He pulls me to the edge of the psychotic abyss
"Jump" he says "you fucking worthless bitch
And take your children with you" he says
It's a war in my head
I attack with words and my paintbrush
Fred keeps stabbing me
Laughing at me
"Do this, do that?" he says
"Do it
Do it now
Do it or die," he says
Who is Fred?
Is he my mother?
My sisters
My husband
Is he real?
What is he?
"Go away Fred," I say feebly
"Shut up Fred," I say quietly
"Leave me alone" I say silently
Got to sleep, I say
Got to sleep now

"Please let me sleep
There's nothing left Fred
I have nothing left to give
You have taken everything from me
My dignity
You told me to strip
I did it
You told me to run
I did it,
You told me to write to all those people
I did it
I listened to you

Now you want me to do
The unspeakable
I won't do it
I won't."
I go to my room and build a spaceship out of Lego
Just as I did when I was small
And home was a hostile, messy, shouting place
That spaceship will take me to the moon
Mr Dinosaur, Mr Mouse and Miss Ladybird
They will protect me and the children, too
We will hide in a warm crater on the moon.

"You will never find us
Stay in your dark cave
Burn down the trees
Pull out the flowers
Trees and flowers they will always grow
Because these hands
Will keep on planting them
Even if you chop them off
So go on then
Spew your shit and
Eat it"

CHAPTER 14

Where I Am Now?

A book is never really complete, I don't think – ever. Since submitting my first draft to Dr Tim Read I have been writing notes in spidery, frenetic scrawl and fragments of poems. Ideas surge into my brain and there's a compulsion to include everything, I could, disturbingly, be working on this book forever.

Wrestling With TrActor

Bewilderingly, I've had inconsistent contact with TrActor, the organisation I was, initially, very effusive about, which is important to reflect upon. It is somewhat ironic that, although enthusiastic about me writing and publishing this book, I have hardly seen Dr Thys, during, what could be described as, the most testing period of my life. I told him candidly that I might be critical of him and TrActor in the book. He said that was "ok". Perhaps Dr Thys has too many patients and not enough time. I know that he is not the enemy.

Dr Thys requested that I come in for a consultation but I did not know when I could find the time to get to TrActor, have the consultation and do the school run. When I sent my son to Sweden and baby to Manchester, for a much-needed break, I finally had a small window to go and see Dr Thys. He was running late; I became unsettled sitting in the waiting room, sent a disgruntled text and was on the verge of walking out. A few minutes later he came down. During the consultation he doodled, I kept on gulping down water; the emotion welled up into a massive ball that lodged in my throat. It was awkward, words began to tease out and I asked if I should send him the latest version of the book; we even cracked a joke; most important of all he said:

> "We are supposed to help people with psychosis, bipolar disorder and schizophrenia. We didn't help you in the way that we should have, but we have learnt a lot from this experience."

It was a small relief to hear this admission.

Dr Thys wondered if I might reconsider taking medication and I said:

"Listen, if you leave a woman with two children in prolonged solitary confinement she will eventually go insane. I know what I need, the help just isn't out there."

I left, cycling in the rain. It was cold, dreary – not how summer is meant to be – but the weather reflected my mood. My plants took a pounding, my delicate blooms were drowning, the rain hammered the world into submission, and I had to keep on going even if I was emotionally drenched.

We (my husband, myself and our two children) all saw Dr Thys together a month later. Sitting uneasily in his office, the first thing my son said was "Fred" in a protracted, deep voice and we broke into awkward laughter.

Sent up to see two mental health social workers, Peter and Marcus, when I saw them, I thought *I don't have the energy to talk to someone new.*

It also bothered me profoundly that they were men, I couldn't envisage inviting them into my home, talking to either of them honestly about any of the complex issues I was facing, nor did I want to. With a history of sexual assaults, how could Albertine and her team even assign them to me? I've always had female mental health social workers. It seemed a totally unsuitable and incongruous allocation.

"Things have changed at our organisation we can't baby sit or anything like that," Marcus said tersely. I was taken aback.

This wasn't even what I was asking for. Feeling tired, I became agitated. I needed occasional, practical assistance and someone to talk to that I could trust when my husband was absent.

"I would like to stick to Jean Pierre, he's professional and I'm at ease with him. I've never allowed him into my home. I don't need anyone to talk to or visit. He knows me, you don't."

"I'm sorry he's busy with other patients. You could try to get to know us," Peter added.

Getting to know them would be too exposing like taking off all my clothes in front of strangers at a bus stop. We'd waited six months for this meeting, only to realise TrActor couldn't help me in the way I specifically required. Not wanting to stay a minute longer, we left abruptly, defeated and unsupported.

Recently and, somewhat, reluctantly I attended a private view of *Return to Sender* organized by TrActor and KAOS at the WIELS, Contemporary Art Centre in Brussels. Dressed up in a bright floral frock, tottering in my Diane Von Furstenberg heels, and carrying my trusty purple hat for extra protection, I was nervous upon arrival. The blurb at the back of the slickly designed catalogue read, "*Return to Sender* wants to break down barriers between 'insiders' and 'outsiders' in art and mental health." My postcard sat snugly amongst the hundred other postcards as if part of one big family, or a group of maverick misfits that had found a temporary home.

Lieven was the first to greet me followed by Dr Thys. Initially, I was terse and we parted company awkwardly, then an hour later I approached him and we spoke again. Dr Thys came out with his now, predictable, "sorry" for not replying to my emails because he had been very busy. He also said that the inability of TrActor to come to my aid was nothing to do with me, it was "politics." *Aagh bloody politics*, I mused, *the bane of my life and that of the world*. A platitude, I know, but a pertinent one.

At the private view I also saw someone I hadn't seen in a couple of years, Krijn. He was starkly changed, gone were his thick black locks, his head was shaved, he had put on weight and his teeth had yellowed. For the last two years he had been in a mental institution, recovering from a breakdown. We sat down and he told me, enthusiastically, how they even had chickens there.

"Are you better?" I asked concernedly.

"Not really" he said, "but I only go back to the hospital twice a week now."

I joked, "Can I come, too?"

Krijn said adamantly, "You are too elegant and delicate and would be eaten alive."

He was speaking rapidly without pausing for breath talking about his father, his mother, a duck that had been raped that was the subject of a play he'd written, and his childhood traumas. I saw Mike, his husband, a charismatic tower of stoic strength. How hard it must be for him to witness the rapid deterioration and even slower rehabilitation of his partner? *Why does Fred always attack the good ones?* Before I left, he told me how he remembered observing me at the private view of my exhibition at KAOS in 2012. Working on the scroll, lost in another world, "It was sublimely beautiful to see and very calming," Krijn said.

We are drowning in a sea of selfishness, ugliness and misery. There are too many crashing waves in this world and not enough rocks to stall them. You have to paint your own piece of heaven to get through the days and stay afloat. I wanted to say.

When I got home I read Dr Thys's words in the catalogue and they confirmed that we were, and always have been, on the same page. Dr Thys wrote:

"The rhythm of the hand holding the pencil or pen, putting the pieces together, or dipping the brush in the paint: (the postcards are) a work that leaves you lucid yet musing, a kind of hypnotic concentration where many things happen half consciously, yet result in coherent art."

He ended with a quote from the American artist Dan Graham,

"Many great artists and writers seem to be borderline 'schizophrenic'... I may be, and probably am, in these fuzzy areas. Maybe it beats taking LSD."

Talking to Dr Thys was a relief and reading his thoughtful words reassuring.

I want to honour my promise and complete the Scroll II project with the patients at TrActor, but then it is time to move on and cut my inchoate roots to this city – a decision that is consolidating.

I met with Lieven and Mike. We ate cake and discussed the project, dates and logistics, even though my mind was elsewhere. The theme of Scroll II will be one of psychological warfare: an attempt to visualize the monumental petty wars we fight in our heads just to make it through each stultifying day resulting in a tapestry of the internal torment, mirrored by the violence that people inflict senselessly upon others. The patients will be

Image 52. *Bosnian War Part 1* (oil on canvas, size 16x14 inches, 2013). When the Bosnian war broke out, I was deeply affected and began a series of works aged 21. Naively, I exhibited them instructing the gallery that they were not for sale; the gallery owner subsequently sold them all, I was distraught. This oil painting was recreated from a photo of the original (now sold) collage and ink painting. I am in the process of recreating the whole series in dedication to my close friend from Bosnia who still suffers flashbacks from the horror of a war that remains unforgotten for many.

encouraged to express their mental affliction through uninhibited mark making, they can scratch, scrape, even spit at the paper if that's what they feel compelled to do. The point is to unleash *the stuff inside* onto the naked skin of the scroll. Then I will examine each mark and respond accordingly interweaving senseless images of war collaged directly onto the scroll.[67] I am returning to the theme that I was interested in when I did my Bosnian war series of paintings two decades ago – a precursor to my *Sorrow on a Scroll*. My education at the LSE is finally fuelling my art. All art is political. It has to be if it is to be worthy of any merit or credence.

My tenuous relationship with TrActor and Dr Thys makes me reflect on past relationships, many of which – both professional and personal – have ended up deteriorating, drifting, detaching or imploding – am I the problem then? The impact of my mental health condition on the children is a constant source of anxiety and something I work at improving every day. I call the Brussels CHS Helpline frequently. Describing myself as a *"PAT – aholic"*, reaching out for the phone has become habitual. As I talk, often, I draw, paint, cook or bake, while dumping everything that is swarming in my head. The various Pats I speak to have become my *everything* – the closest thing to friends. My definition of a friend is someone you can rely on and call on anytime, someone who will listen and lend an empathetic ear. Sometimes it's easier to talk to a stranger than my husband or the family. During one visit, relations with my stepfather combusted with an almost tragic predictability, although later we patched things up. When my husband returned from abroad, I was constantly triggered. Eventually, I achieved a semblance of calm by metaphorically gluing my lips together to avoid any nastiness seeping out. During both occasions, I called the Helpline several times a day to get through it.

Wrestling With Fred

Fred is an unwelcome part of the family that I can't be rid of because we are conjoined. He's part of who I am and here to stay. I have to make him a benign presence, dare I say, a force for good.

During this testing time, I wrote to Dr Tim Read explaining how Fred's voice was becoming increasingly intrusive forcing me to partake in various *risky self-destructive* behavioural patterns that were getting out of control; Fred's veneer of invulnerability was waning, the casual aplomb with which he was behaving was brazen, I was becoming increasingly scared of the consequences since my attempts to curb the behaviour were flimsy. As my decision-making powers became more impaired, due to untenable levels of sleep depravity, I was no longer in control, reduced to an automaton, a vessel inhabited by Fred, doing everything that he instructed. Dr Read was, naturally, very concerned and told me about avatar therapy, pioneered by Professor Leff. I wrote to Professor Leff asking to participate in the current trials.[68] The treatment comprises seven sessions. A computer programme creates a visual image of Fred, according to my description, and gradually Fred's hostile voice transforms into an amiable one.

On reflection, I've already visualised Fred in his multiple guises. He is not always cruel and he pushes me to be proactive and productive. Without him I wouldn't be able to work with the same fervour. For example, he might badger me incessantly to make a piece of art or write a poem, when I would rather watch rubbish TV, so he has a specific utility. He resembles one of those tyrannical gym teachers, contorting a child's body until he screams in agony to achieve perfection, or a farmer demanding his workers keep on picking cotton even if their hands are blistered. It makes working a chore, not a pleasure, creating a climate of tyranny in the home rather than peace. Perhaps I don't want Fred to become cuddly and nice, because I don't know anything different. He comes and goes, taunts and spits; it would be preferable if I could turn down the volume of his deafening rants, though. Lately, he's been creeping up far too much due to overwork and tiredness.

Dr Leff eventually responded and I put myself forward for the treatment. Believing my fate was in the hands of a computer, determining selection randomly, I recently received a call and have been offered the treatment as part of another trial in 2015. I am buoyed because this is my last shot at turning Fred into a friend. Better to try than not.

Having decided to toss the classification of schizoaffective disorder in the bin, I will not be defined by a label. Actually, I don't even know what it means anymore.

People might have a problem with my *ways* sometimes. I can't keep up with Fred's demands, but it's what I am used to and I won't apologise for doing things or behaving in a manner that is deemed strange. Strange is fine. Yet, I am still prone to psychosis, given a sufficient dose of sleep deprivation, stress and prolonged isolation, therefore I can't completely disregard the diagnosis.

Often I am being tested by an over energetic toddler who is missing his father, with Fred to contend with and prolonged fatigue; part of me wants to prove to everyone, especially my husband, that I can find a way to keep Fred away from the children. I must, in the long run.

I have been developing strategies, which include getting a daily dose of fresh air, tending to my garden, listening to music or the radio, and having *fun* sartorially to divert my mind from dark thoughts, and arranging childcare so that I can go out occasionally for some much needed social interaction. If Fred still tries to break me, I try:

1) Walking away
2) Calling the CHS Helpline when I am unable to cope[69]
3) Writing
4) Painting
5) Cycling
6) Meditation
7) Breathing
8) Resting
9) Pilates and/or Yoga
10) Shutting up
11) Staying hydrated and fed
12) If I have a lapse in mood I try to apologise immediately, explaining the situation to my eldest son as clearly as possible.

Implementing the above is my way of punctuating life with self-generated fleeting moments of joy, calm, health and peace. It doesn't just happen, you have to grab it, steal it and work for a *balanced* existence.

There is a new strategy: simply lying next to my son and talking to him, even if I am tired and want to be alone. I do it because he needs that closeness. This evening he stroked me, gave me a kiss and said, "I like you very big".

"Don't you mean very much?" I replied.

"Yes, very much, and I don't want to go to Sweden on my own, I only want to be with you."

I tried to ask him why he liked me, he couldn't give me an answer and then he said, "Go away Fred, go and fly away like a helicopter." My son paused before continuing, "Fred is in the forest with his Mummy. His Mummy is good but Fred is bad and he has a baby in his tummy – a baby caterpillar."

I told him that Fred had planted a worm in my head, to which my son replied, "Yes, Fred has planted hundreds of caterpillars in my head, too, and my brain hurts. We need to lock him up in a cupboard with a key and make him very small. Look, this is how small we have to make him," he said making a tiny triangle with his hand. "Go and make caterpillars on the sun Fred and not in my head or Mummy's head."

My son doesn't appear to be afraid of Fred. He's even suggested that we eat Fred in one of my tofu noodle soups. I said I would prefer to eat him on toast with lots of butter, but that actually it would be better not to eat Fred at all because he probably wouldn't taste very nice.

Is talking openly about Fred the right approach? Is it even age appropriate? I don't know, but what is the alternative – to buckle under the strain of Fred's rants? I have tried to explain very complicated mental health issues in an imaginative, simple and honest way that my son will understand. He has even suggested hitting Fred in the face with his neon green ball until he's dead. I told him that was not the way and that maybe we had to make Fred our friend, since I didn't think he had many. My son looked at me and I could tell he almost felt sorry for Fred. Could I keep him at bay through these stories? Just about. If I continued like this Fred might just put down his sticks, and stop pummelling the walls of my mind.

Is There Light Then?

"Not long to go now
Been well the last few days
Maybe there's nothing wrong up there?" she ruminates.

The baby is snoozing
Looks utterly peaceful,
Arms flung back
Breathing softly,
Grunting occasionally
She looks at him
And it gives her pleasure
"Is this happiness?"

The baby starts to groan, to murmur
A small hand reaches out to touch her
Coils his curious fingers around her arm
Opens and unclasps them one by one

His skin is burning
As if scorched by an angry sun
She sits up feeling his head with the back of her palm
Red hot it is and she panics
His temperature is almost 40 degrees
He's flushed pink like a rose petal
Yet he manages to muster a weak smile
She holds him close
And thinks of life without this little bundle of magic
Those soft thighs and wise, soulful blue eyes

Life would be finished

All night he suckles
All night she is awake
By morning Fred is knocking at her door
He kicks it down and stands before her
Screaming abuse
She ignores him as he skulks and stares
Hissing and spitting
"You have to get him to hospital, you have to do it now."
It is the voice of Sophie, The Cloud Catcher,
Sophie is the one that keeps her dreaming
That makes her notice things like a full moon
Or an unfurling leaf
A flower that is sad, a flower that is flourishing
Sophie makes her see the beauty
Hiding in the folds of the small
Sophie's holding her hand now
It's been too long since Sophie spoke to her
Sophie is the one who tirelessly tends to the flowers in the garden she is
    trying to grow in her mind
Fred tramples on those tender blooms
The weeds start coming at her with their
Fangs
Ripping out those buds one by one
She can't breathe, she starts to panic, but Sophie doesn't let go of her hand
She calls a friend whom she can trust
"Don't worry, I am coming," her friend says
And she does
Taking her baby to hospital
He's still burning up, not eating or drinking
At least he's safe

She tells her other son
"Fred is in the room, but I'll lock him back in the cupboard."
"OK" her son, says calmly
"You are not scared are you?"
"No I am not scared...go away Fred, leave my Mummy alone," he shouts.
She cycles home
Eyes sore with fatigue
Fred makes her work
As soon as she walks through the door
Hours of gardening
Hours of cleaning

Hours of drawing
He doesn't want her to sleep
He doesn't want her to eat
She thinks she might collapse
That the children are better off far away from her
And her body and mind are giving up
The pediatrician calls, "You have to come to the hospital now"
She loathes hospitals and panics "I can't, I haven't slept, I have another
    son..."
"You aren't the only mother with two children...
How can you look after your baby if you haven't slept?"
Fred wants a fight, his fists are raised, he's about to swear
Sophie stops him
Fred is not happy
She's not sure what to do
"If I go to the hospital, Fred might burn it down with his uncontrollable
    gob"
Sophie tells her, "Call Dr Thys, he will know what to do?"
They've not spoken, now, for months
He picks up the phone, immediately
He's friendly
Trust is, tenuously, re-established
And she's glad
She vomits her story in seconds
"Don't worry," he says calmly
She waits,
Paces up and down
Eats a little
Feels sick
Then she gets a call,
"I have spoken to your psychiatrist, your baby has a viral infection. Why
    don't you rest and you can pick him up in a few days?"
"OK,"
The woman sounds
Friendly and understanding
Her friend says, "I can take you to the hospital"
"Really, you would do that?"
"I am not alone then, there are people who care." And she can barely
    believe it.
"Be proud of yourself," someone once told her, "be proud of everything
    you do for your children."
Stricken by

Thorny thoughts
Fred tells her to do this and do that,
Cracking his whip
He never gives up, but she won't listen
She will go to bed instead

It's a luminous, balmy evening,
The sun has not set,
The birds are singing
Her flowers are in full bloom
Her son ate a home grown strawberry and asked
"Can I give it a hug?"
She puts both her children
To bed with a smile

They are safe
Safe from Fred
There is a smudge of light then
She can just about see it.
It flickers, but it does not fade.

The Ongoing Wrestle With Life and Family

Mentally, I am preparing for a big move and the start of a new life in Asia, leaving the temporary home that was Brussels and laying the memories of a past life in London to rest. Finally we will all be together again as a family trying to build something special. It will be a daunting challenge, but an adventure, too.

With my eldest son currently in Sweden with his grandparents and the baby in Manchester with my family, being doted on, I have been given a small window of repose to sleep, work and reflect.

Calling home, seeking tales of happiness, nobody picked up. I was discombobulated but undeterred. Later I skyped my sisters, they both said my baby was beautiful and a very special little boy. I hadn't seen them in such a long time; it was almost surreal, like a short film playing out with my parents in the background and my beaming baby making a beeline towards the computer screen. Seconds later the mood changed, my middle sister was angry with me, sparked off by something said and done the previous night. Seeing Fred mirrored in her face, her eyes ablaze, I watched the verbal evisceration of my mother. In that instant I wanted my baby back, but I let her vent, listened and, when there was a chance, I spoke to my middle sister calmly and diplomatically, knowing she was upset, telling her that I was happy she was spending time with my baby and that I knew she loved him.

When I next spoke to my mother she said, "We are all in pain," and relayed how my little sister had cried out of fear for our family and worry for my mental welfare. Infected with multiple Freds, could we ever recover or properly move forward? I called my little sister, reassuring her that I was ok and even attempting to have a longer conversation – a tiny step towards repairing years of inconsistent contact.

I decided to call my nephew. He was friendly, sounded happy to hear from me, and we talked with ease.

I'd had more communication with my entire family in that single hour than in the last five years. It was overwhelming. My parents have forged a bond with my baby son, more so than I ever had with my own grandparents. At least he has met the family, smelt, touched and listened to the sound of their voices and received a bit of love from them all – that was, surely, a good thing.

In the early hours of the same night, I spoke to with *Bagpuss* Pat, she told me "I have four more decades of life than you – and with age it improves. I've finally settled into myself." Will it take decades, then, for Fred to go bald, lose his teeth and become impotent? Or will my former adversary eventually become a reluctant ally, that badgers but can no longer bite and draw blood.

I must stick it out because I want to age into an elegant old lady with long silver hair, like Dadu – reading books, painting, growing fragrant

Image 53. *Dadu Reading in Barisal* (oil on canvas, size14 x16 inches, 2012). Inspired by Vermeer's use of light, I wanted to elevate a mundane and transient moment. It's also a scene my children will never witness, since Dadu's passing in 2010, other than through this painting.

flowers and sweet, home grown tomatoes – all the stuff that makes life bearable and good. [70]

Putting the baby in the sling, we did some gardening together. I told him that flowers need an abundance of attention, otherwise they will die. He was enthralled with the coruscating colours and watched my fingers beavering away. He's sleeping now, as the tomatoes and strawberries blush on this hot, sunny day. It was reassuring to sketch his foreshortened foot while observing the soft folds of his creamy skin. I know that he loves me. I can tell from the way he gurgles, giggles and eagerly ambles towards me. And if I leave the room he cries, searching intently, with bright wide eyes. I've also found new ways to comfort him. Recently he's been shuffling up to rub his cheeks against my lap before venturing towards the breast for a tentative suckle or, sometimes, painful nibble. The breast is always there if he wants it. Now he is sleeping through the night (with only the occasional short outbursts of crying), he no longer sleeps in my bed, preferring his cot in the newly created nursery. Right now the arrangement is working and I am just trying to follow his lead and listen to what he communicates in that sweet babble of his.

A little while after their return from Sweden, my husband and eldest son kissed me both on the cheeks, as they prepared to embark on their big Asian adventure leaving my baby and I behind to join them later. They have found an airy, bright flat, with room for a capacious new studio to paint on a larger and more ambitious scale.

Will I be tempted to move away from the small to the gigantic or oscillate between the two? I can get consumed with *feminist* concerns related to the body, sexual assault, motherhood and the perpetuation of female stereotypes and everything to do with the mind. But the world is a big place with big issues and big ideas. I want to chew on those and escape the myopia of my internal preoccupations that can seem inconsequential and trite at times. Undecided where I stand, the masculine ego in me (that is Fred) is tempted to compete with the heavyweights and tackle themes seldom confronted by a woman. It is enticing to make large scale, politically portentous and dramatic work. Lately I have been dreaming of monumental works that assault the senses and transport consciousness to other realms, but there's nothing inherently wrong or demeaning about working small. Just think of Alberto Giacometti's miniscule sculptures of emaciated, gaunt figures, which he stashed in his pockets; they are as powerful, if not more so, than his larger works.

Working and dreaming is good for my mind

What does matter is that I miss my son.

My husband sent a photo of our boy donning his smart new uniform for his first day at school. His shoes were mirror shiny and he looked excited rather than fearful. How I longed to be there.

My baby went to sleep peacefully without a fuss this evening at 6pm, latching on again – the sense of relief was immeasurable, after our temporary separation. A small step towards how it once was – or maybe not, either way I don't mind as long as he's settled and content.

"We will be ok," I said. "I will try to go to bed early and focus only on you – nothing else."

Only the baby until the end of the year; we will do simple things like play with bricks, make ink paintings, read pop-up picture books, go for short excursions on the bike, repot the plants, or amble about and create a mess. I won't freak out – just tidy up at the end of the day.

We celebrated his first birthday, just the two of us; I made a cake and umpteen balloons laid out to surprise him. One year, then one step, then one word and he will be off. What a mammoth responsibility I have towards this baby boy. May he grow up to be a kind, thoughtful and generous man and may the *happy* genes prevail.

A new life looms. It is time to put the past to rest, to let it go, and grab the present with both hands, embrace a future that is going to be different, exciting and new. Do I even dare to hope that life will get better?

Fred will become quieter, smaller, and even slightly friendlier.

I must eat and go to bed soon. Started four new oil paintings, two portrait studies, and I've just finished my latest postcard below.[71] Will I complete the 1,000 Fred has demanded? Must I? Yes, I think so because making them, slowly over time, gives meaning to life and some small pleasure, too. Imagine 1,000 of them hung together on a huge white wall, like a massive, extended family, connected by each mark made by two pairs of hands – imagine that.[72]

Torrid rages continue to brew. Fred pins me to the floor, making me weep in frustration. Mia paints away my sorrow and dazzles in red. Sophie

Image 54. *A World of Trees, Planets and Butterflies* (pen and ink on postcard, 2014)

Image 55. *Lady in the Pink Lake* (oil on canvas, size 16x14 inches, 2011)

tries to rescue my battered soul, arming me with a pen and a brush and I try to find the person I once was – that calm, thoughtful, hard working girl with dreams of being a prolific artist, caring mother, genial wife, good friend, loyal sister, kind daughter, and serene being, like the lady gliding across a lake in Bangladesh, shrouded in a pink sunset mist.

She's in there somewhere, waiting patiently inside to re-emerge whole again.

Biography

Filmmaker, author, writer and artist, Q S Lam completed her BSc (econ) and MSc (econ) at the London School of Economics before embarking on a Channel 4 sponsored MA at the Northern Media School in Directing and Screenwriting, and a BA in the Practice and Theory of Visual Art at Chelsea School of Art and Design. She dropped out in her second year. She has exhibited and screened her films in London, Brussels, New York, Paris, Bangladesh, Jakarta, Kuala Lumpur, Rome, India, Pakistan and Frankfurt. She has shown at the Whitechapel, ICA and Hayward Gallery and completed over 90 group/solo shows and screenings of her films.

She has produced and directed sixteen films to date including shorts and one-hour films. The Arts Council, BBC and British Council have

Q S Lam

funded her films and books. These include *From Briarwood to Barishal to Brick Lane*, *Old Meets Young*, *Hidden*, *Connecting Kids*, *Avenues* and *The Cloud Catcher*. Chipmunka Press published her first volume of poems, *Eternal Pollution of a Dented Mind* and the novel *Gungi Blues* in 2008.

Q S Lam has been running Pigment Explosion, an arts organisation specialising in international and local art projects since 1999. She is a mother of two children and works and resides in London and Brussels. She is relocating to Asia with her family at the end of the year.

She has started a blog: https://www.tumblr.com/search/artmotherhood andmadness

Notes

1   Toying with the idea of letting Frederick Vladimir Pucco, the nemesis in my head, be the author of this book, my publisher Dr Tim Read wrote, *I don't think Fred is the author (he) is ... a fragment of the complex and thoughtful person who wrote the book.* I fully realise that it won't be that hard for anyone to work out who I am, yet Q S Lam offers a small umbrella of protection and anonymity.

2   Kusama's paintings sell for astronomical figures. Embraced and lauded by the art world and represented by Victoria Miro Gallery, she has collaborated with fashion houses such as Louis Vuitton with lavish gala dinners held in her honour. Her commercial success and drive to be among one of the greatest living artists does not detract from her continued mental health struggles. I wonder if any of it would have been possible without the dedicated team who support her. In 1973 she left New York, broke, depressed and lonely to return home to Japan only to be vilified by the Japanese press for her controversially sexualised installations. What would have become of her if she'd not admitted herself into the mental hospital in 1975? What would have happened if her doctors hadn't allowed or encouraged her to paint? Without people supporting a fragile mind, art alone probably cannot save you.

3   Quote from the Belgian artist, Michael Borremans.

4   Pigment Explosion specialises in local and international art projects, often working with marginalised groups who have limited access to the arts.

5   It apparently took 110 lorries to transport the work of renowned German artist Anselm Kiefer from his old studio to his new one.

6   Babies can now be removed at birth on the grounds of *emotional damage*, but what constitutes this is very hard to quantify. Although the protection of children is a priority some *good* mothers are being unduly penalised because of their mental health issues.

7   Quote from the photographer Francesca Woodman who committed suicide aged 22.

8   When these visions started, I requested a mental health social worker to visit me weekly to discuss them openly.

9 I am working on strategies to change this.

10 Current research shows there are at least seventy identified genes so far that may cause a predisposition to mental illness. We are all born with some of these genes, but specific people and families are more genetically loaded than others. The genes must have some evolutionary advantage – conceivably creativity – otherwise they would have been bred out.

11 When I met him, he was a gentle, dignified man with a long white beard and creamy skin.

12 I was the first one to call him Daddy when I was a toddler and as far as I am concerned he's my father, but to avoid confusion I will refer to him as my stepfather throughout the book. It sounds strange though.

13 Fragility encompasses various facets that combine together to create a mental fracturing. These facets include: an impulsive control deficit that can be harmful to us and/or others; impaired judgment; and chronic, sustained disordered moods that impact profoundly on the quality of life.

14 At aged 11, I had a serious fall from a bunk bed and landed hard on my head. There was a bang followed by a white flash of light – it was almost blinding. I am not sure if that knock shifted the tectonic plates in my brain and in turn unleashed something that began to ooze between the cracks, but things certainly were not the same afterwards in terms of behaviour patterns.

15 I didn't harbor any specific ambition to be a model; people (usually random strangers or scouts) told me I had the potential to do it. When you are young, impressionable and insecure, it's easy to fall into things. After enduring taunts at school and at home about my appearance, (my stepfather said I looked like an "Ethiopian", because I was so thin), maybe modelling was a way of escaping the insults and reinventing myself. In retrospect it provided the foundations for the creation of Mia, which I am not sure was necessarily a good thing.

16 Expected to get A grades in History and English Literature, I obtained As in Art and English Literature and a B in History. The grade A in Art, unfortunately, didn't count.

17 She never forgets to send one – the last card was huge and pink with a cuddly bear on the cover – they always make me smile.

18 Sadly the relationship has faltered again into almost non-existent communication.

19 I've since told her to let herself off the hook and that there's nothing to forgive anymore, it's the past, the past is dead, "Let's grab today by the scruff of the neck and live in the now" I say.

20 I am working hard to reverse the damage.

21 I increasingly dreaded those huge family gatherings, sitting outside, talking about trivia – as if plunged into an Ingmar Bergman movie – cast as the tortured misunderstood one: a crooked line in a Swedish family of straight ones.

22 To be sectioned entails a compulsory admission to hospital for a person who is considered to be sufficiently unwell that they present a risk to themselves or others.

23 Skyping remains problematic for me because of the prospect of being seen and scrutinised, but I am working hard to embrace it as an effective means of keeping the lines of communication open and free flowing. I can always opt to turn off the camera.

24 A word that would crop up with some frequency and was used to describe my case by mental health professionals.

25 These people were a group of male Bangladeshi artists/writers that were supposed to be participating in the same show.

26 To qualify this, men from different nationalities have sexually harassed me, but these are the incidents that continue to stick at the fore of my mind.

27 I've been contemplating executing fine drawings of each *famous* person I've collided with and scrawling the story behind that collision in tiny handwriting, maybe directly over their well-known faces. The concept behind the work is to highlight the inflated levels of value and interest attached to the cult of celebrity, displacing the role of history, *essential* culture and eroding minds (especially young ones). On second thoughts, can I be bothered?

28 She is dealing with bereavement and the medication, although the dosage has been increased, is not working. So, what now?

29 Once I called and said it was impossible to talk with the TV on in the background, to which she replied "but *Eastenders* is on…it's almost finished." I told her to carry on watching and hung up. From thereon I refer to her as *Eastenders* Pat.

30 On reflection, I believe *Eastenders* Pat has her own Fred inside her head and maybe she, too, has suffered from mental health issues. Often what I was hearing speaking back at me was pain shredded through her voice.

31 Denis Campbell, in a recent article in the *Guardian,* 8th July 2014, asserted that the NHS offers "patchy" and "at times dangerously inadequate care" to women who suffer maternal mental health problems. He added that, despite the vital role of perinatal mental health services there remain "shocking gaps" even though "suicide is one of the leading causes of death for women" during pregnancy and post birth.

32 There is continual debate over whether cannabis deepens depression, or alleviates it, or hastens the onset of schizophrenia, or causes psychosis.

33 Signs of psychosis are: mania, rapid speech patterns, a fanatical zeal for order, frenetic work activity, flight of ideas, inability to sleep, amplified sounds, identification of patterns related to numbers/people, illusions of grandeur, overinflated anger towards specific people, (mainly family members), vividly disturbing visions, and acute paranoia. When full blown psychosis occurs, all the symptoms are woven together to create a seamless other universe, where only you have the messianic power and answers to solve the world's problems and crack the code. This perceived power gives you the mandate to shout and force those around you to listen and obey. The psychotic state can be enticing and infectious: when you are in it, part of you never wants to leave. Some people never come back.

34 Assisted suicide is legal in Belgium.

35 In my case, Fred has tried to become a pseudo ally, when he blatantly wants me dead, Sophie always endeavours to help, while Mia creates mischief and discord.

36 All the current language available to describe what is occurring in my head seems woefully inadequate.

37 *Dorbushor* is the Bengali word for unbearable.

38 The night I met Tracey Emin, she was sitting at the end of a long, majestic white table. Mourad Mazouz, the owner of Sketch, and my friend the philosopher were also seated around the table. I had just done a modelling job, my hair was flowing in soft waves by the hair stylist, I was wearing a big hat, a black dress that clung to the body and pointed, red suede heels. Tracey has always commented on my sartorial taste and appreciated it. As the conversation ensued she said, "You are the first Bangladeshi I have ever spoken to" which seemed rather strange since she lived in east London, home to thousands of them. She said, "You're lovely" and gave me her email address. It was fascinating to talk to her while I was drawing at the same time. I thought it was obvious that I was an artist but she asked, "What do you do?" It touched me when she said my drawings were "beautiful". "This is how I draw" she said and proceeded to draw in my sketchbook.

39 I am so very content with my two sons, I am not suffering from "gender disappointment". The desire for a girl is not due to a hankering for all things pink or girlie. At a time when women are grossly subjugated in many parts of the world and female infanticide is rife, I am in a position to raise a *potential* daughter into a fearless, strong and

independent woman. There are not enough of those in the world and this is my dream, at least.

40 It's also hard to love if you don't love yourself and if there is a voice in your head constantly screaming horrible insults.

41 Or am I being unduly hard on myself, inflating my mental health flaws? Things can get grossly skewed.

42 A few months later I received a standard letter absolving St Elisabeth of any culpability and defending their stance.

43 Recovery from psychosis is a protracted, uncertain process, like a wound that is trying to heal but keeps on getting infected with pus.

44 The visions might involve harming the baby or both the baby and myself. Other times they are violent visual projections i.e. fearing harm from strangers, or hazardous objects such as a car running over the children.

45 www.d-mer.org According to the website "Dysphoric Milk Ejection Reflex is a condition affecting lactating women that is characterised by an abrupt dysphoria, or negative emotions, that occur just before milk release and continuing not more than a few minutes"

46 Family Help is a service offered to new mothers, providing practical support and care for your baby during the first eight weeks postpartum.

47 With limited resources, Family Help have to meet the needs of other new mothers. The fact that they couldn't extend Wendy's help was nothing personal, she was simply required elsewhere. Although they have since offered to send Wendy to me in the event of a cancellation, I never know when that will be.

48 Since my eldest son left for Asia with my husband, I have found Fred's voice to be less intrusive and life is, ostensibly, good with my baby. We have a routine, I follow his rhythm. After Wendy left I have become more self-reliant, enlisted the help of my friendly neighbours, who babysit on occasion. Dare I say it, everything is going well and I am enjoying this special time with my baby more and more. Long may it continue. Was it the strain of being alone with two small children that proved to be my mental tipping point? Yet I am acutely aware that these good phases never last long before Fred comes stalking.

49 My husband is rational, calm and logical, which is why it's helpful to have him present when I am unwell, but sometimes this is not possible when he is abroad, for example. Throughout my book I described my brain as "hot" without realising that I was making an implicit reference to The Limbic System, which is the portion of the brain that deals with emotions, memories, stimulation and impulsivity. I am convinced that the "cool" part of my brain – the prefrontal

cortex– that contributes to logical, rational thinking, modifying social behaviour and decision making is, usually, dominated by a limbic system that has gone askew.

50 Before my relocation to Asia I decided to make a trip to Manchester with my eldest son. Returning home after all this time was strange and sublime. Seeing my mother's lush garden, eating her homegrown blueberries was heart warming. My son said, "Nanu your house is so beautiful" as he marveled at her collection of precious things, from tiny pigs to her twenty odd umbrellas fanning out like a giant rainbow patterned flower. I saw two of my paintings, an etching plate, rescued by my mother, and dusty, broken objects saved from long ago. Her plants stood majestic like loyal, ageing guards and her orchids, all in full bloom, greeted me each time I went to wash my hands at the kitchen sink. Although the visit was painfully short, it was poignant and memorable reminding me of the importance of family. It was emotional saying goodbye, my son cried long and hard and my mother gave me an awkward pat on the back, which I appreciated as a warm, albeit tentative, gesture of maternal affection. I would like to go home again to make up for the wilderness decade. As my parents age time with them becomes ever more precious.

51 Any mother who is alone with a child, harbouring suicidal ideations has a responsibility to inform someone who lives close by and give them a key to their residence, as long as the trust has been established. If tragically the mother succumbs to the voice in her head, the baby can be reached and kept safe.

52 Although extreme and highly unusual, such cases become headline news, sticking in the public consciousness, reinforcing erroneous stereotypes about maternal mental malaise.

53 An article, *Thinking of Ways to Harm Her* and *After Baby, an Unraveling* appeared in the New York Times on 17th June 2014. It described forms of perinatal illness citing it can occur, not just during the initial weeks but also in the first year post-birth.

54 Maternal mental illness can strike anyone. Postnatal depression is relatively common with one in ten women suffering from the condition. Postpartum psychosis is rare, with a high risk of recurrence. Those who have suffered previous psychotic episodes should be monitored closely. It is difficult to treat a condition that comes in many forms and at different times for women, both with and without a history of mental health disorders. The support structures are just not readily available to all women.

55 In this instance, medication to stabilise her condition could have helped. Although not a proponent of medication myself, it is obviously beneficial in some cases.

56 Growing up surrounded by tall, old, leafy trees I remain mesmerised by them. This love of nature, the clouds and the elements contributed to the formation of Sophie the Cloud Catcher, my guardian, my ally, and the notably softer voice in my head.

57 Once my big sister smeared her faeces all over the sofa, my late father just cleaned it up without saying a cross word.

58 During rare phases of persistent sleep deprivation, it is preferable to take half a pill to aid sleep rather than descend into a psychotic state.

59 On one occasion, as I paid for some groceries, a fellow was standing behind me talking in very loud Swedish on his mobile phone. My brain couldn't tolerate the sound and I ran out. Perhaps, then, it is the language and not, specifically, the person that instigates the negative response. Since the psychosis, I have become extremely noise sensitive.

60 My husband has now requested that I no longer have any email contact with his family, since, when I am unwell, I can write with inappropriate candour that has damaging consequences. But this suggests inroads will never be properly made towards them properly understanding my condition, this is only possible through openness.

61 Unfortunately the fragile reattachment with my biological sisters is already showing signs of faltering.

62 My grandmother would let all seven of her children suckle her long after her milk dried up. My mother often recounts how incredibly close she was, to both her mother and grandmother.

63 Recently, I reinstated Marta. Still apprehensive around her, I would say she feels just as awkward and intimidated by me. She needs the job and she's a good cleaning lady.

64 Fred is always cracking the whip, bellowing for me to do more and whatever I do, it is never enough. His demands remain insatiable.

65 Mindfulness is now the buzzword to keep well, with the NHS providing *Mindfulness* courses to teach patients strategies to handle their conditions independently. MPs in the UK are even enrolling on such courses. It's being used by the US armed forces to combat post-traumatic stress disorder and being taught in schools to aid concentration. Must I, then, persevere to reap the benefits?

66 The school run has come to an end – I can breathe a huge sigh of relief, no longer having to fight Fred's voice commanding me to tear through red lights.

67 Some gleaned from the internet by Lieven and I, others from my imagination, or taken from personal newspaper clippings collected over the years.

68 The therapy won't be available for another two years on the NHS.

69 The efficacy of this strategy depends on who is on the receiving end of the phone.

70 My stepfather's mother *Dadu* is depicted in the house in which he was born.

71 Running to collect my baby son from the gym crèche I damaged my leg. At the *Return to Sender* private view, I stuck a plaster on the wound, painting it in blue nail varnish beforehand to colour co-ordinate with my dress. When I got home I stuck the blue plaster on a postcard and began to transform it into a work of art, a departure for me, but perhaps a comment on the wounds we carry within and without and the unique methods we employ to heal them.

72 In the BBC4 documentary *Polka Dot Superstar: The Amazing World of Yayoi Kusama* the artist said "I'll paint 1000 or 2000 (more paintings)…I'll paint and paint and paint and then I'll die." Creating art is an inexplicable compulsion that comes from a visceral place deep within.